The Atlantic Papers
Volume Three

The Atlantic Institute is a private international organization which promotes co-operation among the Atlantic nations and Japan in economic, political, social and cultural affairs. Its work extends not only to the relationships of those countries between themselves but also with those of the East and of the developing world.

The Atlantic Papers

Volume Three

Published for The Atlantic Institute

Lexington Books
D.C. Heath and Company
Lexington, Massachusetts
Toronto   London

Table of Contents

Latin America in Transition

Its Relations with the Industrialized World

Galo Plaza

Secretary General of the Organization
of American States

Introduction

John W. Tuthill *

Among the problems of the day that require urgent and imaginative attention is the relationship of North America, Europe and Japan with Latin America. Other issues may loom larger within the priorities of the highly industrialized countries, but continued neglect of this relationship can transform a difficult problem into a major crisis affecting the security of the entire free world.

Within the developing world there is no other major region that is growing as rapidly—both in terms of gross national product and population—and at the same time facing such a mass of economic and social problems as Latin America. The political lurching of certain Latin American governments to left and right and the widespread resurgence of nationalist feeling is a manifestation of popular dissatisfaction with current conditions and a sign of determination to change them.

The governments of the industrialized countries seem to have entered an era of neglect regarding Latin America not by design but almost without their being aware of it. Latin America has recognized this lack of policy and has rejected the unstated assumption that what is good for northern highly industrialized countries is necessarily good for Latin America.

Many problems are crying for a solution. Too little progress has been made to improve Latin American access to the markets of the industrialized countries. True, a coffee agreement exists, but little concrete progress has been made on a number of other tropical products. Agreement has been reached for a global system of tariff preferences by the developed countries on exports of processed goods from the developing countries, including Latin America. While some observers are sceptical of the trade effects of the global preferential system in favour of the less-developed countries, at least it is a step in the right direction. But when will the agreement be put into effect by the northern nations—and, especially, when will the U.S. Congress act?

In the meantime, the European-African regional discriminatory system not only exists but will probably soon be expanded to include additional

---

* Director General of the Atlantic Institute and former American Ambassador to the O.E.C.D., to the European Communities and to Brazil.

3

African countries. Thus the current discrimination against Latin American trade in tropical products will probably be increased while some limited relief for trade in processed goods remains merely a hope.

With respect to the exports of the temperate Latin American countries, mainly food exports such as meat, the restrictive policies of the European Community have not changed. Through a mechanism of levies, subsidies, and price supports, these countries have reduced imports from third world countries to their own residual needs, leaving producing countries as marginal suppliers. The current shortage of meat is an example of how these policies adversely affect not only the producing countries but also, in the end, the industrialized world which finds it difficult, and at times impossible, to produce what is necessary to satisfy the continuing increase of consumption.

So, despite all the conferences, the statements of good intentions and the pronouncements of public figures, far too little has been accomplished of a constructive nature in the field of trade. Latin America clearly needs vast additional resources from abroad if it is to achieve the growth goals that it needs and that its peoples expect. If these increased resources are unlikely to become available as the result of a substantial increase in exports earnings, what then is the prospect for the flow of governmental aid and foreign investment? It is poor.

Led by the United States, the total flow of governmental aid from the affluent northern countries is declining while the need is increasing. Prospects for a substantial increase in foreign private investment are not good, especially in view of recent policies towards private foreign investment instituted by the Andean Common Market.

There is a clear determination in Latin America to exercise more national —or regional—control over investments and development plans. Such a posture need not necessarily conflict with an adequate flow of government subsidized and privately financed funds, technical assistance and know-how. The governments of the industrialized nations and private enterprise interested in Latin America should however pay increased attention to this growing ferment. Past policies should be reappraised and, where necessary, revised in order to seek agreement with Latin America on methods which can meet rational nationalistic aims and, at the same time, legitimate needs of foreign entities with capital to invest.

Not only is the present relationship between the northern industrialized countries and Latin America unsatisfactory, but in addition the governments of the northern nations show no sign of changing their current preoccupation with other problems. European nations are giving their attention primarily to European problems.

This situation is complicated by the fact that the European Common Market itself is only evolving slowly in terms of its ability to act as a unit. It is not easy to negotiate with the European Community on relatively uncomplicated matters. It is considerably more difficult to negotiate a group of complex Latin American-European trade, industrial, agricultural, financial and—basically—political problems. It is not easy to obtain the atttention of the Europeans on such problems as these, although as a result of the recently formulated Declaration of Buenos Aires, the Latin American countries, acting as a unit, have set forth their aspirations regarding their trade and financial relations with the countries of the EEC. The initial response from the Community is rather encouraging.

For different reasons, it is also difficult to gain the attention of high government officials in Canada and the United States regarding Latin American problems. Aside from Vietnam, the U.S. Government is facing a wide range of internal problems which demand most of the attention of senior officials. These internal problems, in turn, have helped recreate a wave of protectionist sentiment in Congress, industry, labour and agricultural circles. For the first time in 40 years, protectionist interests in the United States seem once more to be getting the upper hand and to constitute a serious threat to a rational resolution of foreign economic issues.

Japan, after years of a heady economic expansion, aided and assisted by the luxury of a small defense budget and moderate aid expenditure, has not yet reconciled her positions on foreign economic policies with her key international role.

In the light of these circumstances, the Atlantic Institute, with the support of the Organization of American States, the Inter-American Development Bank, ADELA and many private individuals and organizations, decided to launch a survey of the overall relationship of Latin America with the northern industrialized countries. Many, and perhaps an excessive number of, surveys have been made of the Latin American relationship with the United States. The Board of Governors of the Institute felt that, while recognizing the basic importance of that bilateral tie, an overall, long-range survey including Canada, Europe (East and West), and Japan as well, would emphasize the broader framework that is necessary for balanced Latin American development. It is believed that this should encourage re-thinking both from the northern industrialized countries and from Latin America. It his hoped that this might contribute to arresting the drift of events, and aid in the search for constructive initiatives for the future.

To assist and advise in the project, the Institute has enlisted the help of an international steering committee. Victor Urquidi, President of the *Colegio de México* is the Chairman. The other members are: Hermann Abs, Chairman of the Supervisory Board of the *Deutsche Bank;* Rubens Costa, President of the *Banco do Nordeste do Brazil;* Lincoln Gordon, President of the Johns Hopkins University; Ernst Keller, President of ADELA Investment Co. SA; Antonio Ortiz Mena, President of the Inter-American Development Bank; Saburo Okita, President of the Japan Economic Research Center; Aurelio Peccei, President of Italconsult; Raul Saez, former Finance Minister of Chile and former co-ordinator of the Committee of Nine, Alliance for Progress; Walter Sedwitz, Executive Secretary for Economic and Social Affairs, Organization of American States; Sir Geoffrey Wallinger, Director of the Bank of London and South America. Adalberto Krieger-Vasena, economist and former Minister of Economy in Argentina, not only joined the steering committee but agreed to be the Project Director, heading a small team at the Institute's headquarters in Paris which includes Miguel Kuczynski of Peru, on leave of absence from the International Monetary Fund; Javier Pazos of the Ministry of Planning, Caracas, Venezuela and Gerald Olsen, Executive Secretary of the Project, seconded to the Institute by the U.S. Department of State. From the Atlantic Institute, John Tuthill, the Director General and Pierre Uri, the Counsellor for Studies, are also members of the steering committee. A Canadian member will also be appointed.

The steering committee will maintain close contact with, and invite to its meetings, other distinguished participants such as Roberto de Oliveira Campos, Felipe Herrera, Javier Marquez, Edwin Martin, Raul Prebisch, Carlos Sanz de Santamaria and Emile van Lennep.

On 16 November, 1970 the Institute took advantage of the presence in Europe of Secretary General Galo Plaza of the Organization of American States, inviting him to speak at a luncheon meeting of the Participating Members of the Institute. His speech was received with interest by a group of prominent European bankers and lawyers. Subsequently, he supplemented that statement and brought various facts and figures up to date. It was felt that there was no better way of launching the project than by a statement of policy by Señor Galo Plaza, whose distinguished accomplishments in Latin American and world affairs reflect his wealth of experience and knowledge.

Dr. Krieger-Vasena has added a commentary regarding the objectives and points of emphasis of the Latin American project which he is directing. In addition, this document includes as appendices: (1) the Declaration of Buenos Aires; (2) the Consensus of Viña del Mar; (3) several tables and charts.

The Atlantic Institute together with the Organization of American States feels that this revised and expanded statement by Señor Galo Plaza warrants wide distribution. Therefore, it is with pleasure that they present it in the conviction that it not only will arouse considerable interest but also will be relevant to the Institute's study which should be published in 1972.

Latin America in Transition and the Northern Industrialized World

Galo Plaza *

T he outstanding characteristic of Latin American life today is change. The region is undergoing a relentless process of accelerated transition encompassing every aspect of human endeavour.

The task confronting Europe is to learn to understand the nature and scope of that change, and to adjust to it, rather than to insist that the potent young civilization of the New World shape its own future in the image of traditional values and concepts. It is useless to attempt to place Latin America into a mould: it won't fit.

Every country of the region has its distinctive profile. But all countries of Latin America have one thing in common: they are in the throes of transformation, more pervasive, dramatic, and fundamental than at any other time in history. Change in Latin America is of course only part of a world-wide pattern, especially in the countries of the Atlantic community, but it is quicker, more radical, more explosive, and more permeated with ideology. This dynamism may be discomforting to those who do not really understand it, but it is by and large constructive and creative.

Contrary to stereotype, there has always been change in Latin America, as indeed everywhere else in our western world. What is different now is the pace of change, and the prospect that it will come faster and faster, affecting every part of the social fabric: personal values, morality, religion, and, especially, politics and economics.

After more than a century and a half of national independence, the Latin American countries are still in the process of developing their political institutions to serve this integral development. Let us not forget that the Latin American countries of the nineteenth century were little more than outposts of European and North American culture. But imported political

* Señor Galo Plaza is currently the Secretary General of the Organization of American States. He was formerly the President of the Republic of Ecuador and has also served as Cabinet Minister, Ambassador and U.N. Representative in Lebanon, the Congo and Cyprus.

7

patterns were often inconsistent with the Latin American reality. This factor may have contributed to delay the present vigorous spurt of development, conceived in terms of economic growth plus social justice.

We are witnessing in Latin America today a kind of Hegelian synthesis between various doctrines and ideologies, which are being selectively adapted to national requirements. As the measure of popular participation in the shaping of society increases, through education and mass media of communication, the countries of Latin America are emerging into integrated nationhood.

The prime engine of change

At the risk of oversimplifying, one could say that the prime engine of change in contemporary Latin America is one of the region's greatest assets: the people.

Latin America is young. Fifty-three per cent of the region's people are less than 20 years old. Each year some 2.5 million young people join the labour force and become eligible to vote. Each year some 2 million of these young people flock to the cities to seek their fortunes. As they crowd together in the sprawling slums of our great cities they become increasingly aware of social injustice, cultural backwardness, a lack of economic advance and opportunity. The demonstration effect is devastating. They learn to aspire to a new life, to become aware of the fact that it is within their power to advance towards their goals, and that only tradition—or inertia—stands between them and fulfilment.

In the final analysis change comes from youth, no matter what their walk of life. It comes from a more and more educated youth. Education brings change. And indeed, all history is perhaps an inexorable race between education and catastrophe.

The Church in Latin America has been a force for social change and structural reform for some time, especially under the inspiration of Pope John. Today, it is an integral part of the Latin American transformation; and there is reason to believe that it will provide in the near future a more powerful ideological force towards reform than many of the imported "isms".

The forces of change generated by the people of Latin America are no mere imitation of a foreign original. There is a growing awareness in our region that political and economic development depend essentially on internal effort, national ideals and traditions, and local customs and institutions.

From the vantage point of the North American or European public it may often appear as if Latin America were now engaged in a simple process of taking sides between East and West, that is to say between oversimplified, overpolarized positions in the cold war, or between the dogmas of either free enterprise or statism. Latin America balks at this false dilemma and shies away from any all-out traditional ideological identification.

Latin America more and more looks towards Europe and other continents for mutually beneficial relations to parallel those our countries have had with one another and with the United States. In this sense, Latin America is not, nor will it ever be, the private domain or the backyard of any power.

The pragmatic approach

The Latin Americans of this generation, many of whom studied in European and North American centres of learning, are essentially pragmatic. Pragmatism is being substituted for rhetoric in our changing Latin America.

And from our vantage point, it often seems that the American foreign investor or the European banker is more of an ideologue than we are when it comes to problems of development and change. Ideology should not be the deciding factor in collaboration between Latin America and what the Atlantic Institute has called the northern industrialized world. The decision to co-operate should be pragmatic, based on reciprocal benefit, on enlightened self-interest on both sides, on the practical merits of each case, on open-mindedness and understanding, not unreasonable prejudice or fear.

Pragmatism should lead Europe and with it the northern industrialized world to view with interest rather than with concern the new phenomena of change in Latin America.

There is a widespread tendency in current European parlance to lump Latin America together with the so-called "Third World", assumed to extend to all developing, non-industrialized countries, most of which happen to be south of the equator. Latin America, however, is not truly a part of the Third World; it is the bridge to it. It is the only viable intermediary, not tainted with the rancid taste of colonialism, between Western Europe and the United States on the one hand, and the Afro-Asian bloc on the other. Whoever has followed closely the emergence of the "Group of 77" at the first UNCTAD Conference will have been struck by that fact. The average per capita income of Latin America is over three times that of Africa and Asia. The per capita GNP of some large countries in our region comes close to that of many highly industrialized nations. The future course of Latin American development may provide the pattern for that of other regions of the developing world.

Latin America—a developing region on its way to industrialization— is part of the Western community, as much as any less industrialized part of Western Europe. In 1970, countries accounting for 2/5 of all of Latin America's population (Argentina, Chile, Mexico, Panama, Trinidad & Tobago, Uruguay, Venezuela) had a per capita GNP of $ 600 or more. These are figures comparable to those applicable to Portugal and Spain, countries whose cultural background Latin America shares and in whose heritage it is steeped.

9

There seems to be in Western Europe an idea that the Monroe Doctrine in the economic field is still very much in effect, and that the United States discourages European and Japanese economic penetration in Latin America. In my view, this idea is mistaken. It is so mistaken, in fact, that sometimes I fear it is used as an easy justification for remaining aloof from involvement in Latin America's development effort. Quite on the contrary, it should be obvious to everybody that it is in the interest of both the United States and Latin America to promote an increasing participation of Canada, Europe, and Japan in the economic development of Latin America and to encourage closer over-all ties with these countries.

Clearly, it is in the enlightened self-interest of the northern industrialized world, and particularly of Europe, to expand its foothold in the potentially enormous market of Latin America. To do so it will have to buy more from the region, on a more diversified basis and on better terms. Let us recall that in only two decades the Latin American market will have roughly the same income and market possibilities as the European Economic Community today, even at the still rather modest growth rate of the past ten years.

A new political maturity

What, we may ask, has been the major change in Latin America's posture towards Western Europe? I think it is a change in the degree of political maturity. Over the past five years or so the countries of Latin America, regardless of their individual forms of government, have gradually developed a new unity of purpose and posture *vis-à-vis* the outside world. Such documents as the Charter of Punta del Este in 1961, the Socio-Economic Act of Rio de Janeiro in 1965, and the Protocol of Buenos Aires in 1967, which amended the Charter of the Organization of American States, all incorporate essentially Latin American ideas and principles regarding economic development and social progress. More recently, in 1969, the Latin American countries as a bloc drafted the Consensus of Viña del Mar, embodying their demands and aspirations within the context of their relations with the United States. Even more recently, the Declaration of Buenos Aires, approved in July 1970 by the Latin American countries acting again in unison, provides the institutional backing for a united position *vis-à-vis* the European Common Market.

Another landmark of special significance is the creation in February 1970, within the OAS of the Special Committee for Consultation and Negotiation (CECON), dedicated to the consideration of trade matters and to a concrete, product-by-product approach to widen market access for Latin American exports. At the November 1970 meeting of this Committee in Washington, Latin America made itself unequivocally heard on the issue of rampant U.S. protectionism, in which its objectives coincide fully with those of Western Europe. In the strongest possible terms Latin America voiced its alarm over impending trade legislation in the United States, pointing to the grave consequences of the threatened new policies on Latin America's development possibilities and on world trading relationships in general.

Latin America has stopped being a sphere of influence; it is now an influence in its own right, because it is united and certain of its own strength and potential. It is ready to initiate dialogue with Europe, or with any other region, to further its interests.

Economic performance

Political and economic development are intertwined. The fact is that Latin America can assume a much more influential stance internationally than before because it has indeed undergone profound change in its economic development. As a region, it is on the threshold of take-off. At the national level, it has in some cases reached it and in others it is well on its way. As we are bracing ourselves for the Second United Nations Development Decade, our region's performance is impressive, surpassing that of other developing regions of the world.

In 1970, Latin America had a real growth rate in its gross product of 6.6 per cent, almost the highest during the past decade. While the average annual increase in per capita GDP for 1961-65 was 1.9 per cent, the 1970 figure was 3.6 per cent (see Table 1). For the third consecutive year since the beginning of the decade, the region exceeded by a comfortable margin the minimum per capita GDP growth rate of 2.5 per cent that was established as a goal in the Charter of Punta del Este in 1961. This level was attained in half of the Latin American countries, including those with the largest population. More than 80 per cent of Latin America's population last year lived in countries where the GDP increased by over 5 per cent. It is thus well within the realm of possibility that Latin America may soon attain an annual growth rate of 8 to 9 per cent, postulated in Raul Prebisch's report * as a minimum needed to ensure the absorption of a rising labour force, and come to grips with one of Latin America's most urgent problems over the next decade: urban unemployment.

This encouraging performance over the past two years was in large part due to the favourable markets for Latin America's traditional exports, underlining the importance of trade to the region's growth. The value of all exports grew as indicated in Table 2. Yet we should not forget that windfalls in exports—either because of a good harvest or good prices, or perhaps the sudden discovery of oil—do not automatically mean growth. It is the use to which the proceeds are put that is decisive.

But a rise in export receipts, though a necessary prerequisite for rapid economic and social development, is not enough to cause achievement of

* *Change and Development: Latin America's Great Task* (Inter-American Development Bank, Washington D.C., July 1970).

this goal. In former times this often was frittered away in sumptuary imports and other unnecessary expenses. It is to Latin America's credit that this is no longer the case. In recent years changes have occurred over the area which assure that this improvement in the performance of the external sector translates itself into a greater domestic effort.

Far-reaching fiscal reforms and improvements in the tax administration have considerably increased the resources at the disposal of the public sector for purposes of economic and social development. The taxation of imports has been modified almost everywhere to make this an effective tool of planning and development. During the last decade eight more countries have introduced a universal, progressive income tax so that now the great majority of them has effective legislation of this type. Reform or improvement to increase the yield and effectiveness of sales or turnover taxes has taken place in more than half of the area. Tax administration has been technically improved and made more equitable in every country.

The private sector too, in recent years, has shown a spirit of great dynamism. Manufacturing production increased by about 60 per cent in the decade just coming to an end. Total investment has grown from $ 14 billion in 1960 to about $ 23 billion in 1969. Let me stress that about 90 per cent of the $ 175 billion invested in these ten years has been financed domestically.

The goals of development

We must always distinguish between genuine development and economic growth as a statistical abstraction. Growth is a prerequisite, but it must be accompanied by an appropriate income distribution, the evolution of new social institutions, and advances in education, health, and popular participation in the process of change. The over-all picture in Latin America on these counts is far from rosy. The problems are still almost overwhelming, and we must attack them relentlessly.

As we move into the next Development Decade it will become increasingly clear that high growth rates by themselves, without a feeling on the part of the masses that they share and have a stake in the addition to a nation's wealth, will be meaningless. By the same token, even low growth rates requiring sacrifice, and some temporary deprivation, will be acceptable if the governments and policies are genuinely concerned about social reform and justice. It is the quality of life—not just quantity—that will determine the degree of social and political stability in the world over the coming years, in the developing and developed countries alike.

It appears, however, that Latin America is being expected to emulate the glorious feat of Baron Munchausen, who lifted himself and his horse out of the river by pulling on his wig. Despite the impressive self-help efforts of Latin America, there has been among the developed countries a growing

12

weariness with foreign assistance. Uncertainties on this score have induced our countries to assume an increasingly introverted posture.

Let us not delude ourselves. We are confronted in Latin America with nations of boundless energy, a new political maturity, but with an increasingly disaffected and alienated youth. The challenge is to confront realistically this enormous problem of social psychology and to avoid therapies that could prove disastrous.

In Latin America we have shown the world what we want, and that we are firmly resolved to get it. And we are taking the proper steps to achieve our goals, on a new and high plane of political and economic maturity as a developing region.

Latin America is calling upon Europe to assist it during this process of all-pervasive change—not just as a humanitarian gesture or as a political lever, for neither is appropriate—but as a common problem, the solution of which is vital to both parties. Action is called for on several fronts: trade, private foreign investment, the external debt, financial cooperation, and scientific and technological exchange. To be able to develop coherent action will require a systematization of the dialogue with Europe. I should like to comment briefly on each of the foregoing fields for action.

Restrictions to trade

The problem of trade is, perhaps, of paramount importance for the future. Latin America's problem is dramatized by an almost relentless deterioration in its share of world trade. Since the early fifties the region's participation in world exports has dropped by more than half, from almost 11 per cent to a little more than 5 per cent in 1969 (see Table 4). In 1950 Latin America's participation in the United States market—excluding Cuba—was 28 per cent. By 1969 the share had dropped to less than 12 per cent.

The blame for this state of affairs is not just Latin America's. The region's exports—especially manufactures—are increasingly hampered by quotas and other restrictions. In Western Europe, discrimination against temperate zone products has had harmful effects. General and intensifying trends to protect domestic producers and keep out competitive products from abroad have discouraged investment and risk capital in export industries, thus closing the vicious circle.

The GATT standstill provisions of November 1963, under which no new restrictions were to be imposed on imports from the developing regions, have almost become a dead letter and all kinds of "non-tariff" restrictions are being used and abused to lessen inroads by foreign producers.

The proposal to establish a generalized system of trade preferences has dragged from one meeting to another and from one committee to another for six years. Only now are we beginning to see some hope that the system

13

will go into effect. And before it does, another full year may have elapsed and it may be riddled with all kinds of exceptions.

Latin America is not resigned to the role of a raw materials supplier, exposing its economies to the proverbial fluctuations in world markets because no way has been found to introduce viable stabilization schemes, except for coffee.

Thus every effort must be made to reduce and eliminate the intricate network of open and hidden restrictions and discrimination in Europe. The establishment of the system of trade preferences must be accelerated. The standstill must be observed. And, in line with the Latin American proposals in the recent Declaration of Buenos Aires, we need a systematic mechanism for consultation and negotiation with Europe on trade and related matters, similar to the arrangement worked out within the OAS with the United States.

A liberal trade policy is not an act of charity, emanating from compassion. A liberal trade policy that allows countries and regions to buy more from one another, assuring an expansion of world trade and a better international division of labour, is the best guarantee of continued high levels of income and employment in the northern industrialized world.

Private foreign investment

Another major ingredient in the relationships between Europe and Latin America lies in the thorny issue of private foreign investment. It is clear that conditions affecting the latter have radically changed during the last decade. A significant document in this regard is the Report on the Seminar on Foreign Private Investment in Latin America, held in Medellín, Colombia, in June 1970, under the joint auspices of the Organization of American States, the United Nations, and the Inter-American Development Bank. The area of agreement reached at Medellín by a distinguished assembly of representatives of the private sector from Europe, Canada, Japan, and the United States was relatively small. It is hoped, however, that further off-the-record discussions at the highest level will be pursued, under the aegis of other inter-American agencies such as the International Chamber of Commerce and the Council of the Americas*. This underscores our desire in the OAS to avail ourselves of every conceivable means of fostering a dialogue between Latin America and the northern industrialized world.

It is paradoxical that Europe should regard Latin America's attitudes towards foreign private investment in the same light as it has for a century, when world conditions have been so radically altered. Europe is apprehensive about the climate for private investment in Latin America in the aftermath

* The OAS, IDB and Italian-Latin American Institute (IILA) jointly sponsored a Round Table on Foreign Private Investment in Latin America, held in Rome from 25 to 29 January, 1971.

of recent political events in certain countries. I believe that this view is inconsistent when European nations are boldly creating joint ventures and investing heavily in countries of the Soviet bloc, where they have far fewer guarantees than those they seek in Latin America, and which the governments of the region are generally willing to provide. A developing country's sovereign decision as to whether it wishes to attract foreign private investment is solely its own. When the decision is in the negative, the country must pay the price. Capital-exporting countries must respect the rights of Latin American countries to exercise that policy option.

On the other hand, the countries that seek foreign investment must give investors an unequivocal idea of what to expect. We at the OAS hope to be able to assist in the establishment of appropriate guide-lines and policies, and to work towards acceptable codes of conduct under which foreign capital would be welcomed and would operate effectively.

The emphasis Latin America increasingly places on capital plus managerial skill and effective transfer of technology tends to favour Western European and Japanese investors, because of their political palatability, cultural empathy, and technological compatibility.

In Latin America we are very much aware of the inventiveness of European businessmen. The creation of ADELA, whose success in our region has led to its emulation in Asia, bears testimony to their ingenuity in denationalizing foreign capital, thus freeing it from any political connotations. The question of foreign private investment in Latin America poses a challenge, not a threat, to this entrepreneurial creativity, the very epitome of pragmatism. ADELA is, in a sense, a truly multinational corporation. It is, now necessary to explore other means to help us tap the dormant riches of our region to mutual benefit. Within the inter-American system we are anxious to participate in further dialogue with Europe.

One tentative possibility that has been discussed is that of developing some procedure for chartering multinational enterprises under the auspices of international organizations such as ours.

The contemporary role of the multinational or transnational enterprise cannot be overemphasized. I venture to say that as we move into the last quarter of the century the question of the compatibility of multinational giants with the economic and political aspirations of individual countries will loom very large. It is precisely in this field that the Atlantic Institute, together with us in the inter-American system, may wish to take the initiative for a systematic exploration of new ideas.

Because of the importance of private foreign investment in Latin America's development, I wish to stress that the positive aspects of this factor far outweigh the negative ones. Most of our countries are pursuing policies and defining the rules of the game in a conscious and deliberate effort to attract investments from abroad, offering all the reasonable safeguards. While there has been nationalization, settlement on adequate compensation either has been reached or is in process. And while there may be further nationalization, especially in the extractive industries, these still constitute a very small proportion of the 16 to 18 billion dollars of direct private foreign investment in Latin America today. Let me stress, moreover, that from the United States alone, gross additions to direct investment in Latin America still amount to more than 500 million dollars annually, a rapidly increasing proportion of which goes into manufacturing and commerce, much in the form of joint ventures or as minority holdings (see Table 5). These investments, which now amount to almost half of the total,—geared to the local market—more and more are regarded not as foreign but as "naturalized" foreign enterprises, forming an integral part of the local business panorama, with major proportions of profits being reinvested locally. Little, if any, xenophobia or threat of takeovers faces those enterprises.

Debt-funding and development assistance

Another major problem concerns the monetary burden of Latin America's external debt. Much of the debt, in the form of suppliers'credits contracted in previous years at high interest rates and short maturities, is now beginning to fall due. At the same time, rising interest rates in the capital-exporting countries tend to intensify and prolong the problem.

To many Latin Americans the entire matter of financial flows seems like a cruel joke; funds flow out of a creditor's pocket, as new loans and credits, just to come back again into another pocket in the form of debt service and amortization. While gross financial flows may expand, real resource transfers lag behind. It is estimated that in 1969 the gross capital flow to Latin America totalled between 2 and 2.5 billion dollars, but between 1.8 and 1.9 billion dollars are believed to have been paid out as service on external debt, some fifteen per cent of exports.

At the meeting of the Inter-American Economic and Social Council in February 1970, the decision was taken to deal with the problem through our Inter-American Committee on the Alliance for Progress, in collaboration with the World Bank. A careful study on the debt issue is now under way, the results of which were the subject of informal discussions under the auspices of the Atlantic Institute in March 1971. We hope that ways can be found to assist countries in easing the debt service burden in an orderly and systematic fashion, and without jeopardizing their credit standing. This will require concerted and collective action and a new imaginative approach to the problem, based primarily on development considerations.

Closely related to the question of Latin America's external debt is the availability of new official development loans and credits as well as lending conditions. A noteworthy feature in this respect is the marked shift of US assistance from bilateral to multilateral forms of development assistance. As indicated in Table 7, the latter type of authorizations by 1969/1970

($1.57 billion) had grown to twice the amount of the former ($780.5 million). Only five years earlier the opposite relationship had existed. It can be expected that this trend will soon be also reflected in disbursements.

Over the last decade official lending to Latin America—in the form of gross disbursements—has averaged about $ 1.5 billion annually (see Table 6). This is not enough especially in view of the rising debt. Moreover, the hardening of loan conditions as world capital markets tighten makes it ever more difficult to finance social infrastructure projects. A major new thrust is needed, along the lines suggested in the Pearson Report. It is essential that the developed countries commit a proportion of their GNP to development assistance and untie it completely if there is to be real co-operation between developed and developing countries in advancing human progress.

Science and technology

A fundamental factor in the current transition of Latin America towards industrial modernization lies in the adaptation of science and technology to development. If underdevelopment has any advantage at all, it is that of enabling nations undergoing a process of accelerated change to skip the intermediate stages of scientific and technological research. In Latin America today, in various OAS-supported centres of excellence, intensive work is proceeding on the adaption of imported technology to the environment, or, as my friend Felipe Herrera, former President of the Inter-American Development ment Bank, has described it, the making of a *tecnología mestiza*. This is a field in which the nations of Western Europe, whose researchers enjoy in our region the highest measure of respect, could produce a marked impact. Education, science and technology are fields eminently ripe for co-operation between Europe and Latin America through the flexible instrumentalities of the OAS. I am glad to note that we already have an excellent working relationship on these matters with the OECD member countries and its Secretariat. This, however, is but a drop of water in the ocean of Latin American needs.

If we are to make effective use of our greatest resource—our people—we must organize cadres of specialists and managers who can put technical knowledge to relevant use in the context of Latin American development. I am thinking of a massive effort such as that undertaken by Japan during the Meiji period, when she telescoped history in order to plunge into the industrial civilization of the nineteenth century. To repeat this astonishing performance under current conditions, we need and seek the help of the northern industrialized world. The facilities of the inter-American system are at its disposal in order to help to untertake this great task in the most efficient manner possible.

17

Towards dialogue and action

When Latin America wishes to have a dialogue with Europe, there are several European forums to which it can turn. Our own Inter-American Committee on the Alliance for Progress meets periodically with the Development Assistance Committee (DAC). We also participate in meetings with the Council of Europe and the OECD. The Declaration of Buenos Aires focus on the Commission of the European Communities as an interlocutor. The Atlantic Institute also provides an excellent medium for frank discussions on matters of common interest.

On the other hand, when European sources wish to take the initiative of proposing a dialogue with Latin America, which we would welcome, their choice of official forums is essentially limited to the inter-American system. The Organization of American States, the world's oldest regional agency, provides the most appropriate ground for such a dialogue. We are willing to explore jointly with the spokesmen of the Atlantic community the possibilities for concrete action on each of the issues I have outlined, as well as on any others which may be relevant.

In addition to providing a multilateral forum for discussion, the inter-American system can play a useful role as a channel for European interest, goodwill and pragmatic action in Latin America. There are definite advantages, in terms of economy and efficiency, if not of political expediency, in the use of the multilateral machinery, in order to avoid overlapping and duplicating of effort. The OAS would be happy to consider the possibility of European participation in regional arrangements of various sorts, including an increased measure of involvement in our technical co-operation programmes, as well as those on educational, scientific, and technological development.

Even the most coldly pragmatic observer of Latin America today is struck by the stupendous vitality of the peoples of our region, by their great achievements in domesticating nature, their feats of engineering, and their massive efforts to build an infrastructure for the world of tomorrow.

Self-help has been the keynote to our development, and it has generated an introspective attitude, an alienation, a disaffection of youth, that can and should be remedied in favour of a broader perspective of interdependence.

The northern industrialized world can ill afford to be a passive bystander to the dynamic process of development taking place in Latin America today. Latin America wants and needs the developed world's co-operation, on terms that respect the region's freedom of action and enable it to improve the quality of life of its people.

We wish to forge a grand new design within the Atlantic space, with Europe as an active partner, so that we may win the battle of underdevelopment and enrich our Western civilization in the dynamic continent of Latin America.

Postscript

Adalbert Krieger-Vasena *

T he Atlantic Institute, in its study of Latin America and the industrialized countries, will examine the current state of relations and make proposals for adapting them to changes that are foreseen in the industrialized countries as well as in Latin America.

In order to do this, the study will begin with a realistic examination of the current situation in the various Latin American countries. We will attempt to identify the most important positive and negative factors, deepen the analysis of them and clarify those questions that now appear contradictory to public opinion in the industrialized nations. These apparent contradictions originate because the economic development which has clearly occurred in the majority of the Latin American countries in recent years, brings with it unsettling changes in the existing order. The conflict between economic growth and traditional society will be analysed also, in order to try to discern the directions it may take in Latin America in the course of the next decade.

The industrialized countries have adopted a "waiting" attitude towards Latin America which makes it more difficult to estimate what their future lines of action towards these countries will be. With the possible exception of the United States, which for a long time has been part of the Inter-American System, the other industrialized countries of Europe, the Soviet Union, Canada and Japan appear satisfied to adapt their policies to the events of the moment rather than take a major interest in future relations with Latin America, even over the relatively short span of the next decade.

The lack of interest in Latin America on the part of the industrialized countries is demonstrated by the small amount of daily information about the region they receive, and this frequently causes distortions. Only certain information to which entities and enterprises already established in Latin America have access is more precise.

Because of the type of daily information received, when Latin America is discussed it is only in terms of political crises or grave economic problems.

* Director of the Atlantic Institute's Latin American Project and former Argentine Minister of Economy.

19

The economic growth of recent years is not noted—only the political contradictions, and of course violence when it occurs.

The industrialization process has advanced markedly in much of Latin America in the years since World War II, making it the most advanced among the regions which are part way to development. The form that the continuing industrialization process may take and the means by which economic development may fulfil the aspirations of the general population will also form an essential part of the study.

The region has reached a point in its development which makes it impossible to maintain a satisfactory forward rate of industrialization on a precarious base of primary material exports. Also, the external debt has reached a size which makes it illusory to think that external finance, whether in the form of government assistance or private capital, can be a principal solution to the balance of payment problems in the coming decades.

If Latin America is to play a full part in international affairs and not become progressively isolated because of political tendencies, which already can be observed, a higher level of participation in world commerce must be re-established. This requires not only a considerable internal effort on the part of Latin America to accelerate the economic integration process, assimilate technology and modern organization techniques, and promote the export of new products, but also a decision on the part of industrialized countries to begin a process of rationalizing international commerce based on a more efficient location of economic activity.

Specifically, the industrialized countries should arrange to accept a larger aggregate value in Latin American primary products, and private foreign investments should play an important part in the opening of new markets for Latin American manufactures. This would be the best political and economic guarantee for foreign firms and for the industrialized countries, who in the long run would benefit from a new organization in the world economy in which Latin America could contribute to well-being at a level in keeping with its capabilities.

Much of Latin America has reached a level of economic maturity that should permit it to participate in the world economy in market terms and not as a region needing outside assistance to attain its development. This tendency has been reflected in CECLA (Comisión Especial de Coordinación Latino Americana), where Latin Americans have strengthened co-operation among themselves in order to present a more cohesive point of view to the rest of the world.

The effect that this incipient Latin American activity will have on the industrialized nations is clearly of great interest for the work of the Institute which attempts to support objective and realistic courses of action in order to contribute to a better mutual comprehension between Latin America and the industrialized countries.

Declaration of Buenos Aires
July 1970

I

1. Member countries of the Special Latin American Coordinating Committee (CECLA) in an extraordinary meeting at ministerial level in Buenos Aires, Argentina, have examined the relations between Latin America and the European Communities and have noted with concern the progressive weakening of the traditional links existing between both areas. Consequently, being aware of the importance of their relations with the European Communities and considering the special significance they attach to them, the member countries have decided to propose to the Council of Ministers of the European Communities some measures of joint action which would lead to a new policy of cooperation and, in this way, reverse counter tendencies which are contributing to a gradual weakening of relations between both regions.

2. This proposal is based on a long-standing human relationship with deep cultural, political, economic and social roots which it seeks to preserve and strengthen. It has, besides, special significance on confirming the existing possibilities for the establishment of full and close collaboration between Latin America and the European Communities.

3. Latin America has today its own values, a concept of life based on man and a great potential of human and material resources which constitute real and positive contributions towards the peaceful progress of humanity. Consequently, it can become a stabilizing factor in economic and political international relations and give new impetus to the economic and social promotion and development of man.

4. Fully aware of its objectives and problems, Latin America has found in CECLA a vigorous expression of its unity, enabling it to project itself to other areas of the world as a single voice and to engage in a frank and responsible dialogue capable of leading to the establishment of efficient formulae and mechanisms in order to obtain fairer and more equitable international cooperation.

5. The Latin American countries reiterate their conviction that their future is basically dependent upon their own efforts and on their determination and capacity of creating internal conditions which will make possible the achievement of the welfare and social justice objectives to which their peoples aspire. They are, consequently, not only determined to persevere in their efforts to attain development in keeping with criteria and values of their own reflecting their national identities, but also to assert the Latin American personality and continue the economic integration process.

6. These efforts have been hindered by the unfavourable conditions in which international relations are being developed. Owing to this, Latin America believes that it is necessary to try to change and improve them and, to this end, it has proclaimed at Viña del Mar the principles and objectives of its common stand.

21

7. The international community has undertaken specific commitments designed efficiently to strengthen cooperation between developed and developing countries.

8. The European Communities, in turn, have recognized the great political and economic importance of their relations with Latin America in adopting decisions and making recommendations, both in the Council of Ministers and in the Commission and also in the European Parliament, for the purpose of promoting greater cooperation between both regions.

9. Furthermore, the Chiefs of State of most member countries of the European Communities and some of their ministers have announced the intention of their countries to take into account Latin American interests when the time comes for the definition of a Community policy with regard to Latin America.

10. Latin American countries have maintained friendly and mutually beneficial relations with each of the Member States of the European Communities. In many cases, these relations have been formalized by means of bilateral agreements of a commercial nature and for financial, technical, scientific and cultural cooperation. However, the progress of the process begun with the Rome Treaty, the integral implementation of a common trade policy and the possible participation of other countries in the aforementioned process, make it imperative now for Latin America and the European Communities to agree urgently on measures for the implementation of new cooperation policies, adjusted to present circumstances in both areas and in keeping with the commitments assumed by the international family of nations and the aforementioned decisions of the European Communities.

11. Finally, member countries of CECLA consider that the progressive formation of systems of association or any other exclusive preferential mechanism should not lead to a fragmentaiton of international cooperation nor to the enforcement of practices prejudicial to Latin America, which would interfere with the effective prevalence of the principles of justice and equality in relations between countries.

12. Consequently, in view of the preceding considerations and for the purpose of:

a) Becoming aware in both regions that the nature of the economic, political, social, and technological problems which will arise in the 1970 decade require new and imaginative solutions adequately reflecting the changes taking place in contemporary society.

b) Implementing and strengthening in their mutual relations the principles approved by the international community regarding relations between developed and developing countries in order to promote permanent action which, by means of specific measures, would contribute substantially to eliminate the negative characteristics of the present-day international economic structure.

c) Placing on an institutional status at a high political level the dialogue between Latin America and the European Communities in order to:

  I. Study and make decisions on matters related to their relations, thus making possible the achievement of the mutually agreed to objectives of the system to be adopted.

  II. Establish a framework of reference which would facilitate the dynamic development of bilateral, regional and sub-regional relations between Latin America and the European Communities, and

  III. Agree on solutions, including the conclusion of sectorial or global agreements in the fields of commerce, financing, transportation and scientific and technological cooperation.

13. Member countries of CECLA propose to the Council of Ministers of the European Communities to adopt jointly the following measures:

a) The establishment of a system of cooperation leading to a strengthening of their mutual relations and inspired on principles of justice, equity, international solidarity and mutual respect. To this end, agreement must be reached on the objectives, the policy and general characteristics of the system, as well as on its mechanisms for consultation and negotiation.

b) To hold, as soon as possible, a meeting at ministerial level for the purpose of arriving at decisions on these subjects.

c) To begin, as soon possible, so as to prepare the meeting properly, preliminary talks at ambassadorial level between representatives of Latin American countries, member countries of the European Communities and of the Commission.

At the same time, member countries of CECLA, fully ratify the principles and objectives of the Latin American Consensus of Viña del Mar, which will be a basis for proposing solutions applicable to relations with the European Communities.

Reaffirm that CECLA is the appropriate forum to cooordinate and present in a uniform manner before the European Communities the interests of its member countries without prejudice to the bilateral, sub-regional negotiations which are deemend necessary.

Resolution

Whereas

1. It is the unanimous desire of Latin America to seek closer relations with the European Communities and such a desire has been stated in the « Declaration of Buenos Aires ».

2. It is pertinent to determine immediately the areas and some of the points of greater interest that Latin America deems convenient to examine together with the European Communities within the framework of the system of cooperation to be adopted.

3. The Latin American countries expect that the European Communities will adopt the same attitude.

4. In various proceedings of organisms of the European Communities, especially in a communication sent by the Committee to the Council on 29 July, 1969, mention was made of important factors for the establishment of possible cooperation between the EEC and Latin America.

5. The topics submitted at present have been presented without prejudice to further elaboration at the opportune moment.

6. To this end, it is convenient to convoke a meeting of CECLA at the expert level.

7. Without prejudice to the proposed system of cooperation, certain measures could be adopted which would immediately contribute to greater cooperation with Latin America.

Member Countries of CECLA Agree :

1. To draw the attention of the European Communities to some of the topics of greater interest which Latin America considers convenient to study together with the European Communities.

Trade:

— Improvement of conditions of marketing and access of commodities and of manufactured and semi-manufactured goods produced in Latin America ;
— Fulfilment of status quo commitments ;
— Study of the repercussions in Latin America caused by the common agricultural policy ;
— Improvement of conditions referring to the cost and distribution of the transportation of goods traded between Latin America and the EEC.

Finances:

— New characteristics for operations regarding the financing of the development of Latin America, which would ensure most favourable treatment and would lead to:

I. An intensification of the flow of financial resources from EEC member countries to Latin America and an improvement in the terms and conditions.

II. Attending to the special requirements of less-developed countries of the area.

III. The assignment of resources to promote the financing of Latin American exports.

IV. Making use of the resources of the Inter-American Development Bank and of other regional and sub-regional organizations.

Scientific and Technological :

— Collaboration for the improvement of the scientific and technological infrastructure of Latin America.

— Improvement of conditions for the transfer of technology.

— Industrial and technical collaboration.

— Financing of pre-investment in studies, research and projects.

2. To draw also the attention of the European Communities to the interest of Latin America in the following subjects, which can be the object of immediate action in keeping with the principles established in the « Declaration of Buenos Aires ».

a) The early establishment of a system of general non-reciprocal and non-discriminatory preferences for manufactured and semi-manufactured goods from developing countries, widening the scope of the offer submitted by the Community to OECD and UNCTAD, in keeping with a presentation made by the Latin American delegations before the Special Committee of Preferences of UNCTAD.

b) Special consideration of bilateral, sub-regional and regional transactions and negotiations of Latin American countries.

c) An extension of credit operations for development of the European Investment Bank to Latin American countries, either directly or through the Inter-American Development Bank and other financial regional or sub-regional institutions.

d) Adoption by the EEC member countries of adequate measures to facilitate access to their capital markets of Latin American countries, as well as of their financial organizations in conditions which would ensure a most favourable treatment.

e) The granting of technical assistance in those fields in which the European Community is particularly apt, such as economic integration.

f) Support in the United Nations of proposals by developing countries for developed countries to make definite commitments with regard to the aims and objectives of the Second Decade for Development.

g) Support in UNCTAD of the recommendations made by the Sea Transportation Committee regarding assistance for the promotion of merchant fleets of developing countries and recognition of the right of those nations to greater participation in the transportation of foreign trade goods.

h) Support in UNCTAD of the recommendations of the Commodities Committee, especially with regard to fulfilment of the agreement of Resolution 16 (II).

3. To carry out opportunely a new meeting of CECLA at a technical level to perfect the preparation on the part of Latin America of the planned meetings with the European Communities. And, to this end, request their advisory organizations to begin without delay the study of documents which can contribute towards the achievement of that aim. The CECLA meeting will be convoked by the government acting as pro tempore Secretariat of the organization.

Consensus of Viña del Mar
May 1969

The member countries of the Special Committee for Latin American Coordination (CECLA), meeting at the Ministerial Level at Viña del Mar, Chile, to examine the conditions surrounding international cooperation and the way in which this influences our external situation, and to propose new approaches that will take due account of current conditions in this hemisphere, have agreed on the following common position for establishing jointly with the United States of America new bases for inter-American economic and social cooperation.

In the Declaration to the Peoples of America, the Charter of Punta del Este, the Economic and Social Act of Rio de Janeiro, and the Declaration of the Presidents of America, the Governments of Latin America and the Government of the United States spelled out obligations and programs of common action that incorporate the aspirations of the Latin American countries to promote the development and progress of the region. Up to the present time those obligations and programs have not enjoyed adequate implementation and attention.

The Member States of the Special Committee for Latin American Coordination (CECLA) reaffirm the validity of the principles and purposes contained in the aforementioned instruments and the necessity of full compliance with the commitments and action specified therein.

Furthermore, they reiterate the principles contained in the Charter of Alta Gracia and the Charter of Tequendama, of which acceptance by the United States and support by that country *vis-à-vis* other industrialized nations will represent a positive contribution to the efforts of the Latin American countries to arrive at more equitable standards in the international community.

Notwithstanding the fact that the solution of the problems of development has been a matter of predominant concern in the international community, the decisions, recommendations, principles, and action programs thus far adopted, although valuable in themselves, have not been sufficient. Therefore, the member countries of CECLA believe it to be imperative to agree on more effective forms of inter-American and international cooperation.

The concepts stated in the following paragraphs, which have no antagonistic or negative import, are the logical consequence of the long process of reaffirmation of the characteristic values of Latin America and taking stock of its common interests.

I. Nature and Substance of Inter-American and International Cooperation

1. The member countries of CECLA affirm the individual personality of Latin America. The process of development of the region and the changes that are at work in each of its countries, joined with the changes occurring in the world at large, demand far-reaching changes in the terms and conditions of relations between Latin America and the other members of the international community.

Inescapably, therefore, the Latin American countries must try to reach solutions fashioned according to their own criteria, reflecting their national identity.

2. Determined to overcome underdevelopment, they reiterate their conviction that economic growth and social progress are the responsibility of their peoples and that attainment of national and regional objectives depends fundamentally on the effort of each country, supported also by closer cooperation, coordination, and harmonization of policies and attitudes among the Latin American nations, which factors find relevant expression in the decision of the Presidents of the countries of Latin America to move to a common market.

3. The achievement of those objectives depends in great measure on the recognition and assumption of their responsibilities by the international community and, in particular, the countries that today carry greater weight in world decisions.

Acceptance of those responsibilities and fulfilment of the duties deriving from them are indispensable for the most rapid and fullest use and mobilization of internal resources and, consequently, for wider and more complete inter-American and international cooperation to supplement the individual effort of each country. These factors will likewise contribute significantly towards the process of Latin American economic integration.

4. During the last decade, inter-American and international cooperation for the development of Latin America has fallen far short of satisfying the aspirations of the countries of the region as defined in important forums and in inter-American and world documents. The resolutions, decisions and declarations of the Bogota Conference in 1948; the Act of Bogota in 1960; the Declaration of the Peoples of America and the Charter of Punta del Este in 1961; the Charter of Alta Gracia in 1964; the Economic and Social Act of Rio de Janeiro in 1965; the Protocol of Buenos Aires and the Declaration of the Presidents of America in 1967; the Action Plan of Viña del Mar and the Charter of Tequendama, both in the same year, and the Declaration of Santo Domingo in 1968, all inspired by the ideal of Latin American unity, have sought to actuate in a coherent and progressive manner far-reaching reforms in the economic and commercial relations between Latin America and the United States, as well as between the developing countries in general and the highly industrialized nations. They are based on principles of cooperation, solidarity, respect for national sovereignty and the self-determination of peoples, and the need for a more just international division of work that will favour, and not obstruct as in the past, the rapid social and economic progress of the developing countries.

5. As the present decade nears its end, the economic and scientific-technological gap between the developing world and the developed nations has widened and is continuing to widen, and the external obstacles that act as a brake on the rapid economic growth of the Latin American countries not only have not been removed; they are on the increase. The persistence of those obstacles manifests itself with particular intensity, for example, in the tariff and non-tariff restrictions that impede access to the great world markets under equitable or favorable conditions for the raw, semi-processed, and manufactured products of the aforesaid countries; in the progressive deterioration of the volume, terms, and conditions of international financing assistance, which is practically offset by the burden of service on existing debts, with the resultant serious impairment of the Latin American countries' capacity to import; in the disturbances stemming from the functioning of the international monetary system; in the conditions of ocean transport, that shackle and raise the cost of Latin America's foreign trade; and in the difficulties of transferring modern technology to the countries of the region, difficulties which slow down its use, its adaptation to their particular requirements and the modernization of their structures of production.

6. The situation described demands, on the one hand, fulfilment of the general commitments contained in the Charter of the Organization of American States and the Economic Agreement of Bogota; in the Act of Bogota, the Charter of Punta del Este, and the Economic and Social Act of Rio de Janeiro; in the Protocol of Buenos Aires and the Declaration of the Presidents of America; and, on the other hand, it requires a new plan of inter-American and international cooperation for the realization of the aspirations of the Latin American countries. The majority of those aspirations have been identified and defined precisely and presented clearly to the rest of the

26

world. Their attainment might have made it possible to solve or prevent many of the problems that those countries have faced, and to lay sound foundations for effective international cooperation.

7. Specific operative measures, which will be set forth in detail below, must be adopted; they must be designed to remove the external obstacles that hold back the rapid development of the Latin American countries.

Those measures must be based on the principles already accepted by the inter-American and international communities, that guarantee the political and economic independence of the countries concerned. Care must be taken to keep particularly in mind the principles of the juridical equality of States; non-intervention in the internal affairs of other States, that is, no kind of action that interferes with the personality of the State and the political, economic, and cultural elements that constitute it; respect for the validity of treaties; the sovereign right of every country to dispose freely of its natural resources; and the fact that economic cooperation cannot be made subject to political or military conditions; and furthermore, the concept that no State may apply or encourage coercive measures of an economic or political nature to force the sovereign will of another State in order to obtain advantages of any kind from it, but on the contrary should make every effort to avoid the adoption of policies, actions, and measures that may jeopardize the economic and social development of another State.

8. The principles of solidarity underlying inter-American cooperation in the political field and in matters of security should necessarily be applied also in the economic and social field. Their non-observance in this regard can disrupt relations among the countries and imperil their peace and security.

9. The effectiveness of the measures that have been and may in the future be taken depends to a considerable extent on the adaptation of the machinery of inter-American cooperation to the political and economic requirements described above and will lead to attainment of the ends pursued.

It will be necessary for the organizations and agencies of cooperation within the hemisphere and world systems to vitalize their action and redirect it towards the central development goals. This action must likewise be based on a full knowledge of the economic and social situation as it prevails in each country, and on respect for the decisions and national programs adopted by each government. A continuing evaluation of programs and their results is also a necessary requirement for greater efficacy in cooperation.

10. These common goals should be complemented by coordinated and effective action on the part of the Latin American countries in the various international forums, institutions, and agencies of cooperation of which they form part. In this way the solidary action of Latin America will have greater weight on a world-wide scale and will lead to attaintment of the ends pursued.

II. Proposals on Operative Measures

11. On the basis of these statements, principles, and affirmations, the Latin American countries, in jointly proposing a dialogue with the United States, have decided to convey to it their principal aspirations with respect to international trade, transportation, financing, investments and invisible items of trade, scientific and technological development, technical cooperation, and social development, with a view to achieving, through appropriate action and negotiation, solid advancement in inter-American cooperation. In these areas they believe it necessary:

A. Trade

12. To insist on effective compliance with status quo commitments with respect to basic products and to manufacturers and semi-manufacturers. To reiterate the necessity for the functioning of the machinery of consultation contemplated in UNCTAD and GATT prior to the adoption of measures that may mean retrogression

in the treatment of imports of Latin American products. To perfect such machinery at the inter-American level, in accordance with the Declaration of the Presidents of America.

13. To continue action in favour of the elimination of customs duties and other non-tariff barriers (such as quantitative, security, health, and other rules and restrictions) which affect the access and marketing of basic commodities. To negotiate with the United States schedules for the elimination of such restrictions in that country's market for Latin American products of special interest, jointly identifying the existence of such obstacles. To promote the holding of a round of special negotiations in GATT for basic commodities that were not properly considered in the last round of negotiations.

14. To emphasize the vital importance of complying with the calendar set by UNCTAD II for agreements on basic commodities which will incorporate provisions guaranteeing equitable and remunerative prices for Latin American exports; respect for commitments established in existing agreements; the conclusion of new agreements, and, in so far as necessary, the broadening of their spheres of action.

15. To review and require the modification or the non-inplementation of policies of encouragement for the uneconomic production of basic products that may prejudice the sale of Latin American commodities on the world markets, and a periodic review of such policies.

16. To carry on joint efforts for the elimination within a fixed period of time of the discriminatory preferences that prejudice the selling of Latin American basic commodities in the markets of certain developed countries, suggesting the adoption of measures or action that will facilitate or induce the renunciation of such preferences by the developing countries receiving them.

17. To demand the effective functioning of consultation machinery in regard to the marketing of surpluses and the disposal of reserves, and that it operate with respect for the general principles already accepted in this field, likewise preventing the disruptions in Latin America's flow of trade caused by the AID-tied loans and the dumping of surpluses.

18. To review the existing bilateral and multilateral systems of food aid, for the purpose of substantially expanding the multilateral programs on the basis of the principles approved in CECLA Resolution 9/68M.

19. To reiterate the urgency of putting into force the system of general, non-reciprocal, and non-discriminatory preferences in favour of the exports of manufactures and semi-manufactures of developing countries within the time limits provided and with due observance of the calendar of programmed meetings. In this regard action should be considered that will enable the countries of relatively less economic development to make full use of the advantages that may result.

20. To eliminate, according to a jointly agreed schedule, restrictions on imports of manufactured and semi-manufactured products of importance to Latin America, tying this in closely with the system of general preferences. In this connection, to give special attention to the problem of the application of escape clauses, which requires the adoption of adequate criteria and machinery for consultation. To avoid in this context the application of discriminatory practices of any kind.

21. To identify jointly industrial sectors or branches in which the adoption by the United States of measures for the modification, within adequate time limits, of certain productive structures might help to improve and expand trade in the United States market for manufactures and semi-manufactures of special interest to Latin America. The effect of such measures would be reviewed periodically.

22. By means of greater technical and financial cooperation, to strengthen, expand, and make more flexible the national and regional mechanisms for the promotion of exports, systematizing Latin American trade information and seeking the cooperation of official and private organizations in the United States in order to intensify and diversify Latin American exports; and also facilitating the supplying of zones or areas with products originating in the same area.

23. To emphasize the importance of active United States support of the proposals of Latin America with respect to other areas, as agreed in the Declaration of the Presidents of America. Compliance by the United States with its own commitments will considerably strengthen the value of such support.

B. Transportation

24. To prevent, as far as possible, increased operating costs that occur outside the Latin American area from being reflected in increases in ocean freight rates that may affect exports of particular interest to the countries of Latin America.

25. To advocate reductions in ocean freight rates in inter-American trade when a reduction in the operating costs occurs for the vessels in the ports, on the basis of the effective improvement of each port, instead of the average productivity of an aggregate number of ports.

26. To recognize the right of the Latin American countries to adopt measures for the development of their national and regional merchant marines. Provided that such measures of support are based on equitable sharing of the cargoes generated by the various currents of trade, national or regional, as the case may be, they will not be considered discriminatory and shall not be cause for decisions that would annul them.

27. To increase inter-American bilateral and multilateral, financial and technical cooperation for the expansion and modernization of the merchant marines of the countries of Latin America and, in accordance with their own programs, the development of their maritime industry and the improvement of port facilities and other elements of the infrastructure of transportation in general.

C. Financing, Investments and Invisible Items of Trade

28. Inter-American financial cooperation, which characteristically supplements domestic efforts, should be governed by the following basic premises:

a. It should be a real transfer and be granted in accord with national development policies and plans, since it will guarantee an adequate and sustained volume of financial resources and the right of the receiving country to determine its priorities, thereby improving the efficacy of the exteral financing in the face of situations that require an overall approach;

b. Lending countries and international financing agencies should base their cooperation on economic and social criteria that respect the receiving country's concept of development;

c. It is indispensable that external financial cooperation should not be made subject to conditions that limit the national capacity to adopt decisions in the field of the receiving country's basic economic policies;

d. Preferential attention should be given to the countries of relatively less economic development in the area;

e. Provisions or criteria that tie the use of loans to the purchase of goods and services in specific countries or of specific origin should be eliminated;

f. It is imperative to strengthen a genuine multilateralization of external financial cooperation. By virtue of their multilateral nature the international financing agencies should avoid allowing possible bilateral programs between countries to influence their decisions;

g. It is necessary to create effective machinery that will make it possible to liberalize external credit, reduce interest rates, and broaden the volume and terms of loans, taking into account circumstances such as the pluriennial nature of certain projects or programs; and to propose the creation of an

Interest Equalization Fund, whose resources, as well as those required by other possible mechanisms, should be provided by contributions from international financing agencies and developed countries;

h. Greater participation by public agencies in the channelling or use of external financing is desirable, and

i. Measures are required to ensure that the terms of external financing are no less favorable for Latin America than they are for other developing areas of the world.

29. It is considered indispensable that external financing be completely freed of elements that impose special conditions, because of their multiple effects on the economy of Latin America, such as: the artificial creation of trade currents, including those resulting from application of the additionality concept; the requirements for an excessive component of local expenditures and investments; the creation of superfluous agencies; possible undue influence on internal decision; the compulsory use of specified ocean shipping lines, and the making of purchases on the basis of inadequate lists which represent high costs and distort the trade of the region. As a possible temporary solution the use of AID loans or other similar funds for purchases in Latin America is envisaged.

30. To emphasize the need for resuming U.S. financial support to the International Development Association, and support to Latin America in facilitating the use of its credits by all the countries of the region, by changing for this purpose the standards of eligibility and by not tying such credits to specific conditions.

31. The access of the Latin American countries and their regional and sub-regional organizations to the capital markets of the United States should be facilitated, by decreasing costs and giving greater flexibility to the administrative and other requirements that now make such access difficult.

32. Available funds should be increased and improvements made in the utilization of the mechanisms for financing Latin American exports, taking into account the need for such credits to be granted under terms and conditions that will make it possible to maintain and improve the competitive position of Latin American products and their trade on international markets, including the use of soft loans when the matter depends basically on the financing terms. In this sense it is considered important to revise the conditions for the use of Inter-American Development Bank funds, in order to expand pre-shipment credits, provide for the availability of financing for exports of manufactures and semi-manufactures, and not limit them to trade among Latin American countries.

33. It should be agreed that private foreign investment should not be considered as assistance, nor should it be computed as part of financial cooperation for development. Private foreign investment, subject to national decisions and priorities, should operate in favour of the mobilization of domestic resources, generate income or prevent expenditures of foreign exchange, promote savings and national technological research, represent a real technological contribution, and participate as an element supplementing national investment, preferably associated with it—these being factors that have not always prevailed. Concern is expressed at the global magnitude of the flow of external financing that it (private investment) has originated, and at the excessive use of local financing resources, the effect of certain marketing agreements that disrupt competition in the internal or external markets, and the possible resultant effects on the economic development of the region.

34. Interest is expressed in increased international cooperation in the financing of multinational projects and the extension of such cooperation to projects for the promotion of economic integration, this being a reflection of decisions of the integration agencies in their specific field. This cooperation should be provided in conformity with the Declaration of the Presidents of America.

35. Insistence is placed on the necessity for greater participation by Latin America in the discussions on the reform of the international monetary system, including those that may take place outside the sphere of the International Monetary Fund and, particularly, within the so-called Group of Ten. The prompt ratification and activation of the provisions on Special Drawing Rights and the search for mechanisms

that will make it possible to obtain additional financing for development at the opportune time are considered matters of importance.

36. The importance of expanding tourist travel to the Latin American countries is pointed out, by avoiding the adoption of measures that would obstruct it and supporting by means of technical and financial assistance the improvement of services in this field and of the tourism infrastructure.

37. All countries making up the inter-American system should be included in the annual country reviews made by CIAP, in order to study the execution of commitments undertaken, including those national policies that may impinge on the economic development of the Latin American countries.

D. Social Development

38. It is reiterated that:

a. Their (the Latin American countries) economic development should be conducive to effective social transformation, whose basic goals should be to attain substantial improvements in the standards of living of the population, particularly in rural areas, and to bring less privileged or marginal groups into active participation in the process of economic and social progress and full enjoyment of its benefits.

b. Investments for social development are one way of raising the standards of living of the people, a factor of great importance for the increase of productivity and a better distribution of income; therefore, they deserve preferential attention, taking into account the particular situation of each country.

c. The goals set forth in the Declaration of the Presidents of America on the social development of Latin America can reach full and prompt fruition only if there is a considerable increase in international technical and financial cooperation for social development, which cooperation should be provided on the basis of the programs and policies of each country, with due consideration for national characteristics.

To that end, the financial cooperation should be granted without discrimination and on especially flexible terms; therefore, mechanisms such as the Fund for Special Operations of the Inter-American Development Bank (whose resources should be increased in due course) should be used more widely.

E. Technical Cooperation

39. It is affirmed that the following principles should be observed in the field of technical cooperation:

a. Technical cooperation should be a joint undertaking of the parties concerned. Its volume, processes, and form of coordination should be fitted to the national objectives of each country, according to its economic and social development plans.

b. Technical cooperation should be channelled through the national coordinating agencies of each country or, as the case may be, of regional or sub-regional agencies.

c. Technical cooperation should be directed towards supporting and supplementing the national programs of each country and the agencies in charge of the execution of those programs, but not towards replacing such programs or agencies.

d. Multilateral technical cooperation should be strengthened and substantially increased.

e. Latin American experts should be used in so far as possible in programs of technical cooperation.

31

f. Technical cooperation should not be cut down as the countries of Latin America achieve more advanced and complex stages in their growth; rather it should be adapted to the new conditions in the development process.

g. In addition to the needs and responsibilities involved in the process of national and regional development, technical cooperation should be made available basically on non-reimbursable terms.

F. Scientific and Technological Development

40. For the fulfilment of their economic and social development programs, the countries of Latin America recognize that it is necessary vigorously to promote a process of scientific and technological development, based on maximum domestic effort and supplemented by international cooperation. In this sense the countries of Latin America will adopt a concerted action plan, through a broad program of scientific and technological cooperation that requires the help of international cooperation, especially of the United States.

41. It is imperative to carry out fully the Action Program agreed upon by the Presidents of America with respect to science and technology. To that end, and in view of the fact that scientific and technological development requires resources of an order of magnitude much in excess of the amount currently being invested at the national and regional levels, it becomes necessary to have available special funds for such development, which should be granted without repayment commitments.

On the basis of the complementarity of efforts mentioned, the United States of America should:

42. Support the Latin American countries in respect to science and technology channelling its cooperation in consideration of the goals and priorities set by those countries and through the pertinent national and regional organizations.

43. Adopt suitable methods to improve the transfer of technology to the region. In this respect it should:

a. Contribute to the improvement of scientific and technological information through the training of experts and assistance in setting up national information centers, which would make it possible to create regional scientific and technical information machinery, including information on patents, trademarks, licenses, etc.

b. Intensify assistance for improving the region's scientific and technological infrastructure, by means of the following measures, among others: increased exchange of scientists; promotion of cooperative programs of research on problems of importance to Latin America; strengthening and supplementing the necessary physical facilities for scientific and technological research.

44. Improve the transfer of science and technology among the countries of Latin America, for which purpose it should:

a. Substantially increase its financial support of the multinational projects contained in the Regional Program of Scientific and Technological Development; and

b. Support the efforts for cooperation among Latin American countries in relation to teaching and research, among both State and private organizations or universities.

45. Assist in the efforts of the Latin American countries to speed up the establishment of their own science and technology, for which purpose it should:

a. Encourage research work in the Latin American countries by United States concerns that have branches or affiliates there, using national or regional scientific and technological ability.

b. Study, within the framework of Latin American national or regional programs, the execution in Latin America of certain specific scientific and technological research programs of interest to the region that are presently

32

being carried out in the United States by government or para-government bodies;

c. Support the national development programs prepared by the countries of Latin America to encourage scientific and technological development; and

d. Support national efforts towards integration of the action of the entrepreneurial, governmental, university, and technological research sectors in order to increase the capacity for original research.

46. It is also necessary to agree between the countries of Latin America and the United States on joint international action to promote the region's scientific and technological development. In that regard the United States should:

a. Collaborate in the review of existing international conventions on patents, for wider access, with assurances of equitable, non-discriminatory treatment, to industrial knowledge and processes and of eliminating restrictive practices, thereby making possible the more effective use of the benefits of science and technology covered by the said instruments, as well as the rapid and effective utilization of such benefits in industry in the aforesaid countries. The cooperation of the United States in this field should include facilities for wider access, with assurances of equitable, nondiscriminatory treatment, to industrial processes that are subject to licenses, and to contracts for technical services. To this end it is necessary to promote on an urgent basis a joint study of the problems involved in the transfer and absorption of technology where patents are concerned.

b. Act jointly with the countries of Latin America in advocating that the international financing institutions and credit organizations in the developed countries grant them loans on advantageous terms for scientific and technological research, within the framework of national priorities.

c. Similarly, advocate that in the financing of development projects funds always be included for the research that such projects may require, using the scientific and technological capacity of the countries of the region.

d. Give its support to the holding (on an urgent basis) of a conference on the application of science and technology to Latin American development.

Tables

provided by the General Secretariat
of the Organization of American States

1. Real Variation in per Capita GDP, 1961-1970

2. Exports of Goods (f.o.b.) by Countries

3. GNP of, and Investment in, the 18 Latin American Countries of the OAS

4. Latin American and World Exports;
   US Imports: Worldwide and from Latin America

5. US Direct Investments in Latin America

6. Loans and Assistance to Latin America:
   Disbursements by Selected Official Sources

7. Credits and Grants Authorized by Selected Sources

Abbreviations in tables 6 and 7

AID	Agency for International Development (US)
IBRD	International Bank for Reconstruction and Development
IFC	International Finance Corporation
IDA	International Development Association
IMF	International Monetary Fund
SPTF	Social Progress Trust Fund
IDB	Inter-American Development Bank

Table 1

Real Variation in per Capita GDP, 1961-1970
(in annual percentages)

	1961-1965	1966	1967	1968	1969 (p.)	1970 (p.)
Argentina	1.3	—1.3	0.4	2.9	5.3	3.3
Bolivia	3.4	4.4	3.3	3.7	2.9	3.3
Brazil	0.1	2.0	1.9	3.6	6.0	5.8
Chile	2.7	5.0	—0.1	0.3	3.1	—0.2
Colombia	1.4	2.2	0.8	2.1	3.1	3.7
Costa Rica	2.4	4.1	3.0	3.5	6.0	6.2
Dominican Republic	—1.1	0.9	0.0	—0.2	4.4	—0.1
Ecuador	1.6	1.2	1.2	—1.6	—3.1	5.9
El Salvador	4.2	3.7	0.9	—2.3	1.6	1.7
Guatemala	2.5	2.2	1.6	2.7	2.8	2.1
Haiti	—1.1	—0.1	—1.2	—1.2	—	1.4
Honduras	1.5	2.2	3.4	3.4	—1.6	3.1
Jamaica	3.3	2.3	1.9	1.2	2.2	n.a.
Mexico	4.0	3.4	3.2	4.0	3.1	2.4
Nicaragua	6.2	1.4	1.9	—	—0.4	0.1
Panama	4.1	3.8	3.8	2.0	2.4	4.3
Paraguay	1.6	2.0	3.3	1.7	1.6	2.1
Peru	2.9	0.4	1.5	—1.7	—1.4	4.1
Trinidad and Tobago	2.1	2.1	2.9	—1.0	—1.6	n.a.
Uruguay	—1.0	—1.2	—8.2	—0.4	3.1	—0.3
Venezuela	4.3	1.1	2.1	2.4	0.2	2.4
Latin America	1.9	2.9	1.5	2.5	3.7	3.6

(p) = preliminary estimate.   n.a. = not available.

Table 2

Exports of Goods (f.o.b.) by Countries

	1967		1968		1969	
	Millions of US $	% increase over 1966	Millions of US $	% increase over 1967	Millions of US $	% increase over 1968
Argentina	1,464	—8.1	1,368	—6.6	1,610 (p)	17.7
Barbados						
Bolivia	155	16.5	157	1.3	168	7.0
Brazil	1,654	—5.0	1,881	13.7	2,269	20.6
Chile	871	0.5	914	4.9	1,038	13.6
Colombia	558	4.5	603	8.1	662	9.8
Costa Rica	143	5.1	172	20.3	195	13.4
Dominican Republic	156	13.0	164	5.1	184	12.2
Ecuador	201	7.5	211	5.0	184 (p)	—12.8
El Salvador	208	9.5	212	1.9	202	—4.7
Guatemala	206	—12.3	233	13.1	259 (p)	11.2
Haiti	32	—15.8	36	12.5	37 (p)	2.8
Honduras	156	3.3	184	17.9	168	—8.7
Jamaica						
Mexico	1,147	—5.0	1,253	9.2	1,448	15.6
Nicaragua	148	4.2	161	8.8	155	—3.7
Panama	109	5.8	117	7.3	137	17.1
Paraguay	50	—7.4	50	0.0	50	0.0
Peru	751	—4.7	846	12.6	867 (p)	2.5
Trinidad and Tobago	245	18.9	245	0.0	234	—4.5
Uruguay	160	—15.8	179	11.9	186	3.9
Subtotal	8,414	—2.5	8,936	6,8	10,053	11.9
Venezuela	2,462	5.1	2,475	0.5	2,536 (p)	2.5
Total	10,876	—1.0	11,461	5.4	12,589	9.8

(p) = preliminary estimate.

35

Table 3

Gross National Product of, and Investment in, the 18 Latin American Member Countries * of the OAS
(in millions of dollars)

Year	Gross National Product	Gross Investment	Investment as % of GNP
1960	74,017	14,200	19,2
1961	78.627	15,000	19,1
1962	81,804	14,900	18.2
1963	84,155	14,700	17.4
1964	89,617	16,800	18.7
1965	93,995	17,600	18.7
1966	98,409	18,400	18,7
1967	102,713	18,900	18.4
1968	108,999	21,100	19.4
1969 (p)	116,041	22,900	19.7

* = Excludes Cuba and Haïti. (p) = preliminary estimate.

Table 4

(A) Latin American and World Exports

Year	1950	1960	1965	1966	1967	1968	1969
World Exports ($ million)	52,200	112,300	165,400	181,400	190,500	212,900	243,500
L.A. Exports ($ million)	5,950	7,950	10,380	11,040	11,030	11,560	12,400
L.A. Exports as percentage of world exports	10.8%	6.3%	6.3%	6.1%	5.8%	5.6%	5.1%

(B) US Imports: Worldwide and from Latin America

Year	1960	1965	1966	1967	1968	1969
Worldwide ($ million)	15,000	21,429	25,618	26,889	33,226	36,052
From Latin America ($ million)	3,171	3,703	4,003	3,878	4,288	4,214
Imports from Latin America as percentage of total	21.1%	17.3%	15.6%	14.4%	12.9%	11.7%

Table 5

US Direct Investments in Latin America
(in millions of dollars at end of year)

	1960	1967	1968	1969
Mexico	795	1,343	1,459	1,631
Panama	405	801	922	1.071
Brazil	953	1,327	1,484	1,633
Argentina	472	1,082	1,148	1,244
Chile	738	879	964	846
Colombia	424	597	629	648
Peru	446	660	692	704
Venezuela	2,569	2,555	2,620	2,668
Other countries	630	1,021	1,093	1,222
Total Direct Investm.	7,432	10,265	11,010	11,667
Of which:				
Manufacturing	20.1%	32.3%	33.6%	34.9%
Trade	9.1%	11.8%	11.4%	11.4%
Mining and Petroleum	52.4%	40.7%	39.7%	39.1%

Table 6

Loans and Assistance to Latin America :
Disbursements by Selected Official Sources
(in millions of dollars)

	Annual average											
	1950/55	1956/60	1961	1962	1963	1964	1965	1966	1967	1968	1969	1970 (p)
A. Development credits and grants	141.9	272.5	502.3	658.1	859.3	883.1	976.7	1,213.0	1,123.6	1,308.1	1,353.5	1,137.0
1. U.S. Government	88.2	190.0	394.5	442.0	446.3	435.0	601.5	741.2	626.2	778.0	671.7	433.2
a. AID total	0.5	32.3	200.5	277.4	347.4	360.2	455.5	578.8	426.3	469.8	381.7	244.6ᵃ
AID grants			95.9	86.8	124.1	118.3	158.3	126.5	77.6	88.7	87.5	..
AID project and sectoral			54.6	92.5	105.4	95.0	129.2	184.9	178.7	185.8	205.3	..
AID program			50.0	98.1	117.9	146.9	168.0	267.4	170.0	195.3	88.4	..
b. EXIMBANK	87.7	157.7	194.0	164.6	98.9	74.8	193.0	258.4	256.2	244.0	293.7	271.9
2. World Bank	59.5	82.8	101.3	157.4	272.0	250.1	146.0	162.4	199.9	308.2	290.5	143.6ᵇ
a. IBRD	59.5	76.7	96.2	138.6	261.0	232.7	162.9	228.2	223.6	218.8	265.9	263.7
b. IFC		6.1	5.1	12.4	3.2	7.9	14.2	9.4	9.5	11.2	22.0	..
c. IDA	..	..	..	6.4	7.8	9.5	15.9	20.8	23.1	14.0	5.8	8.2
3. Inter-American Development Bank		..	6.5	58.7	141.0	198.0	182.2	213.4	241.2	286.1	388.1	426.9
a. Ordinary Resources			3.1	28.1	59.8	106.4	83.1	98.6	111.6	110.1	135.4	151.2
b. Special Fund			2.6	8.6	15.4	24.6	28.6	44.6	69.7	118.9	189.8	244.6
c. Trust Fund			0.8	22.0	65.8	67.0	70.5	70.2	59.9	54.4	58.6	23.3
d. Others										2.7	4.3	7.8
B. Sales of Agricultural surpluses												
1. Food for Peace	..	..	109.7	252.7	237.0	236.6	160.8	141.5	151.7	148.3	137.9	..
C. Compensatory Aid	..	..	682.6	276.6	455.5	139.4	220.6	224.9	159.9	270.5	177.2	124.2
1. U.S. Treasury			65.0	34.5	90.5	18.3	13.4	13.5				
2. IMF			347.4	95.7	231.5	62.5	147.2	174.0	122.7	270.5	177.2	124.2
3. EXIMBANK			270.2	146.4	133.5	58.6	60.0	37.4	37.2			
Total			1,294.6	1,187.4	1,551.8	1,259.1	1,358.1	1,579.4	1,435.2	1,726.9	1,668.6	..
of which: multilateral assistance			455.2	302.8	644.5	510.6	522.4	644.8	620.1	860.6	854.0	..
U.S. official agencies			839.4	875.6	907.3	748.5	835.7	933.6	815.1	926.3	809.6	..

(a) = includes only loans.
(b) = January - June 1970.

(p) = preliminary estimate.

37

Table 7

Latin America :
Credits and Grants Authorized by Selected Sources
(in millions of dollars)

	1960/61	1961/62	1962/63	1963/64	1964/65	1965/66	1966/67	1967/68	1968/69	1969/70
AID	253.8	480.8	559.3	641.5	597.9	694.1	585.4	548.4	341.5	399.6
a. Loans	135.1	189.6	342.8	479.0	441.5	505.4	439.1	433.6	250.8	290.4
b. Grants	35.0	83.8	112.1	93.5	88.7	88.5	95.1	88.7	88.4	—
c. Others (1)	83.7	207.4	104.4	69.0	67.7	100.2	51.2	26.1	2.3	—
EXIMBANK	438.7	62.9	64.9	165.7	151.7	130.9	494.8	301.4	289.0	184.5
SPTF	—	223.8	170.2	131.0	—	—	—	—	—	—
Food for Peace	145.4	128.1	165.1	296.5	101.1	146.5	66.0	228.1	137.0	162.8
Treasury	82.0	125.0	60.0	90.0	76.1	62.5	75.0	4.8	—	—
Others (2)	1.9	10.2	19.2	32.9	33.7	37.9	31.2	31.2	26.0	31.6
Total bilateral	921.8	1,030.8	1,038.7	1,357.6	960.5	1,071.9	1,252.4	1,113.9	793.5	780.5
Total bilateral (Excl. Treasury)	839.8	905.8	978.7	1,267.6	884.4	1,009.4	1,177.4	1,109.1	793.5	780.5
IMF	504.5	296.2	172.5	102.7	254.5	334.0	270.9	331.0	272.9	173.5
IBRD	129.1	408.1	122.8	252.5	202.3	352.7	261.6	376.4	444.8	701.0
IDA	27.4	30.0	11.3	11.6	18.5	7.5	2.0	9.1	11.7	11.0
IDB (3)	70.1	154.9	189.9	130.6	248.6	368.6	456.7	406.1	493.8	681.2
Total multilateral	731.1	889.2	496.5	497.4	723.9	1,062.8	991.2	1,122.6	1,223.2	1,566.7
Total multilateral (Excl. IMF)	226.6	593.0	324.0	394.7	469.4	728.8	720.3	791.6	950.3	1,393.2
Total authorisations	1,652.9	1,920.0	1,535.2	1,855.0	1,684.4	2,134.7	2,243.6	2,236.5	2,016.7	2,347.2
Total authorisations (Excl. IMF & Treasury)	1,066.4	1,498.8	1,302.7	1,662.3	1,353.8	1,738.2	1,897.7	1,900.7	1,743.8	2,173.7

(1) Includes "Supporting Assistance," "Contingency Fund" and "Chile P. et R. Loan".
(2) Includes Funds for the Peace Corps and the Pan American Highway.
(3) Includes only Ordinary Capital and the Fund for Special Operations.

Stemming
World Inflation

Gardner Ackley

Henry Carter Adams Professor of Political Economy
at the University of Michigan

Introduction

'Stemming World Inflation' analyzes a problem which today troubles the economy of all Western countries. With few minor exceptions, the internal price level in the major Western countries increased by from 50 to 100 per cent between 1955 and 1970, and by substantially more than that in some of the smaller ones. Price increases have *averaged* in excess of 4 per cent a year in the West since 1965, rising to nearly 6 per cent a year in 1970. Although inflation is now slowing down in some major countries, it is still accelerating in others. The study presents a comprehensive picture of the causes, the costs, the effects and the possible controls of this worldwide phenomenon.

Rejecting all simple, one-sided explanations for the "endemic disease" of inflation, the author finds its multiple causes deeply rooted in the economic structures of modern Western societies. Against the background of full employment policies followed by most governments, contributing causes include: mistakes in the execution of these policies; the ability of unions and semi-monopolistic firms to push up their wages and prices, in an effort either to raise their own relative incomes, or to protect themselves from the price-raising effects of such push by others or from price rises induced by high demand; downward rigidities of individual prices; institutionalized or legislated "protections" for economic groups ("inherited from the almost forgotten time when full employment was not a commitment of government policy and occurred but rarely"); "the increasing aspirations of every group in our societies for rapidly rising real incomes, and the tendency everywhere for the fulfilment of people's aspirations—in all areas of economic, political, and social life—to be pressed ever more aggressively and insistently"; along with a host of institutional, psychological, and socio-logical factors which heavily influence the responses of individuals and groups to the "objective" economic circumstances, and which may in turn be altered by the process of inflation itself. Moreover, inflation can be imported from another economy in which these factors are operating.

The author critically reviews the whole array of government policies tried or proposed to deal with inflation. Consistent with his view of multiple and deeply-rooted causes is his prescription for the use of a broad range of policies: better fiscal and monetary policies for the more even control of demand; "incomes policies" (including, even, on occasion, temporary or partial price and wage controls); manpower policies; efforts to breack down income "protections" that have no place in a full-employment world; and policies to reduce or slow down the rise of the prices of particular goods and services.

Admitting that there may be some tendency for an inflation to acceler-ate in the absence of vigorous efforts to curb it, the author is nevertheless

41

basically optimistic that a range of effective policies can hold the rate of inflation below the average of the past five years.

Inflation is unlikely to be eliminated, however; at best, it is likely to be reduced to the average rate of $2\frac{1}{2}$ to 3 per cent a year which prevailed in 1955-65. The costs of such an inflation—frequently exaggerated—are probably tolerable. Beyond this rate, however, the costs of inflation rise more than in proportion to its speed. They consist of unjust arbitrary redistributions of income and wealth, of damage to efficiency and possibly to economic growth, and ultimately of social and political tensions which can threaten the stability of the social and political order.

Believing that an informed and concerned public opinion is indispensable for assuring that adequate steps are taken to keep the costs of inflation within the tolerable range, the author has addressed this study to businessmen, politicians, labour leaders, journalists, public officials, and all those interested in improving the performance and thus the chances for survival of Western political, social, and economic institutions.

The author

Gardner Ackley has divided his career almost equally between research and teaching in economics—mostly at the University of Michigan—and service as a public official, much of it intimately related to the control of inflation. He served in the Office of Price Administration during most of World War II, as Assistant Director of the Office of Price Stabilization during the Korean War, as Member of the President's Council of Economic Advisers from 1962 to 1968 and as its Chairman from 1964 to 1968 (in which ccpacity he was President Johnson's principal agent in attempting to hold down wages and prices by "jawboning"); and as U.S. Ambassador to Italy in 1968-69. He is currently the Henry Carter Adams Professor of Political Economy at the University of Michigan.

42

Preface

More and more frequently in recent years, every country of the Atlantic Community has faced the problem of inflation. Its presence has often created or exacerbated internal social tensions and embittered domestic political competition. When it has been suspected or alleged that the inflation was imported from another country, friendly international relationships may have been impaired. Unfortunately, given the conditions of modern social and economic life, there are reasons to fear that inflation is becoming a more frequent and serious—perhaps even an endemic—social and economic problem for most Atlantic countries.

Recognition of the unpleasant experience and prospect of inflation has led the Atlantic Institute—as it has led other governmental and private organizations and bodies, national and international—to attempt to focus informed public opinion on the problem of inflation and on policies to deal with it. The present paper was commissioned by the Institute not primarily in order to add to the body of specialized economic knowledge about inflation, but to contribute to an improved public understanding of the problem, and perhaps thereby to the development of more effective public policies to deal with it.[1]

Writing about inflation for a "lay" audience is not easy. Economists believe that they know quite a bit about the nature and causes of inflation. But many questions remain unanswered; we are not even sure as to all of the facts, and controversies abound as to the correct interpretation of the many facts we have. These gaps in the understanding of the phenomenon of inflation—as well, perhaps, as disagreements on certain basic values—are reflected in frequent and lively controversies among economists (and also among informed public officials) as to appropriate policies to deal with inflation.

In preparing this paper, I have endeavoured to present more than a superficial analysis of the problem and its possible remedies, yet, at the

1. Another recent study with these same purposes—*Inflation: The Present Problem,* a report by the Secretary General of the Organization for Economic Co-operation and Development—was published in December 1970, after the present work was well under way. As the reader will see, I have made frequent reference to this study, and I recommend it most highly, especially to the reader interested in policy questions.

same time, I have felt the need to make the argument reasonably under-standable to any intelligent layman who is willing to undertake the effort to follow it. To do so, I have had to take positions—without presenting all the arguments pro and con, or even, sometimes, indicating that there are other views—on many issues which some economists regard as still highly controversial; and I have had to simplify many highly technical matters into quite non-technical language.

I do not expect that other economists will have much patience with my efforts. Many of them, I know, will regard this paper as dangerously oversimplified, or as just plain mistaken, perhaps in a number of respects. But here I am not writing for them.

Inflation is a current problem of public policy. With or without help from economists, most governments, political parties, interest groups, leaders of public opinion, and concerned citizens are having to take posi-tions on issues relating to inflation. In my view, economists cannot wait until they have reached full agreement among themselves on facts and analysis before contributing to public discussion and action. When they do so contribute, they must take what they believe to be the correct positions on unsettled issues, whether or not all of their colleagues agree, and they must try to make their contributions understandable.

I believe that my analysis is basically correct. I hope that it is reasonably clear and understandable. I have tried as best I can to fulfil both purposes.

My colleagues at the University of Michigan, Professors Warren L. Smith, Harold M. Levinson, and Robert Stern, together with Arthur M. Okun of the Brookings Institution, read all or portions of an earlier version of this study, and made many valuable suggestions for its improve-ment. An international panel of experts was invited by the Atlantic Insti-tute to review the study in a near-final version. At a meeting in London on 4 May 1971, and subsequently by letter and in person, members of the panel provided a wide variety of stimulating and challenging comments and suggestions, many of which have greatly improved the final version. I am deeply grateful to all of these persons for their help. Naturally, however, I alone take responsibility for the findings and views expressed.

I am also most grateful to the Atlantic Institute for commissioning this study, to my secretary, Mrs Jacqueline Parsons, for her patient typing of interminable drafts, and to Miss Janice Benaderet for research assistance.

Gardner Ackley

Ann Arbor, Michigan
May, 1971

An age of inflation

During the year 1970, prices rose rapidly in the twenty-one member countries of the Organization for Economic Cooperation and Development (OECD). (These countries include essentially all of non-Communist Europe, together with Canada, the United States, and Japan. We will often refer to these countries—somewhat inaccurately—as the "Atlantic Community".) On the average, prices paid by consumers in these countries rose by about 5¾ per cent during 1970. In nine of the countries (the United Kingdom, Japan, Denmark, Sweden, Norway, Spain, Turkey, Iceland, and Ireland) the year's increase in consumer prices was 7 per cent or more. In only six countries (Germany, Canada, Belgium, Greece, Portugal, and Finland) was the consumer price rise 4½ per cent or less.[1] Moreover, the advance of prices was only moderately faster during 1970 than in a number of other recent years. No wonder that some have referred to the present as an "age of inflation".

Meaning and measurement of inflation

Although in the past the term has sometimes been given other meanings, today there is general agreement that inflation is best defined simply as "a persistent rise in the general level of prices of goods and services". "Persistent" means more than temporary—lasting over a span of several years—and may connote a price rise which in some sense "feeds on itself". A rise in the "general level of prices" does not mean that every single price rises, nor that all prices rise by the same amount, but only that individual price increases, taking into account both their amount and the importance of the goods and services in which they occur, outweigh price declines.[2]

1. The data compare consumer prices in the 4th quarter of 1970 with the 4th quarter of 1969.
2. If direct controls prevent what would otherwise have been a persistent rise in prices, many prefer to say that inflation nevertheless exists: "suppressed inflation".

45

Movements of the general price level are measured by a "price index number".[1] The price indexes of broadest coverage are those called "gross national product (GNP) deflators" or, because of the method of their calculation, "implicit price indexes of GNP", or simply "implicit deflators". These indexes, which are available (and with some delay) mainly for the larger countries, attempt to measure the average price movement of all goods and services included in GNP: that is, all "final" goods and services produced in an economy. ("Final" goods consist of finished consumer goods and services at retail; new capital goods—currently produced buildings, machines, etc.; goods and services sold to governments; and exports minus imports.) The price index of more limited coverage which is most used and most useful is that for consumer goods and services alone, sometimes— inaccurately—called a "cost-of-living" index. Such indexes are rather promptly available for every country of the Atlantic Community (although not necessarily of equal quality). Their availability leads to their frequent use in international comparisons; unfortunately, especially for this purpose, they are inferior to GNP deflators. The indexes of "wholesale prices" prepared in many countries summarize the movements of prices for a wide variety of *goods* (usually excluding all or most *services*) when sold other than at retail.

Price indexes (often of consumer prices) are used to correct or "deflate" data on money or "nominal" incomes. The resulting "deflated" data are said to measure "real incomes"—that is, incomes expressed in terms of the aggregate quantity of real goods and services they will buy. Measures of the money value of output, when deflated, are referred to as measures of "real output"—that is, they show changes in the "physical volume" of production.

Because of defects of concept or coverage—some of which are, even in principle, unavoidable—the accuracy of any price index is less than perfect, even in those countries which devote the most money and care to their preparation. Measures of real income and real output are similarly impaired. In particular, it is generally agreed that almost all price indexes have a built-in tendency to exaggerate the extent to which prices are increasing. Without going into detail, this "upward bias" arises in part from our inability fully to measure improvements in the "quality" of goods

1. To compute this number, the price of each of a large number of representative individual goods and services in each month, quarter, or year is first expressed as a percentage of what it had been in some recent year (taken as a "base period"). Each such percentage is given a "weight" proportional to the money value of the output which it represents. All of these weighted percentages, for each month, year, or quarter, are then averaged into a single "index number", which thus indicates the weighted average percentage which prices in the particular period are of those in the base period. Such price indexes generally exclude the prices of "productive services"—that is, wage rates of workers, interest rates on loans, profit rates of business—and exclude, as well, the prices of assets—e.g., shares or bonds, existing buildings, land, antique furniture and paintings, etc. (Indexes of wage rates, interest rates, share prices, land prices, etc., are sometimes computed, and have their purposes; but they are not usually considered as direct indicators of inflation.)

sold (an improved quality, sold at the same price, just like a larger quantity sold at the same price, is really a price reduction).[1] Much more important is our inability to measure the improvement in the "quality" of the whole assortment of goods and services available on the market, which arises from the introduction of completely new goods and services, previously unavailable. Whether this bias is of the order of ¼ of 1 per cent a year, or as much as 1½ or 2 per cent a year is a matter of debate among economists.

For this reason, as well as because a small upward creep in prices (as measured) is both extremely difficult to avoid and probably not seriously harmful, some authorities reserve the term inflation for a persistent rise exceeding (say) 1 or 2 per cent a year in the conventional price indexes. Other economists reach a similar judgement, but framed in a rather different way. However they may choose to define inflation, they prefer to emphasize the particular importance of industrial prices—that is, of the price level excluding food and services. They regard the stability of industrial prices as representing a fully satisfactory achievement. In most countries, stability of industrial prices would be consistent with a rise of from 1 to 2 or even 2½ per cent a year in the consumer price index or GNP deflator.

The extent of inflation, 1955-70

Even such minimal rates of price increase (2 or 2½ per cent a year) have been exceeded most of the time in recent years in every country of the Atlantic Community. Table 1 (see page 12) shows the average annual change and the cumulative change in the GNP deflator in each of the principal Atlantic countries over the past fifteen years, along with average changes for these countries as a group. Table 2 (see page 13) shows changes in the consumer price index in each of the 22 countries over the same period. The tables show that the average annual price increase in the Atlantic Community has been a little more than 3 per cent over these 15 years.

Among the larger countries, only Italy, during 1955-60, and the United States and Canada, during 1960-65, had half-decade inflation rates as low as 2 per cent, as measured by GNP deflators. Germany, Canada, and Japan also met this standard during 1955-60, measured in terms of consumer prices. Among the smaller countries, Belgium, Switzerland, Denmark, and Luxembourg, during 1955-60, and Greece during 1960-65, experienced inflation of 2 per cent or less for a half decade, as measured by the change in consumer prices. No country met this standard during 1965-70, either in terms of GNP deflators or consumer prices.

1. Not all quality changes are improvements, of course. Sometimes, especially during periods of inflation, deliberate quality deterioration is a hidden form of price increase.

47

Table 1

Price Changes in Major Countries, 1955-70
as Measured by GNP Deflators

	Average annual percentage increase				Cumulative percentage increase
	1955-60	1960-65	1965-70	1955-70	1955-70
Germany	2.7	3.6	3.4	3.2	61
France	6.5	4.1	4.6	5.0	109
Italy	2.0	5.5	3.4	3.6	70
United Kingdom	3.2	3.4	4.7	3.8	74
Canada	2.6	1.9	4.1	2.9	53
United States	2.6	1.5	4.0	2.7	48
Japan	3.3	5.0	4.7	4.3	88
Average, seven countries *	3.0	2.6	4.1	3.2	61

* Weighted by 1969 GNP

Source : Publications of the OECD and national authorities. Deflators for 1970 are partially esti mated.

Prices rising at 2 per cent a year, compounded, will produce a rise of nearly 35 per cent over 15 years. No country came close to that during 1955-70. The average cumulative rise during this period for the major countries was 61 per cent as measured by GNP deflators and 56 per cent as measured by consumer prices. For all 22 countries, the average cumulative rise of consumer prices was 61 per cent. The United States, with 45 per cent, Germany, with 43 per cent, and Canada, with 44 per cent, had the best 15-year records among the major countries, along with Belgium, Luxembourg, Switzerland, and Greece among the smaller countries.

A longer-term comparison

Inflation at an average rate of 3 per cent a year, although it could still be characterized as mild, nevertheless contrasts sharply with the movement of price levels between the two world wars. Table 3 (see page 51), taken from a recent OECD study, compares the experience of seven Atlantic countries during the "inter-war" period, 1925-1938, and the

Table 2

Price Changes in Countries of the Atlantic Community 1955-70, as Measured by Consumer Price Indexes

	Average annual percentage increase				Cumulative percentage increase
	1955-60	1960-65	1965-70	1955-70	1955-70
Germany	1.8	2.8	2.6	2.4	43
France	5.8	3.8	4.3	4.6	97
Italy	1.9	4.9	2.9	3.2	61
United Kingdom	2.6	3.5	4.6	3.6	69
Canada	1.9	1.6	3.9	2.5	44
United States	2.1	1.3	4.3	2.5	45
Japan	1.5	6.0	5.5	4.3	89
Average, seven major countries *	2.3	2.5	4.2	3.0	56
Netherlands	2.6	3.5	4.9	3.7	73
Belgium	1.7	2.5	3.5	2.6	47
Luxembourg	1.5	2.1	3.0	2.2	39
Norway	2.8	4.1	4.9	3.9	78
Sweden	3.6	3.6	4.4	3.9	78
Denmark	1.7	5.5	6.4	4.6	96
Finland	6.7	4.9	4.7	5.6	126
Austria	2.1	3.9	3.3	3.1	58
Switzerland	1.2	3.2	3.5	2.8	47
Spain	7.8	7.0	5.1	6.7	163
Portugal	2.1	2.6	6.4	3.7	71
Greece	2.3	1.6	2.5	2.1	38
Turkey	14.4	3.7	8.2	8.6	248
Ireland	2.6	4.2	5.3	4.0	81
Iceland	4.6	10.8	12.9	9.4	284
Average, 15 smaller countries *	4.1	4.0	4.7	4.3	94
Average, 22 countries *	2.6	2.7	4.3	3.2	61

* Weighted by 1969 GNP

Source : Publications of the OECD and the IMF.

thing that had happened was the assumption by each government, at the end of World War II, of a responsibility to promote full employment and economic prosperity. This assumption of responsibility was possible only because of a revolution that had occurred in economic knowledge and understanding. The principal tools of intervention on behalf of prosperity (government spending, taxes, money supply) were not new: only they were used in a new way, and with a new consciousness of their power.

But if new government policies are responsible for the vastly superior economic performance, it seems clear that they must also accept some responsibility for the shift from the previous price stability to the inflation—however mild—that has universally arisen. To be sure, if the price of the greater prosperity and faster growth was a mild inflation averaging 3 per cent a year, most people would probably agree that this was a price well worth paying. Still, three important sets of questions need to be raised and are increasingly being raised about this proposition:

1. Are we sure that we can continue to enjoy the benefits of the post-war prosperity along with only a mild inflation? Is there not danger that a mild inflation will accelerate? Indeed, is there not evidence that such an acceleration is already under way?

2. What are the true costs of a mild inflation? Could they not be more serious than we think?

3. Was even the mild inflation of 1955-70 a *necessary* price for the economic achievements of our post-war world? With even better policies, could we have enjoyed post-war prosperity along with something closer to pre-war price stability? Is there any prospect that we can do better in the years ahead? How should we go about trying to improve our price performance?

Much of the rest of this study is designed to throw light on these questions. The question whether we are already experiencing an acceleration of inflation occupies the remainder of this chapter. The costs of inflation are analysed in Chapter 2. Chapters 3 and 4 attempt to summarize the causes of inflation in the Atlantic world and Chapter 5 the methods that have been and may be used to control it. This analysis implies at least tentative answers to the third group of questions.

An acceleration of inflation?

Tables 1 and 2 showed that the average rate of price increase during the most recent half decade—1965-70—substantially exceeded that of the two previous 5-year periods. Of the three 5-year periods, the most recent was the most inflationary in three of the major countries and in eleven of the others. It is interesting to note that, on average, the 15 smaller countries experienced a much steadier, although faster, rate of inflation

Table 3

Inter-war and Post-war Growth, Unemployment, and Prices

	Average Annual % Change in GNP		Average Level of Unemployment, % of Labour Force		Average Annual % Change in Consumer Prices	
	Inter-war 1925-38	Post-war 1955-65	Inter-war 1925-38	Post-war 1955-65	Inter-war 1925-38	Post-war 1955-65
	1	2	3	4	5	6
Belgium	0	4	6½	2½	0	2½
France	0	5½	3	1	0	4¾
Germany	4	6	8	2	—1	2¾
Italy	2	6	4½	5	0	3½
Sweden	3	4	5	2	—½	4
United Kingdom	2½	3	9	1½	—1	3½
United States	1	4	14	5	—1½	1¾

1. For statistical and other reasons, comparisons should not be made between the levels of unemployment in different countries. Minor changes in the level within the same country may only reflect differences in the manner of collecting the statistics.

Source : OECD, *Fiscal Policy for a Balanced Economy : Experience, Problems, and Prospects* (the Report of a Committee consisting of Walter Heller, Cornelis Goedhart, Guillaume Guindey, Heinz Haller, Jean van Houtte, Assar Lindbeck. Richard Sayers, and Sergio Steve, with the collaboration of J.C.R. Dow),December 1968, p. 80. (Sources of the particular data are shown in the original. Although not so indicated, the GNP data obviously are changes in "real" GNP. The changes shown in consumer prices during1955-65 are not in all cases fully consistent with data in table 2, but are of similar orders of magnitude.)

"post-war" period, 1955-1965. The difference in price behaviour, shown in columns 5 and 6, is striking: in each of the countries, the inter-war period was characterized by price stability or a slightly declining price level; in the post-war period each country's price level was rising. Equally striking, however, are the differences shown in columns 1 and 2, and 3 and 4. These data make abundantly clear that the post-war Atlantic world has been an infinitely more prosperous and economically rewarding one: in each of the countries, economic growth was distinctly faster in the post-war period than during the inter-war period—replacing what in some cases was complete stagnation—and jobs were available for a substantially larger fraction of the working force—replacing in some cases mass unemployment.

There can be little doubt that so revolutionary a change, occurring simultaneously in each of the Atlantic countries shown (and surely in the others as well), was no accident. Something new had happened everywhere in the Atlantic world. No doubt there were many economic, social, and political trends which influenced the result. But, surely, the most crucial

Table 4

Annual and Half-Year Price Changes, 1965-70
in Major Countries, as Measured by GNP Deflators

	Percentage change					Percentage change at annual rates		
	1966 1965	1966 1967	1968 1967	1969 1968	1970 1969	I-1969 II-1969	II-1969 II-1970	I-1970 I-1970
Germany	3.8	0.7	1.9	3.4	7.4	6.6	8.0	7.3
France	2.9	2.7	4.8	7.0	5.6	5.3	6.0	5.0
Italy	2.2	2.8	1.5	4.0	6.3	5.3	6.8	6.0
United Kingdom	4.4	3.1	4.0	5.0	7.3	4.9	7.3	9.0
Canada	4.6	3.7	3.6	4.7	4.1	3.3	5.3	2.4
United States	2.8	3.1	4.1	4.8	5.1	5.3	5.4	4.9
Japan	4.5	4.3	3.4	4.2	6.6	7.3	6.6	6.0
Average, seven countries *	3.2	3.0	3.7	4.8	5.7	5.6	6.0	5.5

* Weighted by 1969 GNP

Source : Publications of the OECD and national authorities. Data for II-1970 and therefore for year 1970 are partly estimated.

than the major countries, the average rising only from 4.1 per cent during 1955-65 to 4.7 per cent in 1965-70.

Tables 4 and 5 record the year-by-year course of price increases within the last half decade, together with the most recent half-year changes.[1] They show that the average rate of inflation in each of the past five years was higher than the average for the previous decade. Moreover, there was a clear acceleration in the rate of price increase beginning in 1968 for all countries together, and for the major countries taken as a group. The years 1969 and 1970 were years of the fastest inflation the Atlantic Community has known since the period of post-World-War II reconstruction and the Korean War. By 1970 the average price increase had reached a rate more than twice the average of 1960-65.

1. Annual movements in consumer prices were influenced in several cases by special factors, including changes in rates or systems of indirect taxation. In this period, this was the case in one or more years for the United Kingdom, the Netherlands, Belgium, Norway, Sweden, and Denmark.

52

Table 5

Annual and Half-Year Price Changes, 1965-70
as Measured by Consumer Price Indexes

	Percentage change					Percentage change at annual rates		
	1965 1966	1966 1967	1967 1968	1968 1969	1969 1970	I-1969 II-1969	II-1969 I-1970	I-1970 II-1970
Germany	3.5	1.5	1.8	2.7	3.8	1.5	5.9	2.2
France	2.7	2.7	4.6	6.4	5.3	5.2	6.3	5.0
Italy	2.3	3.2	1.4	2.6	5.0	4.4	5.5	4.5
United Kingdom	3.9	2.5	4.7	5.5	6.4	3.2	7.7	6.9
Canada	3.7	3.5	4.2	4.5	3.4	4.9	3.5	1.6
United States	2.9	2.8	4.2	5.4	5.9	6.1	6.1	5.3
Japan	5.1	4.0	5.4	5.2	7.7	7.8	8.0	7.0
Average, seven major countries *	3.2	2.8	4.0	5.0	5.7	5.4	6.2	5.1
Netherlands	5.8	3.4	3.7	7.5	4.4	1.9	5.1	5.8
Belgium	4.2	2.9	2.7	3.8	3.9	3.9	4.5	2.8
Luxembourg	3.3	2.2	2.6	2.3	4.7	2.0	6.7	3.3
Norway	3.3	4.4	3.5	3.1	10.6	3.4	15.6	7.9
Sweden	6.4	4.3	1.9	2.7	7.1	3.5	9.2	6.2
Denmark	6.7	6.9	8.6	4.2	6.7	5.0	6.1	8.8
Finland	3.5	6.0	9.0	2.7	2.7	1.7	3.4	2.6
Austria	2.2	3.9	2.8	3.0	4.4	3.5	4.5	4.9
Switzerland	4.8	3.9	2.5	2.5	3.6	1.8	3.4	5.8
Spain	6.2	6.5	4.9	2.2	5.7	3.2	5.2	9.3
Portugal	5.0	5.5	6.1	8.8	6.4	7.2	6.7	5.0
Greece	5.1	1.6	0.4	2.4	3.2	1.1	4.1	3.5
Turkey	8.7	14.0	5.3	4.8	6.9	4.2	9.6	8.7
Ireland	2.9	3.2	4.7	7.3	8.2	5.8	8.5	10.0
Iceland	11.1	3.2	14.8	2.4	13.0	17.0	10.0	17.2
Average, 15 smaller countries *	5.4	5.0	4.0	3.9	5.4	3.2	6.3	6.3
Average, 22 countries *	3.5	3.1	4.1	5.0	5.8	5.3	6.4	5.3

* Weighted by 1969 GNP

Source : Publications of the OECD and national authorities.

53

Nevertheless, a pattern of generally accelerating inflation within these five years is not characteristic of most countries individually. In no country was the acceleration of inflation uninterrupted, although it was essentially so for the United States. Outside the major countries, there is almost no suggestion of a trend towards acceleration. In only 10 of the 22 countries was the 1969-70 increase in consumer prices the largest of the five annual changes. The fact that the United States accounts for roughly half of the total GNP of the 22 countries combined, automatically imprints the US pattern rather heavily on the weighted average for all countries, and in the United States the acceleration of inflation was strong and uninterrupted (except briefly during 1967) for special reasons which one may hope will not be repeated. Moreover, to some extent, the pattern of price increase in other countries has been influenced by that of the United States (through mechanisms that are sketched in Chapter 4).

One hopeful development is that price increases slowed down in the second half of 1970 in a number of countries, particularly the major ones, as is apparent by comparing the last two columns in Tables 4 and 5. However, it appears that this largely reflects seasonal elements in many of the major European countries. The data becoming available for the early months of 1971 suggest that only in the United States, Canada, and France, among the major countries, has inflation clearly slowed down since the first half of 1970. The trend is not yet clear for Japan, Germany, and Italy, and it is clearly towards a continuing acceleration of inflation in the United Kingdom. Among the smaller countries, a genuine slowing-down seems indicated only for Austria and Denmark, while price increases apparently are continuing to accelerate in Norway, Spain, Switzerland, and Iceland.

Because of the great importance of the United States—both directly and through her influence on prices elsewhere—the slowing-down of price increases in that country, while rates of inflation are at least no longer increasing in many others, provides some hope that, for the present at least, the trend will be towards lower rates of inflation in the Atlantic Community. It is important to recognize, however, that this modest improvement has been purchased at the cost of substantial unwanted unemployment in the United States, Canada, and the United Kingdom, and a slowing-down of rates of increase of output in most of the other major countries. Relative to rates of unemployment, inflation remains at an unprecedentedly high rate.

If the United States should succeed in getting her recent inflation firmly under control, and were to resume approximately the degree of price stability she enjoyed prior to 1966, it could be that the Atlantic Community as a whole might expect an inflation no worse than the $2\frac{1}{2}$ to 3 per cent rate that prevailed from 1955 to 1965. Clearly, much depends on what will happen to prices in the United States in the next few years.

There is, however, no possible basis for complacency about the outcome. Even with the recent slowing down in some countries, inflation remains at an uncomfortably high rate almost everywhere. Surely, the experience of the past fifteen years, and the analysis which will be developed in the subsequent chapters of this study, strongly suggest that the problem of inflation may now be rather deeply-rooted in the economic conditions and institutional structures of the Atlantic countries, and will not readily be overcome. There are few who believe that price increases in the United States are likely to return to the negligible rate of the early 1960s (a period when unemployment was substantially in excess of US official targets). Indeed, some fear that, once the US economy again begins to expand more rapidly, as is the express goal of current government policy, the substantial rates of inflation experienced in the late 1960s might well return. In that case, there will be no question that inflation has definitely accelerated, and there will be increased basis for fears of still further acceleration.

It is therefore necessary to look with some care at the costs of inflation, which are the subject of the next chapter.

The costs of inflation: myth and reality

I t should be emphasized at once that this chapter deals only with the costs of inflation, *per se*. It is not concerned, that is, with the benefits (or costs) of whatever circumstances may have caused the inflation or been associated with its occurrence. For example, inflation is often the consequence or "side-effect" of an unusually high rate of production, and an unusually low rate of unemployment. We do not try here to balance the benefits of the extra output and jobs against the costs of the inflation, but only to assess what are the costs. The questions (a) whether the costs are a *necessary and unavoidable* side effect of the benefits, and (b) if they are, what is the net balance of benefit or cost can only be considered later.

The myth that inflation reduces real incomes

Popular opinion in most countries, like most journalistic discussion, typically misrepresents—and may well exaggerate—the damage done by a moderate inflation. The popular view is that inflation impoverishes us: that a five per cent rise in prices necessarily represents a reduction of real incomes of roughly five per cent. Yet it is undeniable that the aggregate real income of a community consists of the total physical amount of goods and services it produces. A rise in prices would reduce real incomes proportionately only if the total physical production of goods and services were to decline in the same proportion that prices rose. But this rarely, if ever, happens during an inflation. Indeed, the effects of inflation on aggregate output, and thus on total real income, are complex and indirect.

First, therefore, we need to be clear about what is wrong with the popular view that inflation automatically cuts real incomes in proportion to the price rise.

It is surely true that a 5 per cent rise in prices reduces by nearly 5 per cent the amount of goods and services that any particular money income can buy. What is equally true but not so easily appreciated is that the inflation that raises prices by 5 per cent also raises people's money incomes by an extra 5 per cent, at least in the aggregate, leaving the average person's real income essentially unchanged. To see why this must

56

be so, it is only necessary to start with the inescapable fact that any inflation in the prices that buyers pay has to be exactly matched by the same inflation in the prices that sellers receive. Sellers of goods and services have this extra amount available to pay larger money incomes to their workers, higher prices to their suppliers, and, usually, to increase somewhat their own incomes. The suppliers of the goods and services bought by the first set of sellers are in a similar position. They receive more due to higher prices; their costs, too, including the wages they pay their workers, are inflated; still their net money incomes will typically rise. Their suppliers have the same experience, as do their suppliers' suppliers. Tracing the effects successively backwards, we find that if goods and services are sold at prices which average 5 per cent higher, the aggregate of money incomes—of workers, owners, proprietors, farmers, etc.—must rise essentially by that same 5 per cent, leaving the average real income the same.[1]

If it is a myth that inflation reduces average real incomes, it is also easy to understand how this belief arises. In an inflation, everyone is very conscious of the fact that the prices he must pay have gone up. But fewer are aware—or willing to admit—that inflation has also raised their money incomes. We all like to believe that the unusual gains we have been making in our money incomes are due to our skill, effort, or good management; to the effectiveness of our trade union; or, at the very least, to the fact that fate has smiled on us personally. What has happened to our incomes would have occurred whatever had happened to the general price level. Consequently, almost all of us feel impoverished by inflation; it has robbed us of our just gains. Many individuals, of course, *are* impoverished—those

---

1. There are qualifications and exceptions that must be made to the propositions set forth above, but they are minor and inconclusive in direction. As prices rise, the full amount of the additional receipts from sales will not be received by anyone as income to the extent (for instance) that some of the extra money receipts from the sale of goods and services at higher prices are automatically required to be paid to governments in *ad valorem* sales or excise taxes, but neither were all the money receipts at the lower price level. However, to the extent that progressive income taxes are in use, after-tax incomes will go up less than in proportion to pre-tax incomes, and therefore less than in proportion to prices of goods and services. On the other hand, there is a significant part of the cost of producing goods and services which does not supply income to anyone—namely the depreciation on capital goods in use— and which does not rise along with prices. Under conventional accounting methods, depreciation allowances will not rise at all during an inflation until, (and only to the extent that) new capital goods are acquired at the higher prices. Some businessmen may indeed make mental allowance for the fact that when their existing capital goods come to be replaced it will be at higher prices, and thus recognize that their real incomes are lower than their books of account record them. However, it is doubtful that full "mental allowance" is made by businessmen. To this extent, money incomes— profits and/or wages—rise by more than prices.

Our simplified treatment has also ignored certain other forms of incomes, for example, interest. Interest rates on already outstanding loans are, of course, fixed by the terms of these loans. This stability of interest cost on outstanding loans permits other incomes to rise by a greater percentage than prices; but this is exactly offset by the fact that the real incomes of interest recipients fall (at least until loans come due, and can be renewed, probably, at interest rates that reflect whatever inflation may be occurring or expected to occur).

whose money incomes do not reflect the average extent of the inflation. Others, however, are necessarily correspondingly rewarded. But even the latter tend to attribute their improved position to their own efforts or luck, and resent the price increases that have limited the extent of their rightful gains.

Thus, psychologically, inflation has a real cost, and probably a very substantial one. The economist may be objectively correct in denying that inflation reduces real incomes. But if people *think* their real incomes are cut by inflation, in some very real sense they have been cut. The cost of inflation to a nation thus includes a growing sense of dissatisfaction with the performance of the economy, resentment against the general state of affairs, opposition to those who are "in charge". It leads to the hunt for scapegoats: the "profiteers", the trade unions, the bankers—or perhaps those abroad who are said to have "exported" the inflation.

Redistribution by inflation

Even if inflation does not reduce real incomes on the average, it does somewhat redistribute them; it also tends to redistribute wealth. Such redistributions are arbitrary, accidental, and bear no relation to the social worth or economic contribution of those affected by them. The injustice of these redistributions is a major part of the true cost of inflation; and people's recognition of their injustice provides an additional cause of the heightened social and political tensions which accompany inflation.

The nature of any systematic redistributions through inflation is not altogether clear. To be sure, there appears to be some rough tendency for labour's share of the national income to rise slightly faster than its trend during periods when prices are advancing most rapidly, and to fall slightly (relative to trend) in periods when prices are more nearly stable.[1] However, this association is far from perfect, and may not be related to inflation, *per se,* but to some other factors (imperfectly) associated with inflation, including measures taken to combat it. Neither is there clear-cut evidence suggesting that inflation systematically favours rich over poor; farmers over urban dwellers; salaried workers over wage-earners; organized over unorganized workers; or the reverse of any of these. In some countries at least, the main systematic redistributions from inflation appear to be in favour of the younger and against the older members of the society (because retirement incomes are apt to be inflexible in money terms); and against interest recipients and other property owners who hold long-term contracts fixed in money terms.

1. See, for example, chart C, pp. 20-22, in *Inflation: The Present Problem,* Report by the Secretary General (Paris: OECD, December 1970).

The absence of any clear, systematic redistribution from inflation, *per se,* of course does not exclude that, in particular cases, the forces producing inflation—and the responses to those forces by public policy—may not produce substantial redistributions of income in one or another direction.

Inflation may do its greatest injustice, however, not through any systematic redistributions of income between particular groups or classes or individuals, but rather through redistributions among the various individuals in any or every group or class, some of whom reap windfall benefits while others suffer hardship. To an extent, the more sophisticated in every group tend to gain at the expense of the less sophisticated: some are better than others in figuring out ways to benefit from inflation; others have little idea how to protect themselves from it. As Arthur Okun puts it, inflation benefits the "sharpies" at the expense of the "suckers".[1] It is possible that the average income in the latter category is lower than in the former.

As is the case with real income, inflation does not directly reduce the real value of a community's wealth. But it does tend to redistribute it. It obviously shrinks the value of savings held in the form of cash, bank deposits, bonds, and insurance policies, while increasing the values of land, buildings, and shares. And it decreases the real burden of debts of all kinds. Once again, more skilful or knowledgeable individuals are usually able to arrange their wealth holdings and debt positions to benefit from inflation; the less sophisticated tend to lose. Since persons of small means tend to be less knowledgeable, less able to afford professional assistance, and less able to spread the risks of holding wealth in forms that on the average will appreciate in value during inflationary periods, the wealth-redistributive effects of inflation are more likely than the income-redistributive effects to be systematically regressive.

To be sure, redistributions of income and wealth occur continually, and for many reasons, even when the price level is stable. The benefits and hardships of these redistributions are no different in kind from those that result from inflation, *per se*. But if inflation is occurring, *all* redistributions tend to be blamed on the inflation by those who are adversely affected.

If the rate of inflation were steady, most people could learn to adjust to it, and social policies could rather easily be devised to protect the others. It is one of the many paradoxes of inflation, however, that most of the ways in which people can adjust to inflation are very likely to cause it to accelerate, if many begin to take advantage of them. And the faster the rate of inflation, the more unlikely it is to be steady, and the more difficult it is for public policies to keep it steady. Thus the costs of inflation rise more than proportionately to its rate.

---

1. A.M. Okun, H.H. Fowler, M. Gilbert, *Inflation: The Problems it Creates and Policies it Requires,* The Charles C. Moskowitz Lectures (New York University Press, 1970).

Other costs of inflation

Inflation not only creates unjust enrichment and impoverishment, and generates social and political tensions, but also adversely affects economic efficiency and warps the allocation of productive resources. Every country which has experienced a rapid inflation is familiar with these costs. Inflation, or, certainly, the anticipation of inflation, stimulates excessive indebtedness and the wasteful over-building of capital goods and over-accumulation of inventories. It turns valuable managerial and entrepreneurial time and talent from productive pursuits towards speculative efforts to benefit from rising prices, or protective efforts to avoid loss from rising prices and costs. Some seek to make long-term contracts that have no genuine economic advantage and reduce desirable flexibility; for the same reason others may refuse to enter upon long-term contracts that would greatly enhance productive efficiency. Under some circumstances, it can reduce the rate of saving and of economic growth.

There is argument among economists as to how serious these effects on efficiency may be so long as inflation remains moderate and intermittent. So far, it is difficult to prove that the inflation of the past fifteen years has done severe damage in the Atlantic Community. Most students would probably agree that, so far, it has done no appreciable damage. But if the rate of inflation has truly accelerated, and might accelerate further, the damage to efficiency and even to economic growth could easily become more serious.

It used to be held that inflation inevitably had to end in recession or depression, with all the further very real costs that this entailed. Whatever may have been the inevitability of that sequence in the past, it is clearly not an automatic consequence today. Given the responsibility which governments now assume for the state of their economies, a significant recession can only occur through a deliberate government decision or by miscalculation. Conscious of the very real and substantial costs of recessions, governments rightly hesitate to risk plunging their countries' economies into serious recession in order to produce a better price record. Today, the danger that is principally feared is not that inflation automatically and inevitably brings on a recession. It is rather that, if inflation is not stopped by a recession or in some other way, it will continually build up steam, making it increasingly difficult for government policies to slow it down or even keep it from accelerating. The OECD Secretariat clearly believes that this is a very real danger, which accounts for its somewhat alarmed position:

> *The essence of the problem today is that the cumulative economic, social and political consequences of inflation, which up to now some may have regarded as tolerable, could begin to build up rather quickly. Further, the relation between inflation as the cause, and its effects—*

growing distortion, friction and discontent—may not be either clearly or immediately apparent to large segments of public opinion. This is why such a heavy responsibility lies on informed opinion to stress the dangers in the present situation, and the urgent need to give a higher priority to price stability.[1]

So far, reference has been made only to domestic costs of inflation, but there are also international costs. These costs arise not from inflation, *per se,* but from unequal rates of inflation. A country experiencing a prolonged higher-than-average rate of price increase is likely to incur costs both for itself and, indirectly, for other countries with which it has important economic ties. For itself, these costs are likely to take the form, sooner or later, of balance-of-payments difficulties. These difficulties may well force it deliberately to deflate its economy—reducing domestic production, employment, and real incomes; may force it to adopt controls on foreign transactions which clearly impair the economic welfare of its own citizens and probably citizens of other countries; and may force it to devalue its currency. While undergoing inflation itself, it is very likely to be exporting inflationary problems to other countries; and the balance-of-payments difficulties which may be the consequence of its inflation may require action by a number of other countries as well as itself.

Not all balance-of-payments problems arise from differential rates of inflation, and not all differences in rates of price inflation create such problems. Still, at various times, several countries in the Atlantic Community have experienced severe balance of payments difficulties as a result of their unwillingness or inability to control domestic inflation. And on many occasions a number of countries have had to take actions with respect to their international transactions which they would have preferred not to take because either they—or some other country in the Community—were experiencing inflation.

The nature of some of these international problems is discussed in Chapter 4.

The costs of inflation and the decision to control it

Thus, inflation has costs—very significant and very real costs. In the first instance economic, many of these costs translate into social and political tensions which threaten the stability of the social order. These costs are probably tolerable as long as the rate of inflation is low, averaging say 2 or 2½ per cent a year. Above that level, they rise more

1. *Inflation: The Present Problem,* p. 9.

than in proportion to the rate of price increase. The conclusion that we must therefore make a greater effort to control inflation, and the choice of how to do it, require, however, that we understand the causes of inflation in the Atlantic Community, understand what tools governments have at hand to control or eliminate these causes, and be aware of whatever costs may be incurred by using these tools. These are the subject of the balance of this study. Successful control of inflation requires, however, not only the best knowledge that economists and others can supply. It also demands the political willpower and leadership necessary to ensure that the appropriate actions are taken. For this to occur, an informed and concerned public opinion is indispensable.

Inflation in a single country

T his chapter deals with the initial causes and the continuing mechanisms of inflation in a single country. That is, it ignores the impacts of domestic price changes on other countries, or of price changes elsewhere in the world on its economy. In effect, this chapter assumes a "closed economy": one which has no connections with the rest of the world. The following chapter on "International Inflation" redresses this severe oversimplification.

Economists have traditionally suggested the existence of two alternative kinds of domestic inflation: "excess-demand" (or "demand-pull") inflation and "cost-push" inflation. The implied sharp dichotomy between these two types of inflation turns out to be an oversimplification of reality; few inflations can be unambiguously explained as the result exclusively of one or the other of these mechanisms. Yet the two labels do point to two basic forces at work in the inflationary experience of recent years, and thereby contribute to a more generalized explanation of inflation.

Demand-pull inflation

Given the supply of labour and natural resources available to an economy, and its existing stock of capital equipment, there is at any given time an approximate limit on the total output of goods and services which it can produce. This aggregate productive capacity or "potential output" grows over time, through any expansion of the country's labour force, through its accumulation of capital facilities, and particularly through gradual improvements in the joint productivity of these resources.[1] But at any given time, the aggregate quantity of resources is fixed—as is their productivity. And when they are fully employed, total output cannot be further increased.

1. For some countries, it is possible to measure with reasonable accuracy the trend of growth and possibly even the level of potential output. See *Economic Growth 1960-1970* (Paris: OECD, 1966), Appendix B, pp. 101-113.

So long as the community as a whole attemps to buy an aggregate quantity of goods and services not in excess of this potential output, there need be no upward pressure on the price level. But let the aggregate demand for output exceed potential, and prices will be "bid up" by the excessive demand. Many buyers of individual goods and services, wanting more than is available, willingly pay the higher prices (which sellers quite willingly charge), rather than do without. Producers of goods and services, seeking to accommodate the larger demand, compete with each other for the available labour, natural resources, and productive facilities, in an effort—collectively futile—to expand their employment and thereby their output.[1] In the process, they are willing to pay higher prices for productive services rather than to do without them, especially since the output produced by these services can now be sold at higher prices. In a sense, the bidding up of the prices of the productive resources—and especially the wages of labour—is the fundamental feature of the demand-pull inflation; for it is the shortage of such resources—relative to the over-all demand for output which requires their use—which is the basic cause of the price rise. Plausible empirical measurements have sometimes been made of the size of the "inflationary gap" in an economy—the excess of aggregate demand over potential output—even though, in these circumstances, the level of aggregate demand cannot be directly observed.

Historically, the situations which most resemble the above sketch of excess-demand inflation have usually occurred in periods of large deficits in government budgets, most often occasioned by wars. The government's demand for goods and services at such times is greatly increased, but not enough is done correspondingly to reduce private demands—through higher taxes, tighter money and higher interest rates, or direct controls limiting the private use of resources. Less frequently, situations which resemble the demand-pull type of inflation have been associated with significant bulges in aggregate *private* demands—as for example when there is a widespread boom in the purchase or production of capital equipment, of residential structures, or of consumer durable goods, sometimes as a

1. Current production of almost every individual good or service is usually below its own particular capacity limits, which are based on the existing supplies of whatever specialized labour services or unique capital facilities may be required for the production of that good or service. (These particular limits, of course, can be overcome, in time, by training more workers or building more of the specialized equipment.) The limit on a country's aggregate output, however, falls far short of the sum of the individual limits on each of its many individual outputs. At most times and places, the ultimate limiting factor is the over-all supply of labour. Thus, even when most resources are employed, individual outputs can be rather easily expanded, merely by drawing labour and other resources, as necessary, from the production of other goods and services. But this reduces the ability to produce the other goods by an amount roughly equal (in value) to the expanded ability to produce the goods in question. Thus, whatever the proportions (within limits) in which individual goods and services are demanded and produced, there is a roughly constant value (expressed in constant prices) of the maximum aggregate production that is feasible at any given time.

consequence of a prolonged previous interruption in the production of these goods (e.g., following a war or depression). A significant reduction in potential output through wartime destruction of capital facilities has sometimes been the proximate source of an inflationary gap. For some countries, a large and continuing boom in export demand may have been the source of an excessive total demand.

Whatever the original source of an inflationary gap between demand and potential, the rise in prices which results does little or nothing—at least directly—to remove the excess, and to close the gap. For the higher prices paid to productive resources increase the money incomes—the aggregate wages and profits measured in money terms—of the community. As noted in Chapter 2, real incomes will thus not be reduced by the higher prices. Buyers can still afford to attempt to buy as much as they tried to buy before prices (and money incomes) rose. Thus, the rise in prices that was generated by the inflationary gap does little or nothing to close the gap. If the buyers' demand was originally excessive, it will tend still to be, generating a further bidding up of prices, wages, and profits, in more or less indefinite sequence.

This process will continue until something occurs to eliminate the inflationary gap—to cut back sufficiently aggregate demand relative to potential output. The normal growth of potential output is not likely to do this, for a greater ability to contribute to production is ordinarily accompanied by a corresponding automatic expansion of incomes earned, and thus of demand.[1] Price stability is more likely to be restored by events or measures which tend to limit or cut back the growth of aggregate demand. Such events or measures will not ordinarily similarly limit or reduce potential output.

One such event which tends to restrain the expansion of demand occurs rather automatically as the result of the inflation itself—namely, a disproportionate expansion of tax collections. In most countries, tax receipts tend to be quite sensitive to the money value of total output and income. As prices rise—even apart from any growth in the physical volume of output, although that, too, may be occurring—the amount collected by all levels of government in sales, excise, value-added, and income taxes goes up automatically. This expansion of government revenues will surely be at least in proportion to the rise in the price level, and, if the income tax is an important source of revenue, considerably more than in proportion to the rise in prices.

A disproportionate rise of tax collections means that private incomes, *after taxes,* will rise less than in proportion to the rise of prices. To this extent, real incomes, after taxes, are reduced, and this will tend to dampen

---

1. To be sure, the increment of aggregate demand resulting from the growth of potential output is likely not to be quite as large as the increment of potential output: but the gap is reduced only by any difference between the two, not by the full increment of potential.

the expansion of *private* demand. Thus the expansion of *total* demand will also be dampened, unless all the extra tax revenues due to inflation are immediately and automatically spent by the government. Since the prices which governments must pay for their purchases and payrolls will also rise due to inflation, the net dampening effect of inflated tax collections on the growth of aggregate demand may not be large, but it is sufficiently important not to be overlooked. Often, the expansion of funds appropriated for government expenditures lags somewhat behind the rise of prices, so that higher prices in part reduce the real volume of government purchases, thus further reducing aggregate demand. As will be indicated in Chapter 5, governments may not merely allow this passive dampening of inflation to occur, but may—and usually should—attempt actively to restrain inflation, by raising tax rates and/or cutting back their less essential expenditures.

A second event which can automatically dampen the expansion of demand relative to supply may occur in the monetary sphere. If the central bank fails to expand the money supply as rapidly as prices rise, interest rates will be forced up, making borrowing more expensive and thus perhaps deterring the growth of demand.[1] Whether this automatic effect of inflation on interest rates will occur and how effective it may be depend on the policy of the central bank. If its policy is to stabilize interest rates, it will thereby fail to place any restraint on aggregate demand. On the other hand, if it is determined to fight the inflation, it will not merely passively allow inflation to drive up interest rates, it may actively seek to increase the cost and reduce the availability of credit. Such a response will be discussed more fully in Chapter 5.

If there were systematic redistributions of income as a result of inflation, which altered significantly the proportions of the aggregate income accruing to those who spend a larger-than-average portion of their incomes and to those who spend a smaller proportion, this too could affect aggregate demand. However, as noted in Chapter 2, there is no clear evidence to support the existence of such redistributions. Nevertheless, in particular cases, such redistributions may occur, and can affect demand in either direction.

---

1. As experience with inflation generates the expectation of further inflation, this too should tend to raise interest rates. However, the same expectation of inflation which makes lenders demand higher rates, to compensate for the expected reduction in the value of their loan, makes borrowers willing to pay higher interest rates, because they foresee higher money returns from which to pay the interest charges and meet the principal when it becomes due. Thus the rise in interest rates due to inflationary expectations is by itself unlikely to curb the expansion of demand. Indeed, if borrowers are more alert to the prospects of inflation than are lenders, the expectation of inflation may even tend to enlarge total demand.

Demand-pull as a matter of degree

The implications of this theory of demand-pull inflation for the avoidance or control of inflation seem clear enough: since inflation arises from excessive total demand, it is necessary to avoid allowing an excess to develop; if it has appeared, it must be eliminated. This may be easier said than done; nevertheless, in principle, if policy can successfully avoid or eliminate excessive demand, it can avoid or eliminate inflation. Unfortunately, we have come to see that this theory—as presented above—is seriously oversimplified. We now recognize that having "too much demand" is not an "all-or-nothing" thing. Only during a major war, perhaps, is there a classic "inflationary gap", in the sense that aggregate demand exceeds the physical maximum output which the economy could produce, and thus causes a genuine bidding up of the price of everything. In fact, prices begin to rise long before aggregate demand comes even close to the maximum achievable level of output. The reason for this can be traced to the imperfect mobility of labour and other resources, combined with the fact that the pattern of aggregate demand—its distribution among industries, commodities, firms, localities—is not fixed, but instead is constantly shifting.

What we call the aggregate supply of output actually arises from the productive activities of a vast congeries of individual firms and collections of firms, each of which is subject to some ultimate limitation on its output, and some of which are subject to substantially increasing costs as they approach this limit. Each firm is able to increase its output, after some point, only by drawing into use labour, materials or facilities of poorer quality (at least for *its* purposes), or for which it must pay a higher price in order to draw them from greater distances (geographical or otherwise), or by using its existing resources more intensively and thus past the point of maximum efficiency. Corresponding to the congeries of productive units is a congeries of demands for the particular products of these units, each demand fluctuating somewhat independently of the others, even though most demands rise or fall at more or less the same time, as the tide of aggregate demand surges and ebbs. There is, nevertheless, enough independence in the move-ment of the individual demands that, at all times, individual firms and industries will be operating at quite different distances from the absolute limits on their individual outputs.

Even at a level of aggregate demand which leaves large quantities of labour and other resources idle, some firms—a varying assortment of them—will be encountering rising demand, and some may even be increasing their outputs sufficiently that they find their costs rising, and thus may be raising their prices. For most other firms, demand is inadequate or even declining. But a deficiency of demand either for products or labour services has little impact in reducing prices or wages, unless the deficiency becomes very large. If aggregate demand rises, more and more productive units (but a varying assortment of them) will be pushed into operating

67

under conditions of increasing cost, attempting to satisfy their increased demand by using resources more intensively and by drawing in labour and other resources of poorer quality or from greater distance. Moreover, increased costs of recruitment, training, lowered productivity while learning, and labour turnover are incurred. Thus, in more and more cases—as an alternative to incurring these higher costs—higher wage rates are offered to attract more suitable workers from other employers, other industries, other occupations, or other locations, or higher prices are offered to obtain the more suitable materials or facilities.

At first, the expanding firms and their suppliers primarily bring into employment previously idle resources, or attract resources from other firms which are able easily to replace them by employing previously idle resources. But, increasingly, as aggregate demand expands, the firms that succeed in expanding their outputs do so mainly by bidding away resources, particularly labour, from other producers who are unable easily to replace them, except, again, by stealing from some other firm. Eventually, if the pressure of aggregate demand rises sufficiently, no firm will be able to expand its output except by reducing another firm's output. But long before this point has been reached, prices—and money incomes—will have been rising. These price and income increases, like any others, form the basis for further price and income increases: demand is but little reduced, because money incomes have risen, too. The competitive pressures raising wages and prices thus continue to operate, but from an ever higher base. The effects are identical with those of the simple case of demand-pull inflation, except that now we must recognize varying *degrees* of demand pressure, which create various *degrees* of partial or local shortages, which in turn make producers willing, in various *degrees,* to offer higher prices or wages in order to acquire or to hold on to those supplies of materials, facilities, and labour that are most readily available and most perfectly suited to their needs. Thus the rate of demand-pull inflation is a function of the level of utilization of productive resources, which can be measured, at least roughly, by the global unemployment rate.

There is no magic line crossed in the process of the expansion of demand at which point aggregate demand exceeds aggregate supply; nor is it ever possible for demand to become so great that every unit of idle resources—of whatever quality—is drawn into employment. There can only be a *conventional* line drawn—at a point which someone decides represents that at which the social benefits of still higher production and employment no longer exceed the social costs of the still faster rise of prices that would necessarily accompany a further increase of output. In the United States, for instance, "potential output" is conventionally defined as the level of output which would be forthcoming at an unemployment rate of 4 per cent. The sense in which such an output level represents maximum feasible production—if it is to have any such meaning—is that this is the point at which government policy will shift from a posture of encouraging (or at least permitting) an expansion of aggregate demand, to a posture of attempting to restrain or reduce demand.

Thus the level of aggregate demand is seen as significantly related to the rate of inflation. But it is not an "all or nothing" thing: the higher the pressure of aggregate demand, the greater the inflationary pressure from the side of demand. Moreover, this way of describing the role of aggregate demand focuses attention on factors that may affect the extent to which a rise in aggregate demand causes prices to rise. They are many. They include, in important measure, factors that can be affected by government policies over and beyond policies affecting aggregate demand. Some of these will be described in Chapter 5.

The arithmetic of wages, productivity, and prices

Both to round out this analysis of demand-pull inflation and to set the stage for the analysis of cost-push inflation, we need to understand some basic arithmetic about the relationships among wages, productivity, prices and profits. This rather simple arithmetic is of vital importance not only for the understanding of inflation but also for the development of policies to contain it.

Reference has several times been made to the concept of "productivity", and to its gradual advance over time. In all but the most stagnant economies, there has occurred and continues to occur a relatively steady and gradual increase in the output that can be produced by any fixed inputs of labour and capital resources. This increase of productivity—output per unit of inputs—arises from many sources and the interactions among them: the improving average education, health, skill, experience, and attitudes of workers; better management and organization; and the accumulation of knowledge and improvement of technology, some but not all of it embodied in the new capital goods which replace or displace older, less efficient ones. We can also measure this increase in productivity as output per man hour—i.e., in terms of labour input alone—which is a more convenient and familiar concept. Because the use of capital has typically increased somewhat faster than the number of man hours worked, output per man hour has also benefited from an enlarged use of capital per worker. It has thus increased even more rapidly than the output per unit of total resources used. The rise of output per man hour has ranged, over the decade of the 1960s, from about $2\frac{1}{2}$ per cent a year in the United Kingdom, 3 per cent in the United States, and 5 per cent in Germany, to 10 per cent a year in Japan. To be sure, the productivity per unit of *total* resources used increased somewhat less rapidly in each country, because the use of capital increased more rapidly than the use of labour.

Since any fixed input of resources can produce a rising output over time, an increase over time in the price per unit paid to those resources which does not exceed the increase in their productivity does not raise unit costs of production. Indeed, if the prices of productive services rise by any less than the amount of productivity gains, unit costs will fall.

Suppose, for example, that 100 workers, each working 8 hours a day (i.e., 800 man hours) produce 1,000 units of a particular product. Suppose that the wage rate is $ 5 an hour and the product sells for $ 6 a unit. Total labour costs then are $ 4,000 a day (800 times $ 5), or $ 4 a unit of output ($ 4,000 divided by 1,000 units). Sales revenues are $ 6,000 a day (1,000 units at $ 6), leaving $ 2,000 a day, or $ 2 a unit, to cover the costs of purchased materials and services, depreciation and interest on the capital employed, and profit. These hypothetical data are shown in the column "Year 1" of Table 6.

Table 6

Costs and Revenues in a Hypothetical Firm

	Year 1	Year 2	
		Constant wage rate	Wages increased in proportion to productivity
Output per day	1,000	1,050	1,050
Number of workers employed	100	100	100
Hours worked per day	8	8	8
Man hours worked per day	800	800	800
Wage rate per man hour	$ 5.00	$ 5.00	$ 5.25
Daily labour costs	$4,000	$4,000	$4,200
Labour cost per unit of output	$ 4.00	$ 3.81	$ 4.00
Price per unit of output	$ 6.00	$ 6.00	$ 6.00
Sales revenues	$6,000	$6,300	$6,300
Sales revenues available for costs other than labour costs, and for profits	$2,000	$2,300	$2,100

Suppose that a year later output has risen by 5 per cent to 1,050 units a day, with no increase in man hour employment. That is, productivity (output per man hour) has risen by 5 per cent. (See columns "Year 2" in the Table.) If the wage rate should remain at $ 5 an hour, the labour cost per unit would fall to $ 3.81 per unit ($ 4,000 divided by 1,050 units). Indeed, even if wage rates rise by as much as 5 per cent, to $ 5.25 an hour, unit labour cost will be no higher than before—$ 4 per unit

70

(800 man hours at $ 5.25, for a daily wage bill of $ 4,200, divided by the output of 1,050 units).

If the price of output remains at $ 6 a unit, sales revenues will rise to $ 6,300 (1,050 units at $ 6), leaving $ 2,100 a day, or still $ 2 a unit, to cover purchased materials and services, depreciation and interest, and profit. If prices of purchased materials and services remain unchanged and if the amount of them required per unit of output should remain the same, and if the quantity of invested capital and interest rates should remain unchanged too, not only aggregate profits but even profit as a percentage return on capital would rise, unless prices were reduced. Historically, however, for most economies (although surely not for every firm or industry) the total value of capital in use has grown more or less in proportion with output—i.e., more rapidly than labour input. (This increased use of capital is one source of the rise of output per man hour.) Moreover, the amount of purchased materials and supplies required per unit of output usually declines, if at all, only through an increased use of capital per unit of output. If both the input of purchased materials and the amount of capital in use grow in the same proportion as output (and interest rates are constant), wage rates can advance in proportion to productivity; unit labour costs, unit total costs, and the price level can all remain stable; while aggregate profits advance proportionately with the aggregate value of output and the aggregate income of labour.

It follows, of course, that if wage rates advance more rapidly than productivity, labour costs per unit of output will rise, and either prices will also have to rise, or else profits will be reduced.

During a period of demand-pull inflation, when both prices and wages are being bid up by excessive demand, we typically see wages being bid up more rapidly than prices, and real wages gradually increasing over time, in proportion to the rise of productivity. This, however, is not inconsistent with a simultaneous rise in both nominal and real profits. Nor, obviously, is a "guidepost", or a national wage-price policy, which calls for wages to rise over time in proportion to productivity and the level of prices to remain stable, inconsistent with such a rise in profits. In the most probable case, it would leave income distribution essentially unchanged.

Cost-push inflation

With this understanding of the relationships among wages, prices, and productivity, we are now ready to consider the second "ideal type" of inflation, which is described as occurring even in the absence of any excess demand for goods and services—that is, in the face both of appreciable unemployment and of excess plant capacity. Starting from a situation of general price stability, we can imagine that a strong trade union or several strong unions (more or less simultaneously), or one or more large employer, or even both some unions and some employers, become dissatisfied with their existing (real) incomes and seek to increase them. The unions persuade or force employers to grant exceptionally large wage increases, which raise unit costs (that is, wage increases in excess of productivity gains). Their employers pass along the extra cost to buyers. The same employers—or others—may try to raise their profit margins by lifting their prices faster than costs rise, or even if costs don't rise.

If other workers and employers were willing to accept the reduction of their own real incomes which resulted from these higher wages and prices, the rise in the general level of prices might stop there. But if the initial effort to raise money incomes at the expense of the rest of the community were at all widely based—and thus noticeably affected the average price level—the rest of the community would be unlikely to accept its deprivation. Other unions and employers might possess the same kind of power to raise wages and prices. They would be likely to fight back—perhaps not merely by raising wages and prices enough to restore their original positions, but maybe even by attempting to match the income gains sought by the initiators of the inflation. The resulting more general rise in the price level, however, would frustrate both the efforts of those ambitious to improve their relative positions, as well as the intended protective adjustments of those hoping merely to maintain their positions. This frustration may lead to repeated actions to push up wages and prices, further inflation, repeated frustration, and a continuing spiral of upward pressures on costs and prices. What is essentially happening is that the sum of the incomes desired by those participating in production exceeds the value of that production. The nominal value of the production is thus forced up, through higher prices. But the nominal incomes desired go up in proportion to prices, and their sum continues to exceed the value of the product.

A cost-push inflation may and frequently does arise from the activities of groups already well-off, who desire further to raise their shares of the national income—while other sectors of the society resist the corresponding reduction of their shares. On the other hand, the original source of the cost push can reflect legitimate discontent by segments of society whose income shares are in some meaningful sense unfairly low—while the rest of society resists. In either case the competition for incomes—the pressures for and against a redistribution—creates inflation, usually without any significant redistribution occurring. The important conclusion to be drawn is not that whatever income distribution exists is correct or cannot be changed, but rather that attempting to change income distribution through the process of pushing up prices or wages in the market is (a) likely to be ineffective, and (b) almost sure to be inflationary. Other means are available, and far more effective, should a society conclude that its income distribution needs to be changed.

In a cost-push inflation, those who have the greatest market power (or who are most willing to use it) may, of course, be able to stay somewhat ahead in the income competition at the expense of those with lesser market power. Still, even though the inflation arises from cost push rather than excessive demand, higher prices will still, *on the average,* raise money incomes by the same extra amount. Thus, as we have repeatedly stressed, inflation *per se,* does not directly raise or lower the average real income of the community. The advance of productivity, however, continues to permit both aggregate real income and real incomes per capita to grow, because it permits the average of money incomes to rise faster than the average of prices. Likewise, of course, whether inflation arises from cost push or demand pull, it gives rise to the same automatic forces which tend at least somewhat to reduce aggregate demand: through the effects of higher prices on government revenues and spending, and through their effects on interest rates. However, since a cost-push inflation does not in the first place involve any excessive level of demand, these possible automatic limitations on the growth of demand have no clear significance for this case—at least no clear significance for the continuance of the inflation. They would, of course, tend somewhat to reduce output and employment, even if not the rate of price increase.

The preceding pages have now sketched two alternative theories of inflation—in one of which inflation results from an excessive total demand for goods and services, and in the other of which—even in the absence of excessive aggregate demand—prices are pushed up by the efforts of labour and/or management to raise incomes through a collectively bargained increase of wages (in excess of productivity gains) or an enlargement of profit margins.

These explanations need not, of course, be seen as mutually exclusive. One might easily hold that inflation is sometimes (as surely in wartime) caused by excessive aggregate demand, but that it can also arise "spontaneously", in the absence of excessive demand. Some economists, however, deny that inflation can ever arise except through excessive demand. Despite appearances to the contrary, they hold that there is always excessive demand whenever the price level rises. Or they may admit that unions or large firms with considerable "market power" are able temporarily to force up their own wages or prices, even in the absence of excess demand, but contend that such increases cannot be sustained or generalized unless government policy "validates" the higher price level by measures of monetary or fiscal policy that raise aggregate demand. The author will here simply assert his agreement with the majority of economists—as well as with most businessmen and labour leaders—who recognize that strong trade unions and large firms do have the power in a meaningful sense to "push" up wage and price levels. The "wage explosions" in France in 1968, in Italy in 1969 and 1970, and in the United Kingdom in 1970 and 1971, for instance,

73

clearly occurred in the absence of anything that could reasonably be regarded as excessive demand.

It may very well be true that if government fiscal or monetary policy-makers had not been willing to recognize the new price levels which the new wage rates implied, these wage explosions might have raised prices a little less, and also have reduced employment and ouput somewhat. But in the absence of that government recognition, the wage increases would not have been reversed, prices would not have been restored to their previous level. It would be an incredible distortion to say that the subsequent government policies *caused* the wage explosions and the resulting rise of prices, or that different monetary and fiscal policies would have prevented them.

An alternate form of statement of the argument that inflation can arise only from excessive demand is to say that there is always some level of unemployment so high and of economic activity so low as to stop any inflation. Since government can control the levels of unemployment and activity by manipulating aggregate demand, any inflation must be "caused" by a government decision to maintain "too high" a level of aggregate demand. This method of statement may seem more plausible, but only because it defines the problem of cost-push inflation out of existence.

The apparent way to eliminate the *cause* of any cost-push inflation would be to reduce the "market power" of trade unions and large firms which enables them to raise wages and prices even when there is no excessive demand. Establishing sufficiently "atomistic" competition in all labour and product markets should, in principle, make all prices and wages responsive only to the forces of market supply and demand. However, it is not clear whether such a policy would be economically (to say nothing of politically) feasible. It is probable that it would require the sacrifice of a very considerable part of the economic advantages which accrue from large-scale production; and society might lose a great deal from the destruction of the organizations that give workers a feeling of "belonging" and "participating" in the economic, social, and political processes and decisions of their nation.

To the extent that cost-push pressures arise from basic dissatisfactions with an existing distribution of income (or of political power or social privilege), another remedy—and perhaps the only basic one—would be to alter that distribution through policies of taxation, regulation, social services, and all the other means available to governments.

In the absence of changes that either reduce the aggregate of market power or reduce the pressures to use it to alter an "unfair" income distribution, stopping a cost-push inflation would appear to require either direct controls on wages and prices, or some form of non-compulsory "incomes policy", to curb the competitive efforts to enlarge income shares which are the cause of a cost-push inflation.

Market power as a function of the level of demand

However, just as we must recognize that "too much demand" is not an all-or-nothing thing, so we must recognize a similar qualification of cost-push inflation. The "market power" that permits unions to push up wages or firms to enlarge their margins over their costs "even in the absence of excess demand" is not something which particular firms or unions either do or do not possess. Rather, various firms and unions possess it in varying degree. It can be defined (although not measured) in terms of the effective degree of discretion which firms possess to set one price rather than another, and which employers and unions possess to set one wage level rather than another. Not only is this discretionary power possessed in varying degrees by different firms and unions, but the over-all extent of this power may change from time to time, in part dependent on the extent to which resources generally are or are not fully employed. When aggregate demand is high and unemployment low, unions have more freedom to force large wage-rate increases because

— unions are then more willing to assume the risk of a strike in their bargaining: in the case of a strike, their members (or their members' wives) can more easily get other jobs;

— employers are then less willing to risk a strike in their bargaining: in slack times, any loss of production from a strike could easily be made up later on, or inventories could easily be built up to prepare for it; in prosperous times, a net loss of production from a strike is difficult to avoid;

— employers can then more easily visualize the possibility of a future labour shortage, and can see some possible future advantage in a generous wage level which may make it easier to hold on to their workers; and

— employers can then be more certain of being able to pass along to their customers the cost of an expensive settlement made to buy off a strike.

When times are prosperous, producers find that they have more discretion about the prices they can charge. If they raise prices in an effort to widen profit margins they have less fear that their competitors may not follow their price increase and thus that they will lose sales (their competitors are operating near to capacity and could not easily take on extra business); or if they do lose sales by raising prices, alternative profitable uses for their productive resources are more easily available. Those items in their lines of products which they have regarded as least profitable can more easily be dropped, or their prices raised. Most firms have "target" levels of earnings which are much of the time in excess of their actual earnings. When competition permits it, they seek to achieve these "fair

75

and reasonable" target rates of return. When aggregate demand is high, competition is more likely to permit it.

Of course, recognizing that the extent of market power will vary systematically in relation to the level of aggregate demand does not preclude recognizing that the extent of market power may also change for other reasons—that many structural, institutional, social, and attitudinal factors will also affect the extent to which market power exists—and will be used—to generate an inflationary rise of prices. Indeed, such changes may be of exceedingly great importance.

A more general theory of inflation

Still, there clearly is some systematic element present, which provides a second reason why the rate of inflation tends to be related to the overall level of aggregate demand. A high level of demand not only creates more situations of relative shortage of goods and labour which cause wages and prices to be *bid* up; it also creates more market power which allows wages and prices to be *pushed* up where there is no shortage. Both of these effects may be occurring at once in different sectors of an economy operating at a high level of employment. Indeed, in the "real world", it may be exceedingly difficult to distinguish which force is operating in any particular market. In the last analysis, one can even debate whether these are two different forces, or only two different ways of describing a single phenomenon.

Admitting the possibility that both kinds of inflationary forces can occur calls attention to the "mixed" forms of inflation in which both demand-pull and cost-push forces are present. We can, for example, recognize that an inflationary process may be initiated by forces of demand and sustained by those of cost push, even after the demand forces that initiated the inflation have faded out of existence.[1] Similarly, an inflation

1. One version even explains how inflation may arise from a mere *shift* of demand from one sector of industry or class of products to another, with no excess of aggregate demand. The higher demand for the products or services for which demand has increased raises their prices and the incomes earned in their production; but downward rigidity of other prices and wages prevents any off-setting decline in prices in the areas for which demand is reduced. Thus the general level of prices is raised, and organized workers seek extra wage increases to offset the rising cost of living (some may get such increases automatically through "sliding-scale" or escalator provisions). Indeed, workers generally may seek not only protection from the higher cost of living, but to match the real-wage gains secured by those whose wages benefited from the initial rise in demand. The localized wage and price increase is thus generalized, and an inflationary spiral is initiated. Market forces call for what should be a mere rearrangement of relative prices and wages; but rigidities, and the unwillingness of those who would suffer from the rearrangement to accept the relative worsening of their incomes, convert the rearrangement of relative prices into an upward movement of the entire price level. If the subsequent rise in *other* wages and prices prevents the shift of resources into increased production of the goods initially in larger demand, prices may be further bid up in that area, helping to perpetuate the spiral.

which begins with a cost push could strengthen aggregate demand sufficiently to generate some upward "pull" on prices as well. This could happen if the initial "push" redistributed income from groups having a low propensity to spend in favour of those who would spend much or all of the extra incomes they obtained. Moreover, an initial cost-push rise of prices might generate expectations of further rise, which would cause buyers to step up their spending in an effort to beat the price rise, thus helping to insure continuance of the inflation.

But we have arrived not merely at the recognition of possible "mixtures" of two separate types of inflation. Rather, we have reached a more general analysis of inflation, which can replace the dichotomous approach followed up to this point. This more general analysis incorporates important elements drawn from both demand-pull and cost-push theories, along with other significant considerations included in neither. Some of these other elements have already been referred to, but will be further considered in subsequent paragraphs.

1. *Downward rigidity of wages and prices.* Most wage rates, along with the goods and services, other than farm products and internationally-traded raw materials, are not equally flexible in an upward and downward direction, in response to variations in the strength of aggregate demand. To be sure, there are many industries in which productivity gains are exceedingly rapid, and the trend of whose prices may be downward except during the most inflationary periods. But the reference here is to an asymmetrical response of prices to the strengthening as opposed to the weakening of demand. When demand slackens, firms in many industries resist price declines as long as they possibly can, and prefer to make them, if at all, by giving selective and temporary discounts from standard prices. But when markets strengthen beyond some point, they readily raise their price schedules. Today, outright wage rate reductions rarely if ever occur in most countries. Downward inflexibility arises from minimum wage laws, and from social disapproval of direct action to reduce a worker's pay. Of course, many workers suffer wage reductions when they lose their jobs and can only find another at lower pay. Pay is also frequently reduced by shorter working weeks or the loss of overtime. But these do not reduce basic costs of production as would wage rate reductions.

The asymmetry between the upward and downward flexibilities of wages and prices rests on a very simple and fundamental fact. For any individual seller of goods or labour (or of anything else), a reduction of price or wage means a reduction of real income; an increase means an increase of real income. People like higher incomes, dislike lower ones; they seek the one and resist the other. It is true that a reduction of the whole wage-price level has no effect on real incomes—nor a rise, either. But no individual wage or price reduction (or increase) can ever be accurately described as merely part of a general price level change.

77

Downward inflexibility of wages and prices creates a severe bias towards inflation right from the start. Prices and wages are essentially on a ratchet. They move easily upwards, but rarely and with difficulty downwards. Circumstances that cause an appreciable number of individual prices and wages to rise almost surely cause the average price level to rise: offsets in the form of lower prices and wages are rarely available. Instead, the rise in some prices and wages tends to produce increases in others. This phenomenon of downward price and wage rigidity will be further referred to below.

2. *The pattern of productivity, wage rate, and unit labour cost changes.* Although the advance of productivity over time occurs reasonably smoothly and steadily for whole economies, its advance is likely to be both jerky and unequal in particular sectors, industries, or firms. In the United States, for instance, the advance of productivity has tended for many years to be remarkably rapid in the agricultural sector, considerably in excess of that in any other major sector. Among the non-agricultural sectors, the trend of productivity gains ranges from an average of 5 or 6 per cent a year in public utilities and communications, to 1 or 2 per cent a year in services. Mining, manufacturing, transport, trade, and construction fall between the extremes, in roughly descending order. Somewhat the same ranking holds in other countries, although there are major exceptions. The diversity of productivity trends of course becomes all the wider as we consider finer subdivisions of economic activity—e.g., industries, or even firms, instead of these broad sectors. Within manufacturing, for example, many of the new industries generate rapid productivity gains, while more traditional industries are likely to show gains more like those occurring in the service trades.

What this diverse behaviour of productivity gains implies for the individual trends of unit labour costs, and hence of prices, in the various sectors, industries, and firms that make up the economy depends on what happens to wage rates in different industries and firms. For example, if the average wage rate in each industry should rise in exact proportion to the rise of productivity in that industry, unit labour costs would be constant over time in every industry. Or, if the wage rate in each industry should rise by the increase in productivity in that industry, plus 3 per cent, unit labour costs would rise by 3 per cent in every industry.

This kind of pattern of wage increases is not, however, likely to occur, nor would it, in general, be a desirable outcome if it did. Instead of wages rising in proportion to productivity—industry-by-industry, or even firm-by-firm—there are strong forces tending to impose a considerable uniformity in the movement of wage rates. One reason is that all industries and firms must compete with each other for workers. If the wage rates offered in a single labour market for any particular type and quality of labour differ substantially, those employers who offer the lower wages will have trouble attracting or retaining workers, at least in times of high employment. Moreover, differences in wage rates as among various labour market areas

78

or geographical regions, or among workers of various types, qualities, or skills must bear some relationship to the relative attractiveness of the work and the costs of qualifying for it—at least to the extent that workers are able to change their residence, undertake training, or gain experience that permits them to shift among categories in response to changing differentials.

To be sure, the information which workers receive about the wages paid by various employers, and the associated job requirements, is far from perfect in every national labour market. And workers' mobility as among employers, industries, occupations, and regions in response to whatever information they have as to the opportunities available to them is also far from perfect. This is one reason why expanding firms may need to pay substantially higher wage rates to attract workers from other employments. It also means that wage differentials may emerge and may persist for considerable periods, that would be erased if information and mobility were better. Moreover, one objective of trade unions is to raise wages for their own members, and their unequal effectiveness in doing this tends to create further persistent wage differences, particularly to the extent that the unions are able to control entry into their trade or employment.

Nevertheless, competition does *tend* to make wage rates move more or less together over time, and this tendency is strongly reinforced by concepts of equity or social justice, as well as by the rather powerful forces of imitation and jealousy.

These forces, both competitive and institutional, which cause wages to move more or less similarly over time have several consequences, any one or more of which may be exceedingly important for the inflationary process in a particular economy at a particular time.

a. If some groups of workers receive large wage increases—because of a sharp rise in the demand for their services, because they have increased their ability to exclude others from entering their trade, or simply because their trade union has become more aggressive or effective in its bargaining—this imposes a strong tendency for wages in other industries and occupations to be similarly raised, generating an extra rise in unit labour costs and hence in prices throughout the economy.

b. The forces imposing a tendency towards wage uniformity make it exceedingly difficult for relative wage rates—and thus the distribution of wage income among various groups or classes of workers—to be altered significantly in the market, however unjust or socially inappropriate existing income differentials are felt to be. Efforts of workers or employers to alter wage differentials in favour of one group of workers will be largely frustrated by the extra wage increases demanded and received by others. Successful action to alter differentials may instead require programmes which will effectively alter relative supplies of labour of various types: through special training programmes, special aids to mobility, or the breaking down of artificial barriers against the entry into various trades and occupations.

79

c. To the extent that wage-rate changes tend to be similar in all industries, while productivity trends differ widely (as they do), the trends of unit labour costs in various industries will be quite diverse. If the price level is to remain stable, this means not merely that the general rate of wage increases must be close to the average rate of productivity rise, but also that prices must decline in the industries in which productivity rises by more than the average rate. If, for any reason, such price decreases fail to occur, price stability cannot be maintained. In the first place, mere arithmetic requires that price increases in the industries with less than average productivity gains be offset by price reductions in industries with more than average gains. If the reductions fail to occur, the average price level will rise. Moreover, if wages rise only in proportion to productivity, but the average price level nevertheless increases, the resulting shift in the distribution of real income from labour to owners of enterprises will lead workers to demand larger wage increases, which raise the average level of labour costs. Most particularly, the failure to reduce prices in industries with large productivity gains but wage increases proportional only to the economy-wide average productivity increase, creates large profit gains in such industries, which become tempting targets for trade-union wage demands. If extra large increases are secured in such high-profit industries, they will be copied elsewhere, pushing up labour costs and prices across the board.

3. *Further institutional aspects of the inflationary process.* A great many institutional arrangements, which nominally or traditionally exist for other reasons, turn out to play a significant role in the intersectoral transmission and the perpetuation of inflation. For instance, if firms set prices so as to yield some standard percentage mark-up over specified elements of direct costs, and there is much evidence that they do, this tends to convert every rise in wages or material prices into a proportionate rise in selling prices. Yet when the level of costs is constantly changing, firms may have little choice but to follow such a formula. Following a "pattern" set by the most recent wage increase in another firm or industry (or, perhaps, the *highest* among the recent wage increases agreed on in other firms or industries) is an easy way to resolve otherwise irreconcilable claims in bargaining. It is also a way to guarantee that an inflationary spiral will continue to turn. Yet the development and imitation of wage "patterns" can be shown to play a major role in wage bargaining in many countries.

Institutional arrangements relating to the process of wage determination are exceedingly important in the dynamics of inflation. The tradition of contracts for fixed terms—increasingly two- and three-year terms in the United States—provides a great element of inertia: preserving stability once this is achieved, but perpetuating inflation once this is underway. US labour contracts negotiated in 1962-64 provided a built-in stability of labour costs in many industries for several years afterwards. Similarly, wage contracts agreed upon in 1970 have already provided large wage increases for many workers in both 1971 and 1972; large wage increases in 1971 are built into other contracts negotiated in 1969. Workers negotiating new agreements in 1971 will wish to do at least that well.

The stability of labour costs provided by long-term contracts negotiated during non-inflationary periods is at least potentially compromised if those contracts provide escalator clauses, as an increasing number of US agreements do. To be sure, escalator provisions have no impact on wage rates if prices do not rise. But they quickly spread or generalize, and perpetuate, upward movements of prices that originate elsewhere. Wage rates inevitably respond in any case to rising prices, even without formal escalator provisions. But the response is full, prompt, and automatic where escalator provisions exist, whereas in their absence it is likely to be partial, delayed, and to require negotiation. Moreover, there is no clear evidence that the existence of escalator provisions results in the agreement on substantially smaller "basic" wage increases in multi-year contracts negotiated during inflationary periods. And, of course, escalator provisions are never permitted to operate to reduce wage rates. Their use in the United States and probably elsewhere must be judged to strengthen an institutional bias towards inflation.

Where wage agreements are made for an unspecified term, as for example in the United Kingdom, the institutional forces are different. Such agreements can provide little assured stability of labour costs. Whether a new agreement has embodied a large or a small increase can only be determined by how long it lasts before it is again revised. To the extent that current economic conditions affect negotiated wage changes, the British agreement can be more responsive than the US contract: in a less inflationary environment, reopening of the agreement can be delayed; in a more inflationary environment it can be speeded up and the size of the increase also enlarged. Because of this—in the inflationary environment—the British system seems to threaten a "double-whammy": an early reopening that increases the average size of the last increase, and a large new increase to reflect current and expected conditions.

The structure of trade union organization can also be of great importance in explaining wage movements: the extent of centralization of authority in top union officers versus control by the "rank and file"; the existence or not of competitive unions with the same or overlapping jurisdictions; organization by craft versus industry; the power and influence of national union federations; union affiliation with political parties that may be in or out of the government; and many others.

Systems of centralized bargaining—such as those in the Netherlands or Sweden—permit, indeed, almost require, that negotiators be conscious of the effect of their negotiated wage increase on the level of prices. Thus it is easier for those on the labour side to recognize that much or all of what labour might appear to gain from an excessive settlement is illusory. Whatever extra amount workers may gain in higher wages, beyond some point, will be lost through higher prices. The highly decentralized bargaining practised in the United States, on the other hand, makes the size of any individual settlement essentially irrelevant for the prices the workers will pay. Thus, the interest of the negotiators on the labour side in getting the largest possible increase in money wages is not appreciably compromised by any consideration of its effects on prices.

The belief that what happens to prices is independent of the size of any—and thus of *every*—wage settlement is also nourished by the myth that, since the wage bargain is in the first instance made between a union and an employer, a wage dispute can only be an argument about the division of the "pie" between wages and profits, and not about the division of the "pie" among this group of workers, its employer, and its employer's customers—most of whom are other workers. This myth may be reinforced by economic doctrines which assert that the level of prices depends on competition, or the level of demand, the money supply, or some other outside force. That each group of workers believes or at least perpetuates this myth about the effect of its own bargaining is not strange, for it is obviously so comforting and self-serving a doctrine. What is more difficult to understand is how workers often can appear to believe it with respect to other workers' bargaining—even those much better paid than themselves—and how it can be unquestioningly accepted—at least in the United States—by many highly educated middle-class "liberals" in the professions, government, the universities, and the information media.

If questioned as to who will pay for a large wage increase, an educated and public-spirited US citizen is quite likely to reply that "profits are big enough to absorb it". He will have no conception whatever of how *much* of a reduction in profits would be required for a business to absorb a (say) 10 per cent wage increase, particularly if a similar wage increase is to be paid by the firms which supply its purchased materials and services. And he is likely to have no answer when asked whether he thinks the business will *in fact* absorb the increase without raising prices. The question may not have occurred to him. If it is pointed out that excessive wage increases are in fact not absorbed he is likely to remark on the "greed" of employers.[1]

To be sure, a downward rigidity of selling prices provides some basis for persistence of the myth that wage increases come only out of profits. In industries which experience rapid increases in productivity, such that

1. In the United States, the profits (before income tax) of "non-financial corporations" normally constitute around 15 per cent of the value of the gross national product originating in such corporations, and the compensation of employees around 65 per cent. Given an average advance of productivity of around 3 per cent a year, a 10 per cent annual wage increase would constitute about a 7 per cent a year increase in unit labour costs. If prices were not raised, a 10 per cent wage increase would thus reduce profits from 15 per cent to about 10½ per cent of the value of output, or by nearly one third. Repeated a second year (again without price increase), profits would fall to about 6 per cent, and in a third year to about 10½ per cent.

82

Figure 1

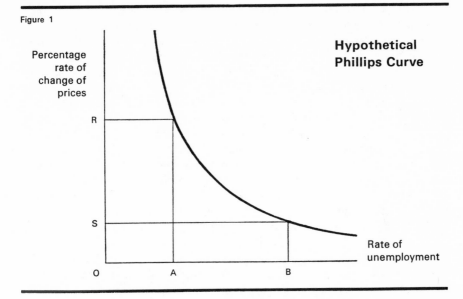

Percentage rate of change of prices

Hypothetical Phillips Curve

Rate of unemployment

moderate wage increases would result in falling unit labour costs, prices are sometimes not reduced sufficiently fully to reflect this, and profit margins are allowed to widen. Although automobile prices in the United States did decline during the late 1950s and early 1960s (mostly through "quality improvements" rather than outright price reductions), they undoubtedly declined by less than unit labour costs. Similarly, the federal agency that regulates airline fares did not require rate reductions to reflect the sharp decline of costs in that industry in the early 1960s. These and similar failures contributed notably to the breakdown of wage stability in the United States in the mid-1960s.

The Phillips Curve analysis

Some of the more systematic portions of the above analysis are frequently summarized in the concept of the so-called Phillips Curve.[1]

In its simplest form, the Phillips Curve idea makes the rate of price increase a function of the extent to which aggregate demand requires the utilization of the economy's productive capacity—as usually measured by the (inverse of the) unemployment rate, or by the difference between unemployment and vacancies. A simple Phillips Curve is graphically reprensented as in Figure 1.

1. Named after the British economist A.W. Phillips, who first cristallized the concept in a well-known article in *Economica* in 1958.

In Figure 1, rates of unemployment in excess of OB would be fully consistent with an acceptable stability of prices—a minimal increase of OS per year. But as unemployment fell progressively below OB, the rate of price increase would step up. Rates of unemployment of OA or below would be associated with rapid inflation at the rate of OR per year or higher; and there appears to be no rate of inflation sufficiently high to reduce unemployment to zero—indeed to reduce it much below OA.

Those who use the Phillips Curve may emphasize either one or the other (or occasionally both) of the two connections sketched earlier between the degree of unemployment and the rate of inflation: either the explanation that as unemployment declines in response to higher aggregate demand, prices must rise to reflect the intensifying competition among firms for increasingly scarce resources, particularly labour; or the alternative explanation that rising aggregate demand enhances the ability of unions and managements to push up wages and prices. However, the presumed level and shape of the curve might well be affected by one's view of the relative importance of demand-pull and cost elements. But either emphasis provides the theoretical support for a public policy that would attempt to avoid or to cure inflation by restraining aggregate demand.

However, the implications of this policy are now very different from those of the simple "inflationary gap" concept. In that situation, aggregate demand needed to be restrained, in order to avoid inflation, only when it exceeded the maximum physical productive capacity of the economy. Such excess demand was completely "non-functional", and there was no reason not to eliminate it. Now, however, it is seen that there is a "trade-off": less inflation implies higher unemployment; lower unemployment requires accepting more inflation. And the choice required may be a most painful one: it may be that the level of unemployment (and the personal hardship and social cost thereof) which a society is willing to accept implies a rate of inflation higher than that society can tolerate. Many think that this is the basic dilemma faced by many countries of the Atlantic Community now and in the years ahead.

If this were indeed the dilemma, the only escape would appear to be either to devise and use policy instruments other than those that operate simply through aggregate demand to deal with excessive unemployment or with inflation, or both; or else to find ways of altering the terms of the trade-off, so that they become socially acceptable. However, some economists believe that the assumed invariance of this trade-off relationship is greatly exaggerated.

Figure 2 presents a simple empirical counterpart of a Phillips Curve for the United States, for the period 1954-1971. Each dot in the quadrant represents one year's experience: measured horizontally, the average level of unemployment during the year, and measured vertically, the change in GNP deflator (for the private non-farm sector of the economy) between the first quarter of that year and the first quarter of the following year. Lines con-

nect each year's observations to the previous and subsequent ones. Data
for 1970 are partly estimated, and those for 1971 are the writer's forecasts.

These data demonstrate some rough conformity to the theoretical
Phillips Curve model. The years 1954, 1962, and 1963—spanning almost a
decade—show almost identical combinations of unemployment rate and
price change. But the rate of price increase during 1958 was more than

Figure 2

US Unemployment Rate and Percentage in Prices, 1954-71 [1]

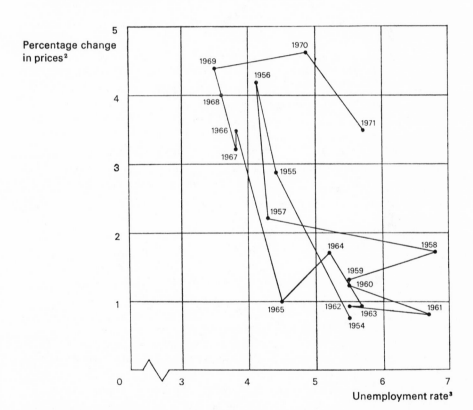

1. Price change for 1970, partly estimated; for 1971, both price change and
unemployment rate are the author's forecasts.

2. Prices are represented by private non-farm deflator; change is measured from
first quarter of the year shown to first quarter of the following year.

3. Average for year.

85

double that of 1961, even though unemployment rates were nearly identical in these two recession years. The price increase during 1955 was almost 3 times as large as that during 1965, with almost the same levels of unemployment; and almost twice as large in 1956 as in 1957, again with very similar unemployment rates. The experience of the years 1955-57 would suggest far more rapid inflation at unemployment rates between 3.5 per cent and 3.8 per cent than was actually experienced in the years 1966-69. And 1970 seems completely out of line with all previous experience shown, as 1971 is almost certain to be. Moreover, observations for post-war years prior to 1954 (although these years admittedly were subject to special factors) bear little apparent relationship to experience during the period 1954-69. Using quarterly data instead of annual, and experimenting with a wide variety of different "lags" between unemployment rate and price change, do not substantially improve the conformity of the relationship to the theoretical model.

The imperfect conformity of observed experience to the theoretical Phillips Curve relationships might have any of several explanations. One explanation is that the Phillips Curve idea, although basically correct, excessively simplifies the rather complex set of forces that produces price level changes in a modern economy. The rate of price change does depend, very importantly, on the level of aggregate demand relative to potential output, of which the rate of unemployment can be taken as a reasonable index. But there are other variables that also must be included in any full explanation of price level changes; and the causal relationships among these variables do not run exclusively in one direction. For example, the level of unemployment mainly explains the rate of change of wages, and thereby of costs and prices. But changes in one set of prices—those which constitute the cost of living—also feed back in helping to determine the rate of change in wages. Prices of farm products and, in most countries, prices of imported goods, which have their own independent causes, significantly affect both the general price level and the cost of living. Changes in prices may also reflect alterations in the rate of productivity advance; changes in the rate of productivity advance also affect the amount of labour required to produce any output and thereby, given the supply of labour, the rate of unemployment. Moreover, each of these relationships may operate with a lag—and possibly a different lag.

Elaborate empirical models have been developed, which incorporate these and other variables, with lags, in a system of equations which simultaneously determines unemployment rates and rates of change in prices. We may call these "extended Phillips Curve" models. It is quite possible to develop such models which are reasonably consistent with past observed experience. Unfortunately, the models so developed have so far proved not to forecast well for subsequent periods. Still, it may be too soon to conclude that the "extended Phillips Curve" approach should be abandoned.

Limitations of the Phillips Curve analysis

Alternative explanations are available, however, for the imperfect conformity of observed inflationary experience either to the simple Phillips
Curve approach or to more elaborate "extended Phillips Curve" models.
The Phillips Curve focuses attention on variations in the rate of inflation
that are primarily associated with variations in the level of unemployment.
This is clearly a relevant dimension for analysis; but it is certainly not
the only possible approach, nor necessarily the one most productive of an
understanding of the total phenomenon of inflation.

For example, the Phillips Curve approach appears to concentrate attention on what may be regarded as the underlying strength of "inflationary
pressures", but pays little or no explicit attention to the inflationary process
which develops from these pressures, and, in particular, to the way in
which each price and wage increase generates others, in endless chain. Yet
it can be argued that, once an inflation is underway, it is or can become
an (at least partially) irreversible historical process. An inflationary spiral,
once well established, appears to develop a life of its own, and becomes
at least in part independent of the strength of the basic inflationary pressures, as these are summarized in the rate of unemployment.

For example, once wage rates have been rising for a time at an annual
rate of 8 per cent, and the price level at 5 per cent, in an economy in which
average labour productivity increases by 3 per cent a year, every group of
workers can clearly see itself falling behind other workers, and behind their
normal experience of annual income improvements, unless their wages, too,
are rising by 8 per cent a year. Every producer whose prices do not continually rise in proportion to his unit labour costs will quickly find his
profit margin squeezed. Yet if his prices rise at a rate which will permit
him to pay 8 per cent wage increases with constant profit margins, he will
not find that he is losing business to other firms or other products. Each
person's or group's adjustment to what has been happening tends to perpetuate whatever inflation rate has been established. That rate becomes the
norm or standard. The inverse—and more hopeful—aspect of this proposition is that price stability, too, tends to perpetuate itself, since no one
falls behind others, or behind his legitimate income expectation based on
past experience, by taking actions consistent with price stability.

Following this approach, analytical attention then needs to focus on
those factors—even temporary factors—which might cause any such
"equilibrium" rate of inflation (or of stability) to be altered, and on how
these factors cause a new norm to be established and to perpetuate itself.
One such factor, of course, might be a change in the level of aggregate
demand.

The hypothesis has frequently been advanced that the longer an inflation at any particular rate has continued, the more firmly established
become the behaviour patterns that cause it to perpetuate itself, and the
more independent these patterns become of changes in aggregate demand.

Thus the longer will be the period of reduced aggregate demand and high unemployment that will be required significantly to reduce any given existing rate of inflation.

These considerations may account for the fact, which stands out so vividly in Figure 2, that inflation in the United States in 1970 was so unresponsive to a substantial rise in unemployment, and appears likely to continue to be unresponsive in 1971. This experience contrasts sharply with the quick reduction of price increases in 1957 in the face of only a small increase of unemployment—perhaps because that period of inflation was relatively short. Possibly illustrating the opposite (and more hopeful) side of the proposition, Figure 2 strongly suggests that the response of price changes to unemployment was gradually adjusting downwards in the United States during 1958, 1959, and 1960, as the cumulative effects of several years of relative price stability began to build up new patterns of economic behaviour. Its more favourable side may also partly account for the unusually low rate of inflation throughout 1962-65, despite a large reduction in unemployment. As chapter 5 will indicate, this effect—if correctly described—creates painful dilemmas for the design of economic policies, whenever inflation has been allowed to develop unchecked for a considerable period.

Another factor which could cause a particular rate of inflation, once established—whether a high or low rate—to be altered would be a change in the degree of trade union aggressiveness or "pushfulness".[1] Trying to understand factors that account for changes in the degree of trade union "pushfulness", independently of the level of unemployment (and of other "objective" factors), may be most important for improving our understanding of the inflationary process. At present, our knowledge of this variable is minimal. An improved knowledge undoubtedly requires analytical approaches far broader than those of conventional economics. As will be noted below, there is reason to believe that a substantial change in this factor may have occurred in the late 1960s in many countries; although, because we do not understand why this occurred, we have little idea whether the change is simply an episode or is likely to continue.

The causes of inflation in the Atlantic Community and the prospects

Forces of aggregate demand and of market power are often described as the alternative or even interacting causes of inflation. Yet the economist's analysis, focusing on these or other factors, does not directly explain what have been the primary causes of the inflation of the past fifteen years in

1. For an effort to isolate and independently to measure "pushfulness" as a factor in inflation, see L.A. Dicks-Mireaux and J.C.R. Dow, "The Determinants of Wage Inflation: United Kingdom, 1946-1956," in *Journal of the Royal Statistical Society,* Series A (General), vol. 122, part 2 (1959), pp. 145-84. (This analysis builds on an earlier paper by Dow.)

the Atlantic Community and of its speeding up since 1965; nor do they directly throw light on the prospects for the future.

Perhaps the causes of the endemic inflation of the modern Atlantic world can be tentatively summarized in the following way. First of all, a generally high level of aggregate demand and consequently a generally low level of unemployment must, of course, be almost taken for granted. Inflation was not, after all, a problem in the West between the two world wars, when economic activity was frequently depressed and unemployment rampant. During those years, governments were not seeking to achieve full employment, and most countries were surely not having it.

Today we know that fiscal and monetary policies can keep our economies more or less constantly at high levels of employment. And, despite periods of relatively high unemployment such as the present one in the United Kingdom, the United States, and Canada, governments have been doing it. Each major country now has a more or less explicit "full-employment" target (expressed in the United States, for example, as an unemployment rate of either 3.8 or 4.0 per cent). Even if there were never any mistakes of policy that push economies into operating *beyond* these targets, some upward creep of prices would be almost inevitable in economies operating more or less continuously at high employment. But, from time to time, in a number of countries, there have been such mistakes of policy—often serious. The failure to raise taxes in the United States from the end of 1965 until mid-1968 was clearly one such mistake.

Nevertheless, it seems incorrect to conclude that inflation is caused simply by too much aggregate demand. As we have seen, excessive demand is, in any case, a relative and not an absolute matter—no unambiguous definition of "excessive" demand is possible. Rather, the problem is a continuing high level of demand *in conjunction with other elements of economic structure.*

In the first place, today's generally high level of demand impinges on economies in which trade unions and large firms possess considerable discretionary power, which, for many reasons, they show varying degrees of willingness to use. It impinges on economies in which there are strong downward rigidities of individual wages and prices, so that there are few price or wage reductions to offset increases. It impinges on economies which have inherited from that almost forgotten time when full employment was not a commitment of government policy, and occurred but rarely, a host of institutionalized or legislated "protections" which create bottlenecks and immobilites at high employment.

In the second place, there are the increasing aspirations of every group in our societies for rapidly rising real incomes, and the tendency everywhere for the fulfilment of people's aspirations—in all areas of economic, political, and social life—to be pressed ever more aggressively and insistently. In particular, in a number of countries in recent years, there appears to have developed an increased aggressiveness, a growing truculence, with which groups of all kinds are pressing their claims for what they regard as their rightful shares of the national income—shares that often add up to more than 100 per cent. To some extent, this new truculence may be the product of inflation, not its cause. Nevertheless, it may also represent the expression, in the market place, of a broader social and political trend in Western society.

In the third place, we have to recognize that inflation is not purely an economic phenomenon. In every country there are significant institutional, psychological, and attitudinal factors which heavily influence the responses of individuals and groups to the "objective" economic circumstances. Psychological responses may well be altered by the process of inflation itself, as well as by other events and developments in the political, social, and international environments.

All of these factors are as much the "causes" of inflation as is the level of aggregate demand; their influence on the price level can fluctuate independently of the pressure of aggregate demand; and—fortunately—some of them, at least, may be capable of alteration through government action.

Given this view of the "causes" of inflation, what may be said about the prospects for an acceleration of inflation? The case for an inevitable acceleration of inflation could rest on any of a number of grounds.

One reason would be an *increasing* propensity for governments to make policy mistakes on the side of the *over*-fulfilment of full-employment targets—or inevitable political pressures to raise the targets themselves. There seems to be little direct evidence to support this. Rather, one could conclude that governments are learning from their policy mistakes, and that public understanding of the need for better management of aggregate demand is steadily improving.

A second theory of why inflation may tend to accelerate is suggested in the recent report by the Secretary General of the OECD, *Inflation: The Present Problem*. It is that, because people know that recessions are a thing of the past, the ability of governments to control aggregate demand through monetary and fiscal policy has been seriously weakened: it now takes progressively bigger doses of restraint to get the same effects as before. While this argument has some plausibility, it is surely, so far, unproved. In any case, there is no reason why the larger doses of restraint might not be forthcoming, if and when necessary.

A third class of reasons why inflation may be found to accelerate involves theories emphasizing price expectations. These are many, and some—such as Professor Milton Friedman's constructions postulating a "natural rate" of unemployment—are rather fanciful. A more plausible version is based on the proposition that the experience of more than minimal rates of inflation—and the continuation of such experience—causes people's, consciousness of past inflation and their expectations of future inflation gradually to build up.

As sketched in the recent report of the OECD Secretary General, the basic argument is somewhat as follows.[1] At low rates of inflation—averaging 2 or 3 per cent a year—most people are not conscious of inflation. Many individual prices are constant or even falling. There are intermittent periods of price level stability. The expectation of future inflation consciously influences the behaviour of few individuals, and their expectations are not held with great conviction. But when the price level is rising at an average rate of 5 or 6 per cent a year, or faster, *all* individual prices are rising, some quite dramatically; even when the rate slows down, it is not to zero. The rate of inflation is high enough to compete with (or to wipe out the benefits of) the return on some forms of investment. Almost everyone comes to be conscious of inflation, and begins to expect it to continue.

This is said to have two effects on people's behaviour that might cause the inflation to accelerate. The first is that their expectations of inflation may cause them to anticipate expenditures that would otherwise have been made later on, thus increasing aggregate demand and causing the price rise to accelerate. This is the basic mechanism of a "runaway" inflation. However, it is not clear that effects of this kind have yet been in evidence in the Atlantic countries. In fact, scientific sample surveys of consumer attitudes all show that the consciousness of inflation or of the speeding up of inflation—at least within the range of our recent inflationary experience—tends to cause consumers not to anticipate their expenditures but if anything to delay them. (The same may not be true of business expenditures.) [2]

However, the second type of effect attributed to inflationary expectations may well be more relevant and more serious. It is that expectations of inflation directly affect the prices and wages that buyers and sellers specify in any contracts that extend more than a short period into the future. Sellers (of labour and of goods and services) demand that an allowance be made for future inflation in the wages or prices which they agree to accept; buyers (expecting an inflation in their receipts) do not resist as strongly. Or sellers demand (and buyers resist less strongly) making their contracts of shorter duration, or to include reopening privileges, or escalator clauses. Existing contracts not for fixed term are reopened more frequently than in the past. The readjustment of prices and wages to changes in other prices and wages occurs more frequently, more fully, more automatically. Inflation may thus accelerate at any given (relatively high) degree of utilization of resources, at any constant (relatively low) unemployment rate.

1. *Inflation: The Present Problem,* para. 5, p. 71.
2. See, for example, George Katona, "The Impact of Inflation on Consumer Attitudes and Behavior," in *The Conference Board Record,* VIII, no. 3 (March 1971), 48-51. Or, for a fuller discussion, taking account of differences in consumer attitudes and responses among various countries, see G. Katona, B. Strumpel, and E. Zahn, *Aspirations and Affluence: Comparative Studies in the United States and Western Europe* (New York: McGraw-Hill, 1971).

Evidence of this phenomenon is far from clear-cut. Figure 2 showed the rate of inflation speeding up in the United States between 1965 and 1969, but this was associated with progressive reductions in the rate of unemployment: these could well be described as movements *along* the ascending branch of a fixed Phillips Curve, not necessarily as points showing progressive movement above the curve. Nevertheless, the further rise in prices in 1970, even in the face of a sharp *rise* in unemployment, could be interpreted as reflecting the effects of increasingly high and definite expectations of inflation.

The hypotheses suggesting an inevitable and significant tendency for inflation to accelerate are interesting, but unproved. Yet some of them are plausible enough to reinforce the view that the inflation problem must be taken rather more seriously than it would be if we concentrated only on the costs of rates of inflation so far incurred.

The basic point of view of this study is that inflations are complex phenomena, with multiple causes rooted in the structures of the modern Atlantic economies. No simple, one-dimensional view of causation can be accepted. We must reject the view that explains inflation entirely by inappropriate changes in the quantity of money, just as we must reject the view that explains it solely by the evolution of collective bargaining institutions, or by any other simple, single line of causation.

Moreover, in an important sense, each inflation may embody the elements of a unique historical experience. How prices and incomes will behave responds to a wide variety of conditions and forces—economic, social, and political—in the society. And each stage in such an inflationary episode depends not only on what happened in earlier stages of that episode, but also on what has happened during preceding inflationary episodes, or what is happening in other countries. For example, the whole character of the inflationary process in an economy that has experienced a runaway inflation will be deeply influenced by that fact.

All of this does not, of course, mean that inflations are complex accidents—acts of God—and that nothing, therefore, can be done to avoid or control them. It only means that simple monistic theories of the causation of inflations—that prescribe simple monistic policies for their control—are wrong or seriously incomplete. The complexity of inflations suggests that a variety of policies may need to be considered for their control. Concluding that the Phillips Curve is not a rigid, invariant relationship, reflecting some basic, inescapable aspects of economic structure, also suggests that social policy may well find many ways to pursue simultaneously—rather than alternatively—the two overriding goals of economic policy in every country: steady high employment along with reasonable stability of prices.

International inflation:
the exporting and importing of price levels

T he preceding chapter has dealt with the causes of inflation in a single country, as though there were no contact between that country's economy and other economies. Yet international economic interdependence is one of the dominant facts of economic life in the Atlantic Community, and this interdependence clearly extends to the processes of inflation. Among the countries of continental Europe, for example, the interdependence of price levels, and hence the interdependence of inflationary developments, differs only in degree from the interdependence of price levels and hence of inflationary developments among the various regions of a single country such as the United States. Through the channels of international trade and payments, it is quite possible for one country to export inflation to others, or for one country to import it from others. The nature of this interdependence needs now to be considered.

The impact of inflation on trade and payments

As a preliminary step to considernig the impact of international trade and payments on the extent of a country's inflation, we first consider the impact of a country's inflation on its international trade and payments. We continue to assume—temporarily—that each country's price level is determined entirely by domestic developments and domestic policies and is thus unaffected by all other countries, price levels. For example, assume that a domestic inflation raises prices at home by 10 per cent, while the average price level elsewhere rises by only 5 per cent. Other things being equal, such a rise in domestic prices relative to those elsewhere stimulates the country's demand for imports and reduces other countries' demand for its exports. It will thereby experience a loss of jobs and profits from the decreased production both of export goods and of those domestic goods whose local markets are reduced by rising imports. We will call this the adverse "competitive effect" of a faster rate of inflation. Obviously, there are favourable competitive effects for the country whose prices rise less than elsewhere.

Given rates of inflation at home and abroad, and resulting competitive effects on the physical volumes of the country's imports and exports, its *balance of trade* will be altered—the difference between the money value of its exports and the money value of its imports. For example, it is conceivable (although unlikely) that a domestic inflation could have only a minor restraining effect on the volume of a country's exports, even though its export prices rose considerably; in that case, the money value of its exports could rise appreciably. Similarly, although prices of goods imported from elsewhere rose very little and prices of domestic import substitutes rose a lot, it is conceivable that the volume of imports would be little stimulated; thus the money value of its imports would rise very little. In that case, the country's balance of trade might actually be improved by its inflation. But normally only a moderate rise in prices relative to those abroad will cause a substantial loss of a country's exports and/or a large increase in its imports. In that case—the usual one—the country's trade balance will be impaired by inflation, perhaps seriously.

As a country's trade balance is reduced as a result of its having a higher rate of inflation than elsewhere, it is likely to encounter balance-of-payments problems. Whether it does, and how seriously, will depend on the previous state of its balance of payments, and on what is simultaneously happening to movements of capital between it and other countries. Other things being equal, however, a country which has a prolonged higher-than-average rate of price increase will almost surely, sooner or later, encounter balance-of-payments difficulties. Thus, it is often said there is a "balance-of-payments discipline" which penalizes countries that are unwilling or unable to avoid inflation. They must ultimately "pay the piper" when their international reserves become depleted to the point that they must create a domestic recession, and/or impose welfare-reducing controls on international transactions, and/or devalue their currencies. Those countries which wish to avoid these costs accept the discipline, and do not permit inflation to develop.

Unfortunately, this discipline is not quite as successful in penalizing "sin" and rewarding "virtue" as here described. In the first place, the sin punished is not inflation, but only faster inflation than other countries are experiencing. The implied "code of ethics" is a highly relativist one—it is all right to sin just so long as others are sinning too.

In the second place, there is the equally serious deficiency that the discipline punishes some who have not sinned (i.e., inflated more than others) and fails to punish some others who have. The statement above was that "other things being equal", a country that inflates faster than others will get into trouble. But other things may not always be equal. A country's balance of trade is affected not only by the "competitive effects" associated with price-level changes. It can also be, and often is, heavily affected by any of a large number of other things quite independent of its price levels—which may be happening at the same time. Suppose, for example, that a shift is occurring in buyers' preferences (both those of domestic buyers and of those abroad) as among different kinds of goods. If buyers' preferences at home and abroad are shifting away from rest-of-world products and towards this country's products, its exports may rise and its imports may decline, even though the home economy is experiencing a higher degree of inflation than the rest of the world. In the case of an unfavourable shift in demand, a country's exports may suffer and its imports may increase, even though its prices are more stable than those abroad.

There is a multitude of factors that can explain a (relative) shift of demand from one country's products towards another's. In addition to autonomous changes in consumer tastes, they include changes in the qualities or styles of the goods produced at home and abroad; the introduction of wholly new products at home or abroad that displace others in buyers' patronage; changes in the structure of aggregate demand (including those changes that arise merely from the growth of average incomes) that cause the demand for one set of products (more heavily represented in the exports of one country) to grow faster than the demand for another set of products (more heavily represented in another country's exports); faster, or slower, economic growth in the economies of its trading partners than at home; a country's entry into a preferential trading community (or such entry by countries that provide its principal export markets); and many more such circumstances. Moreover, prices of *specific* export commodities (and specific import-competitive goods) may and sometimes do change quite differently from changes in a country's general price level. For example, even in a country experiencing more inflation than elsewhere, the prices of the particular goods that account for its principal exports or its import substitutes could fall, or rise less than the prices of directly competitive foreign products, because of differing rates of productivity change, or different competitive conditions in the several markets. Thus, the balance of payments discipline may punish some countries that do not inflate, and may fail to punish others that do.

The exporting of inflation through trade

This analysis of the effects of inflation on trade also helps to make clear the effects of trade on inflation, and how one country's inflation may cause another country's price level to rise.

The international transfer of inflation is directly analogous to what happens within the regions of a single country. Casual observation tells us that prices rise (or fall) at roughly the same rate within all the different regions of a large national market like that of the United States. None can get very far out of line. If prices rise faster in the West than in the East, producers in the East find it more profitable to sell in the West, and the inflow of their "exports" controls the rise of Western prices. Likewise, Western producers find it harder to sell in Eastern markets and are forced either to lower their prices or to lose "exports" to the East. Both these responses, however, increase demand and reduce supply in the East and tend to raise prices there. In somewhat attenuated form, the same process works internationally (among countries whose exchange rates are fixed) to keep their price changes at least somewhat in line with each other. The argument will now be developed more fully as it applies to the international case, although it holds even more strongly within a single market.

Assume that, at first, no country is undergoing inflation. Then domestic aggregate demand increases in one country to an extent that threatens to bring about a domestic inflation. This rising pressure of domestic demand will, however, first increase that country's imports from its trading partners, and might, as well, tend to divert some of its own resources from making export goods to production for the home market.

If supplies of imports from other countries were freely available at constant prices, the availability of the imported supplies might fully satisfy the increased demand in the first country, and thereby cushion its price level from any appreciable inflationary pressure. At the same time, however, this process produces an increased pressure of aggregate demand in the economies of its trading partners. The demand for their exports by the first country has increased, while their imports from that country may have decreased (thus reducing the total supply of goods available in their own domestic markets). If aggregate demand was previously deficient and resources unemployed in some or all of the trading partners, the increased demand pressure may be welcome, and thus helpful to them in attaining full employment, just as their increased exports to the first country are helpful to it in avoiding inflation. However, if aggregate demand is, or once it has become, neither deficient nor excessive in the economies of some or all of the trading partners, a strong and persistent rise of demand in the first country could tip the balance towards inflation in many or all of the countries.

It it thus apparent that trade—among countries just as among regions of a single country—is a means by which the pressure of increased demand on supply, wherever it originates, is spread over a larger market, tending thereby to keep the balance between demand and supply relatively similar in all parts of the larger market area. If foreign goods and domestic goods were perfect substitutes one for another, the pressures of demand on supply in one country would be spread evenly over all parts of the trading area, and no part would experience inflation from excessive demand until demand was excessive everywhere and all regions or countries experienced inflation together. Within a single country this is nearly what happens. However, in the separate country case, imports are even less likely to be perfect substitutes for domestic goods than is the case within a country; and imports never are even imperfect substitutes for some domestic activities (e.g., construction and personal services). Thus, excessive demand in one country can begin to create inflation at home even though some or all of the countries with which it trades are not yet at full employment. Even so, as excess demand raises prices at home, the attendant competitive effects will strengthen its "export" of excessive demand to others, and thereby may begin to engender inflation in some of the countries with which the first country's trading relations are closest.

Competitive effects in trade will occur, of course, even if the first country's inflation is entirely of the cost-push variety; and this too could tip the balance of supply and demand in other countries' markets towards inflation.

There have been many cases in recent years in which inflation has clearly been spread from one country (or group of countries) to others through trade effects. This is clearly most important for neighbouring countries which account for an important part of each other's trade, in a volume which is also large relative to one or both countries' domestic production. Excessive demand in the United States in 1966-68, for example, clearly "spilled over" into Canada and had a significant impact on Canada's price levels. During this same period, the strong US demand for imports from Europe and Japan contributed somewhat to rising aggregate demand and to inflationary pressures in those areas. Germany's boom in 1964-65, and again in 1969-70, clearly had strongly inflationary effects on most of her neighbour's economies. Small countries whose trade is large relative to their GNP are almost sure to import any inflation being suffered by their larger neighbours.

Obviously, the reduction of barriers to trade, both multilaterally through GATT and through the formation of EEC and EFTA, has tied countries' economies even more closely together through trade and has made the exporting and importing of inflation between them considerably easier and more significant. Nevertheless, at least in the case of the larger countries, the effects of other countries' inflation on the balance of demand and supply in the home market will rarely have an impact so great or so sudden that it could not be offset by a country that was seriously determined to avoid inflation, and possessed adequate tools for the control of domestic demand.

Just as countries that inflate more rapidly than others export some of their inflation to their neighbours, so those that inflate less rapidly export some of their price stability to others. Countries with stable prices that are able to let their exports to inflating countries grow rapidly tend to hold down others' inflation. Moreover, especially if a country with relatively stable prices has a large internal market—e.g., the United States or Germany—export producers in other countries, ambitious to enter that market or to expand their sales there, have no alternative but to hold down their costs and prices by every possible means. This effort to stabilize their export prices also may help, to some appreciable extent, to stabilize internal

97

costs and prices in their own countries. Though this means, too, that price stability is "exported".

Thus trade effects pull in the direction of keeping price-level changes in all countries relatively similar. Lower rates of inflation tend to be pulled up, higher rates pulled down. However, the pressures towards price-level conformity can rarely be more than partially effective. If domestic policies together with the "export of price stability" by other countries fail to control a particular country's inflation, and its price level gets too far out of line with others', it may ultimately have to bring its international (although not its domestic) price-level back into line by altering its exchange parity. Or, if a country wishes to and is able to achieve substantially greater price stability than its trading partners, it may ultimately have to revalue its currency upwards in order to avoid importing their inflation.

Other ways of exporting of inflation

Cost-Push Effects. If the prices that must be paid in one country for significant and not easily replaceable imports from another should rise as a result of the other country's inflation, this can set off inflationary impulses in the first country even if there is no change in the aggregate demand for its products. Higher prices paid for essential imported raw materials will raise costs of production and push up the prices of domestic goods made from these materials. Higher prices paid by domestic consumers for such goods, or higher prices for finished consumer goods directly imported, can generate demands for larger wage increases, thus setting off a cost-push spiral. Similar effects may occur as the result of a trading partner's revaluation, or a country's own devaluation.

Such cost-push effects from higher import prices are by themselves unlikely to be decisive, at least in the larger countries. But they can contribute to existing internal cost-push pressures, and intensify an otherwise already difficult problem. Small countries, highly dependent on imports, have no way to resist cost-push inflationary effects from a rise in world market prices.

Labour Migration Effects. The increasingly international labour market that exists in Europe, like that which exists in North America, provides a further means for the spread of inflation. If the pressure of demand in one country raises wages there and pulls in workers from other countries, this tends to create labour shortages and thereby to raise wage costs in the other countries. The large reservoirs of idle or under-employed workers in Southern Europe and North Africa that were available to meet labour shortages in Northern Europe during the 1960s long helped to cushion the latter region against inflationary pressures, without at the same time creating such pressures in the countries losing workers. Once full (or fuller) employment was achieved in Spain and Italy, rapidly rising aggregate demand in

98

the North was no longer so easily accommodated, and inflationary pressures developed more readily both in the North and the South.

The movement of workers across borders in Northern Europe—among France, Belgium, the Netherlands, Switzerland, and Germany—has also on occasion been in sufficient volume to help to transmit inflationary pressures from rising internal demand from one of these countries to another. Because of the large daily movement of workers across these borders, a wage change on one side must be almost immediately matched on the other.

Imitative effects. In today's increasingly unified world, bound together by massive flows of information through press, radio, television, and the direct observation of tourists, there are still other channels for the importation of inflationary tendencies. (The phrase "importation of inflationary tendencies"—rather than the "export of inflation"—is meant to convey that in this circumstance inflation can be imported even from a country where it does not exists!) Workers in countries in which the growth of productivity is slow see the faster gains in living standards being made by workers elsewhere. When they seek to match those real income gains by securing larger nominal wage increases, in the absence of corresponding productivity gains, this can only create inflation. Some argue that this phenomenon has relevance for the United Kingdom.

Other students have suggested that the wage explosion in Italy in 1970 was in some sense influenced by Italian workers' observations of the events in France in 1968. Here the importation (if any) may have consisted as much of the spirit and tactics of political militancy as of the borrowing of an economic objective. If so, the economic impact of the borrowing was nonetheless inflationary. It may be, of course, that both wage explosions (and those in other countries) reflect common social and political trends of wider origin.

On the other hand, some have suggested that, during the early part of the 1960s, the excellent price performance of the United States had a widespread dampening effect on price expectations—and thus, indirectly, on inflation—throughout the Atlantic world, an effect that has now been lost.

Direct investment effects. A country involved in an inflationary boom may find its problems of controlling demand intensified by the participation of foreign entrepreneurs in its investment boom. An inflationary impact is not, however, the inevitable result of foreign direct investment. Foreign direct investment will be inflationary primarily to the extent that (a) it results in a larger total volume of investment than would otherwise have occurred through domestic entrepreneurial activity alone, and (b) this increased total investment is not offset by foreign entrepreneurs' greater importation of capital goods. If foreign entrepreneurs merely make investments that would otherwise have been made by domestic firms, or if their extra volume of investment is matched by their importation of capital

99

goods from their home countries, it need not be inflationary: indeed, in the latter case, it may thereafter be an anti-inflationary influence. Even if foreign direct investment were inflationary in the first instance, the importation of more advanced technology that might accompany the foreign investment could subsequently permit a faster expansion of output with less strain on domestic resources and thus, again, subsequently help to cushion the country against inflationary tendencies.

The impacts of foreign direct investment are many and it raises many issues more important than that of its contribution to inflationary pressures. Nevertheless, under some circumstances it might contribute to inflation, and it is possible that it has sometimes done so in the Atlantic Community during the post-war period.

The impacts of capital flows

Almost no subject in recent years has stirred more controversy than that of the impacts of the international flows of "liquid capital" and "portfolio investment". Such flows have been massive in recent years in the Atlantic Community. They have responded to interest-rate differentials, to speculation over revaluations or devaluations of currencies, and in some instances to tax changes or efforts to escape taxation. They often have been described as a mechanism through which inflation is exported along with the capital. More appropriately, we should call it a means by which inflation is imported along with the capital, for the capital-exporting country need not be one suffering inflation.

However, such flows do not *directly* affect aggregate demand or cost pressures either in the exporting or the importing country. Yet they may do so indirectly if they—along with the financial flows associated with the net balance on trade, tourism, services, and other international transactions—affect credit availability and/or interest rates in either country through altering its domestic supply of money and credit. In some countries—e.g., the United States—the central bank can without difficulty completely insulate domestic monetary conditions from the financial effects of balance of payments surpluses or deficits, and almost invariably does so, mainly through open-market operations. This is not the case in many other countries, and it would require institutional changes to provide the machinery necessary to permit their central banks to accomplish that insulation.

The case for *not* insulating domestic monetary conditions from capital flows would rest on a presumption that all international flows of foreign exchange respond to basic economic forces which make domestic monetary expansion appropriate when funds flow in and monetary contraction appropriate when funds flow out. If a country experiences an increase in international reserves as the result of its own export boom, occasioned by the fact that its price level is "too low" relative to other countries' prices, an expansionary monetary policy might conceivably be deemed appropriate to create the inflationary conditions at home which would restore equilibrium in its balance of payments—although few governments or central banks might reach that conclusion. In the opposite case, however, in which reserves decrease as a result of an import surplus because domestic prices are rising in response to excessive demand, it might well be appropriate if this loss of reserves automatically brought about a deflationary monetary policy. In this case, the balance of payments discipline would be working—quite automatically—in the direction it is supposed to work, namely to restrain an inappropriate inflation.

But none of this has much relevance to those changes in reserves which result primarily from capital flows. If, for example, the importation of capital is attracted by high interest rates which were deliberately raised by a restrictive domestic monetary policy in order to fight a domestic inflation, an increase in the country's money supply arising from capital imports does not thereby become appropriate. Indeed, its effects are precisely counter to the original objective. If the import of capital occurs because another country is using an easy money policy to stimulate its domestic economy, which lowers its domestic interest rates and causes funds to flow out, this fact does not itself make monetary expansion appropriate in countries which are the recipients of such outflows. Nor is there any significant *a priori* case showing that fund inflows or outflows relating to speculation about changes in exchange parities (other than perhaps the country's own) provide any clear guidance as to what internal monetary policy is appropriate.

There was once an economic theory that related to an (even then) probably non-existent world: one in which all prices and wages were perfectly flexible, in which no government needed to use nor tried to use nor would be able to use domestic monetary policy as an instrument of economic stabilization, and in which the international money—gold—was also the sole circulating domestic money. For such a world, there was a theory about how international interest rate differentials reflected only the relative abundance or scarcity of capital and the relative availability of opportunities for profitable investment in various countries; and how capital flows that responded to these interest rate differentials generated price differentials that in turn generated flows of exports and imports that maximized welfare all around. That world bears little relationship to the one we know.

In our world, one or more of several changes would appear to be necessary in order to deal effectively with problems of the international transmission of inflation (or deflation) through undesired flows of capital. One would be for all important countries (or groups of countries participating in a community that seeks to carry out a common monetary policy) to develop effective means to insulate their domestic monetary systems

101

from international inflows or outflows of funds. In this way they could more effectively use monetary policy to deal with problems of domestic economic instability. A quite different solution would be for major countries to co-ordinate more effectively their monetary policies so as to minimize undesired and destabilizing capital flows, while encouraging capital flows that promote balance of payments equilibrium both in countries exporting and countries importing the capital. However, this would require that countries should have and be able to use tools other than monetary policy to deal with problems of internal stability—most importantly, flexible fiscal policies. A third solution would be "floating" exchange rates, or new and easier means for exchange parities to be adjusted frequently and in small amounts. Other solutions are perhaps possible, including direct controls on capital flows, controls on the receipt or payment of interest, or perhaps flexible tax mechanisms. However, the analysis and solution of today's balance of payments problems—which only in part arise from inflation—lie entirely beyond the scope of this paper.

The export and import of price stability

The preceding pages have suggested a number of ways in which inflationary tendencies may be—and often are—transferred across international borders in the Atlantic Community. However, in most cases, this is a reciprocal process: these are also ways in which price stability can be transferred across international borders: the means by which inflation in one country is restrained by relative stability in another. And indeed this has often happened.

Until 1965, and particularly between 1960 and 1965, the United States economy (and that of Canada) constitued an "island of stability" in a world in which many countries experienced strong tendencies towards inflation. Much of the time in the past 15 years, Germany, and, at least in important product lines, Italy and Japan, have also been strong forces for stability, absorbing inflationary pressures originating elsewhere rather than radiating such pressures to others. The reservoirs of unemployed or underemployed labour in Southern Europe were for many years, and to some extent remain, another great force for stability.

Surely, price stability—just as inflation—is an exportable commodity, even though there is now perhaps less of it around to export. But even when there was more of it on the market, it is probable that the international pressures towards stability and towards inflation were not fully symmetrical. Why?

Partly it is merely the "ratchet effect", the fact that wages and prices go up far more easily than down. Today, international variation in price level performance exists only on one side of zero change; domestic price levels do not decline (although a country's international prices may decline through devaluation). Moreover, ratchet effects mean that it is easier for the countries with inflation to export that inflation to other than to import the others' stability.

Second, many of the ways in which one country can export stability to others require that it have a margin of idle resources—so that it can readily increase its exports of goods—and/or of labour—to satisfy excessive demand pressures elsewhere. Today countries are both more ambitious in their employment objectives and better able to achieve them. Thus there are typically (and progressively) fewer circumstances in which some countries are in a position to export stability to others.

Third, the alleged discipline of the balance of payments, which is one instrument through which the stable countries export their stability to others, has increasingly been seen to be a captious and often misdirected master. Countries may have balance of payments difficulties even though their inflation is considerably less than that experienced elsewhere—as was the case, for example, for the United States, between 1955 and 1965. Other countries have experienced more than the average rate of inflation, yet have been saved from trouble through demand shifts or fortunate capital flows. Recognition of these facts has led to the development of new international machinery, and of new attitudes, that have in effect relaxed the balance of payments discipline, even when that discipline is properly exerted on countries which get into trouble through inflation.

Countries experiencing less inflation than others, whether or not this is reflected in an improved balance of payments, surely do not invite inflation nor willingly accept it. But the control of inflation is almost always difficult, unpleasant, painful. If a country's price record up to now has been better than average, and its balance of payments is favourable, it finds it easier to postpone efforts to avoid or control a new impulse to inflation in the hope that the problem will go away, or to relax its efforts to avoid or control inflation once they begin to show partial results. But countries with poorer price records do not thereby find their efforts to control inflation any more pleasant or less painful. They do what they think they can do. And their task is not easier simply because other countries, whose past price records are better, are more relaxed about dealing with their own inflationary pressures. Indeed, the task of the countries in trouble is made *more difficult* by the other countries' reduced ability to export price stability.

The control of inflation

nflation may have different causes at different times, and its nature may be affected by circumstances peculiar to a particular country. This suggests that the particular method which a government may select to avoid or control inflation should be tailored to the nature of its own problems at the particular time. Nevertheless, one main conclusion of the discussion in Chapters 3 and 4 is that it is rarely possible to isolate a single cause or mechanism which fully explains any inflationary episode. All simple, monistic explanations of inflation—for example, that it only results from too rapid an increase in the money supply—are surely wrong. Similarly, no simple, one-dimensional programme for the control of inflation is likely to be the best policy that can be devised.

At a great many times and in most countries, inflation has been associated with an unusually high level of aggregate demand; more effective "management" of aggregate demand is therefore undoubtedly the single most important thing that can be done to improve control of inflation in the Atlantic Community. Nevertheless, tighter restrictions on aggregate demand—i.e., achieving or maintaining a somewhat higher margin of unemployed resources—is not the *only* way, and may not always be the *best* way, of attacking the problem. Alternative—or, rather, *complementary*—strategies to avoid or control inflation may include

a. efforts directly to control, alter, or influence individual wage and price decisions through agreement, persuasion, or compulsion;

b. efforts to alter the structural and institutional factors that cause any particular level of aggregate demand to be translated into a particular rate of price increase (sometimes called programmes which have the effect of "shifting the Phillips Curve"); or

c. efforts to offset or minimize a general price increase through achieving price reductions (or smaller price increases) in particular sectors.

Moreover, the most difficult problems of controlling inflation are not those of choosing one or more of the general principles or strategies of action suggested above. Rather they are the problems of devising or improving specific techniques of action or control in pursuit of the strategies selected, and of developing the political and administrative processes and the level of public understanding which will support their timely and effective use.

Although stress is here placed on the complementary nature of the various methods for inflation control, it is of course necessary to discuss them at least in the first instance seriatim rather than simultaneously. For reasons of space, it is impossible to deal in detail with any of the methods, to cite the experience of particular countries except occasionally by way of example, or to refer to the large available literature on most of these matters.

" Demand management "

There are two important tools which governments have for "managing" the level of aggregate demand. The first, fiscal policy, relates to the impacts of changes in government taxes and expenditures. The second, monetary policy, relates to the impacts of changes in the cost and availability of borrowed funds, or in the prices of financial assets—to the extent that these arise from governmental (meaning, usually, central bank) action or controls. In the case both of fiscal and monetary systems, impacts may be "automatic" or "built-in" on the one hand, or "discretionary" on the other. The built-in effects are largely of a "stabilizing" variety; discretionary changes, on the other hand, can either be stabilizing or destabilizing. In the present context, this means that the automatic effects tend always to dampen tendencies towards inflation, while discretionary changes may either help to avoid or control inflation, or may create or intensify it.

Fiscal policy[1]

Discretionary fiscal policy. The instruments of discretionary fiscal policy are the raising or lowering of tax rates (including rates of compulsory contributions for social security) and the increase or reduction of government purchases of currently produced goods and services, of government subsidies to firms, or of government transfer payments to individuals (including social security benefits). [2] Raising tax rates and reducing expenditures are measures which reduce or restrain aggregate demand. Higher tax

1. An excellent and comprehensive study of fiscal policy in the Atlantic Community was made by a committee of experts appointed by the OECD and was published by that organization in December 1968 under the title *Fiscal Policy for a Balanced Economy: Experience, Problems, and Prospects.*

2. Alteration of the investment expenditures of government enterprises (including nationalized industries) are also usually included as measures of discretionary fiscal policy. Changes in the prices charged by government enterprises are sometimes included, their effects being analogous to changes in excise tax rates.

rates cut back after-tax private incomes and thereby tend to lessen private demand; lower government purchases of goods and services directly reduce the government's contribution to aggregate demand; while lower transfer payments or subsidies—like higher taxes—affect private incomes and tend to reduce private demand. Lowering tax rates and raising expenditures are, of course, measures which tend to expand demand. There are possible combinations, involving simultaneously raising both tax rates and expenditures (or lowering both), which can be exactly neutral in their impacts—neither expanding nor contracting aggregate demand. (Such neutrality would generally require somewhat larger changes in taxes than in expenditures.)

Automatic fiscal stabilization. The fiscal system automatically operates in a partially stabilizing manner even in the absence of discretionary changes in policy. As aggregate demand increases, and production responds, the resulting higher levels of employment, sales, and incomes automatically generate—at constant tax rates—a larger volume of tax revenues. Unless government spending is automatically tied to revenues, this means that tax collections rise relatively to government expenditures, thus dampening the further expansion of aggregate demand. Certain types of government expenditures also provide built-in stabilizing effects—those expenditures that automatically fall whenever aggregate demand is increasing more rapidly than potential output, and that automaticlly rise in the reverse case. Unemployment insurance benefit payments are the most outstanding example of this category.

Built-in stabilizing effects are not uniformly helpful or appropriate. For they dampen increases in demand which would otherwise have resulted in larger—and desirably larger—increases in employment and production, in an economy well below full employment. Yet built-in stabilizing effects can never by themselves completely prevent, but can only reduce, an expansion of demand sufficiently strong to move an economy into the inflationary range. However, as noted in Chapter 3, once prices begin to rise (if the tax system is progressive), the rise in prices also adds to tax collections, and could further tend to choke off the rise in demand. Built-in stabilizing effects also help to protect an economy from a weakening of aggregate demand, causing smaller losses of employment, but can only limit its effects ; never reverse them.

Interaction of discretionary and automatic effects. Neither the magnitude nor even the direction of the net impact of fiscal changes on the economy can be measured by what is happening to the surplus or deficit in the government's budget. For changes in the budget surplus or deficit reflect not only the primary impacts of discretionary tax rate or expenditure changes, but also—indeed, even more—the automatic impacts on revenues and expenditures of changes in the level of economic activity. For example, a recession in private demand may generate a budget deficit (or increase a pre-existing deficit) even if tax rates are simultaneously being raised, the

106

lower levels of production, sales, and incomes more than offsetting the effect on tax collections of the higher rates of taxation. Moreover, even if other forces affecting private demand are unchanged, because higher tax rates tend to reduce private demand, the rise in revenues that would otherwise have resulted from the higher tax rates will be partially offset by the consequent lower level of economic activity.

Objectives of discretionary fiscal policy. The most limited objective for a discretionary fiscal policy is to avoid letting the budget become an independent source of economic instability. In the present context of inflation control, this means reducing tax rates only when expenditures decline, and raising taxes (or reducing another expenditure) to offset the effect of any increase of expenditures. Under this policy, the automatic stabilization effects of the fiscal system would still dampen upswings or downswings in private demand; but no discretionary budget changes would be made in an effort fully or partly to offset the effect on the economy of any swings in private demand. Although there are influential voices (particularly in the United States) which claim that this is the only feasible objective of policy, most governments take the position that this is much too modest a goal for their fiscal policies. Yet it is a striking fact that fiscal performance has too often failed to achieve even this most modest objective. The record of inflation in the Atlantic Community would be much better than it is if governments had always done at least this much. The failure of the United States to raise taxes (or to reduce other expenditures sufficiently) when expenditures for the Vietnam War began to accelerate in late 1965 is only one of the more striking recent examples of this proposition. (Taxes were finally raised only in mid-1968.)

A more ambitious objective is not merely to prevent fiscal policy from itself being destabilizing, but, beyond that, to use it (along with monetary policy) to offset, at least in part, significant changes in the strength of private demand that would otherwise be destabilizing. In the context of inflation control, this means raising tax rates or reducing expenditures (or reducing the "normal" growth of expenditures) not merely to offset increases in government spending, but also to offset (for example) a private investment boom that threatens to raise aggregate demand in an economy already at or close to full employment.

A still more ambitious objective—one accepted by a number of governments in the Atlantic Community—is continually to adjust the degree of stimulus or restraint provided by the budget (and by monetary policy) in such a way as to keep the growth of aggregate demand within a "narrow band" just below the growth track of potential output, maintaining always the highest level of employment (lowest level of unemployment) which is deemed consistent with a "reasonable" stability of prices, and thus skirting always close to—although remaining always within—the borderline of "excessive" demand. Obviously this policy leaves little room for mistakes, at least those which would cause the growth of demand to stray for long over the borderline into inflation. Today, the appropriateness of such a policy objective is being called into question in some circles, as will be indicated below.

The technical problems. This is not the place for an extended discussion of the technical problems of managing aggregate demand through fiscal policy.[1] These technical problems include:

1. *Forecasting and flexibility.* Since there is an inevitable instability in private demand, and there are inevitable lags in taking fiscal action (under the best of circumstances), and further substantial lags before the fiscal action can have its impacts on aggregate demand, it is necessary always to be forecasting the level of aggregate demand (relative to potential output) from six months to two years in advance. Forecasts are, at best, subject to a margin of error; frequently they are handicapped by the lack of adequate, accurate and timely data, and by inadequate understanding of the dynamic structure of basic economic relationships.

2. *Choice of tools.* Because the lags in altering many kinds of government expenditures are rather long; because expenditure programmes, once undertaken, can often be halted or phased back only with great difficulty or substantial loss of efficiency; and because most expenditure programmes are the means for attaining vital political and social ends that are not easily subordinated to stabilization objectives, many economists argue for an increased emphasis on tax rate changes as a major tool of stabilization policy. Choices must then be made between taxes that primarily affect consumer spending and those that also affect private investment outlays. On the other hand, some countries have demonstrated an ability to use expenditure variations most effectively.

3. *Co-ordination and control.* In some countries, problems arise in the control or co-ordination by those responsible for stabilization policy of the activities of the departments or ministries which have the direct responsibilities for various kinds of government expenditures, social insurance programmes, the investments of nationalized industries, etc.; difficult problems also arise if any attempt is made to achieve some degree of fiscal policy co-ordination between central and local governments, whose budgets may be collectively as large as or larger than that of the central government; there are also sometimes problems in the co-ordination of fiscal and monetary policies.

The political problems. Most expert assessments conclude that the technical problems of discretionary fiscal policy—difficult as they may be— are far simpler than the political problems. A government may know what needs to be done and how to do it, yet delay action for political reasons (e.g., a forthcoming election), or because of lack of public understanding and support. Frequently, there is need to take fiscal action before the

1. See, however, the OECD study referred to earlier: *Fiscal Policy for a Balanced Economy.*

problem it is designed to deal with is yet clearly apparent to the average citizen or even to the leaders of public opinion. Under such circumstances, it is difficult to take timely action, especially if the action called for is in the restrictive rather than the expansionary direction. Moreover, any action that may be recommended will sometimes itself threaten to create or reopen difficult political issues—regarding, for example, the distribution of the burden of taxation, or the levels of funding for politically sensitive expenditure or transfer payment programmes. In some countries, executive agencies are able to take certain types of stabilizing action without the necessity of first securing legislative authority. However, even their possession of such authority (e.g., to vary certain rates of taxation) will not guarantee its proper and timely use in the absence of adequate public understanding and support.

Monetary policy

As is the case for the fiscal system, there are both automatic (or built-in) monetary effects, and those which result from the exercise of discretionary policy. A rise in aggregate demand—which might threaten inflation—will be somewhat restrained by the "automatic" or "built-in" rise of interest rates and tightening of credit conditions which will occur if the central bank fails to provide the additional money that is needed to accommodate a rapid rise of incomes and output. As noted earlier (Chapter 3), this built-in impact will be further strengthened to the extent that the increased aggregate demand causes prices, as well as output, to increase. Of course, automatic monetary effects, like those of fiscal policy, can only cushion a rise (or fall) of aggregate demand, not stop it short of the point at which it may produce inflation (or excessive unemployment). Nevertheless, some influential voices (particularly in the United States) advocate reliance solely on these built-in stabilization effects of monetary policy. Their objective would be simply to keep monetary policy from itself serving as a destabilizing influence. They would have the central bank supply only the slow and steady increase in the quantity of money that would be appropriate for a steadily growing, non-inflationary economy. They ask the monetary authorities to abjure any flexibility—not to attempt to offset fluctuations in the strength of private demand, except as those fluctuations would be dampened by automatic stabilization effects. Most central banks consider this far too modest and limited an objective. Yet those critics who oppose the exercise of discretion would claim that discretionary monetary policy has more often had the effect (even though not the purpose) of contributing to instability—to inflation or recession—than of contributing to stability.

Clearly, the performance of discretionary monetary policy has often been far from optimal, judged in retrospect. Most authorities, however, believe that the critics' judgement is unwarranted, and that, in any case, the solution is not to abjure discretion, but rather to learn to use it more wisely and effectively.

The instruments of discretionary monetary policy are many and varied, and differ considerably from country to country. They include the authority to establish and to alter bank "reserve ratios"—the rules which control the volume of deposits (or loans) which a bank may have outstanding in relationship to the volume of its reserves; "open-market operations" (i.e., the sale or purchase of securities) by the central bank, through which the volume of reserves of the banks may be increased or decreased; ceilings or other limitations on the volume of loans which banks may have outstanding (exercised either through formal, public regulations or private "advice" from the central bank); ceilings on the interest rates that banks and other financial institutions can pay on deposits; directives to banks regarding their handling of foreign exchange assets; changes in the interest rates or other terms on which the central bank will lend to (or "rediscount" selected assets of) the banks; and many others. All of these instruments can affect the ability or willingness of banks to lend, or the terms on which they will lend, to businesses or individuals; the interest rates that businesses must pay when they issue new securities to the public; and/or the market prices of the financial assets in which individuals or businesses may hold some part of their accumulated savings. When interest rates fall or credit becomes easier to obtain, the volume of borrowing—and thus the spending of borrowed funds—will be stimulated, and vice versa. Increases in the market prices of financial assets held by individuals or businesses may increase their willingness to spend their own as well as borrowed funds, and vice versa.

Again, this is not the place for an extended discussion of technical problems of using discretionary monetary policy. In part, they are the same as those of discretionary fiscal policy: those of forecasting and flexibility, of choice of tools, of co-ordination and control. Since monetary policy can be changed more quickly and flexibly than fiscal policy, its dependence on accurate forecasting may be reduced (unless, as some hold, the lags between changes in monetary conditions and changes in private spending are longer than the corresponding lags of fiscal policy effects). Moreover, political obstacles may limit the freedom and flexibility of central bank action less severely than they limit fiscal actions. On the other hand, there is considerable support for the view that monetary policy changes are less effective than fiscal policy changes in affecting aggregate demand. In the United States, for example, the effects of monetary policy appear to be primarily focused on a relatively few sectors—chiefly house construction—which means that exceedingly and perhaps unfairly severe changes must be wrought in these areas if there is to be much effect on the economy as a whole. Other countries have effectively protected residential construction from the impacts of monetary policy—and the United States is moving strongly in that direction. But if this most heavy user of borrowed funds is protected from the effects of monetary policy, monetary changes must be quite drastic in order to have an appreciable effect on other sectors.

But perhaps the most serious problem in using monetary policy as a weapon against inflation is that monetary policy also has an important role to play in a country's balance-of-payments policy. Chapter 4 noted that many countries lacked adequate means to insulate domestic monetary policy from the undesired impacts of international capital flows. The other side of this coin is that monetary policy is one of the principal weapons a country can use to influence these flows. There are times when domestic stabilization objectives and international necessities both point in the same direction for monetary policy: high interest rates and restricted availability of credit may be desired to dampen an over-exuberant domestic economy as well as to restrain an undesired outflow of capital (or to attract an inflow). But frequently the objectives point in different directions, giving monetary policy a schizophrenic cast. The development of new international credit institutions (the Euro-currency and Euro-bond markets), which severely restrict the ability of domestic authorities to control monetary conditions within their borders, further complicates the task of monetary policy.

It is beyond the scope of this study to discuss possible solutions to these problems, some of which may require new forms of international co-operation. However, most students of stabilization policy will support a conclusion frequently reached by international organizations—most recently, for example, in the OECD report on inflation of December 1970—that many countries have relied much too exclusively on monetary policy as an anti-inflationary tool. They recommend a greater use of fiscal policy for demand management purposes, not only in order to make the total policy more effective, but also to free monetary policy to be used as appropriate to influence the country's balance of payments.

Demand management and inflation

The OECD Report, *Inflation: The Present Problem,* to which frequent reference has been made in these pages, concludes its discussion of demand-management with the judgement that, "In general, the most important questions relate not so much to the technical aspects of fiscal and monetary policies, but rather to the more basic question of the appropriate objectives to be pursued." [1] It is the view of the authors of the Report that the objectives of fiscal and monetary policies have in most countries been framed too exclusively in terms of minimizing unemployment. They recommend that governments also frame rather more precisely than in the past their goals or objectives for price-level stability, and weigh these objectives, along with the employment objectives, in the guidance of fiscal and mone-

1. Page 36.

111

tary policies. Few, however, would argue that price-stability objectives should take precedence over employment objectives, or even be given "equal" weight (whatever that might mean). For the authors of the OECD report are quite conscious of the facts that (a) it is not politically feasible to pursue anti-inflationary objectives at the price of substantial or prolonged rises of unemployment; and (b) even if it were possible to do so, the somewhat longer-term effects might actually be counterproductive.

People's reaction to going bankrupt or being thrown out of a job may have been different in the 1930s when it could be thought that this was the result of a natural disaster. But today, a serious recession would be clearly recognized to be the result of a deliberate policy being followed by the government. The experience of those few countries which, at one time or another during the 1960s, fell short of their potential growth rates for some period of time, suggests that the undercurrents of social and political discontent thus generated may eventually have rather violent economic repercussions in the form of wage explosions which are difficult to foresee or control. [1]

The major purpose which the report sees for more specific and firmly stated price-stability objectives would be to influence price expectations. But the report admits to the difficulty of doing this so long as the public believes—and correctly—that, in a showdown, the government would never pursue restrictive demand-management policies at the expense of a serious or prolonged rise in unemployment. When inflation has gained momentum and has persisted for several years at a high level, a relatively long period of relatively high unemployment and slack may be necessary in order to alter inflationary expectations. Yet to create and maintain such conditions may be unfeasible, and quite possibly ineffective or counterproductive.

This dilemma points to two clear conclusions for anti-inflationary policy:

1. In the future, anti-inflationary demand-management actions should be taken more vigorously and more promptly, so as not to allow inflation to gain momentum and inflationary expectations to develop. A number of the current or recent serious inflationary episodes have been the result of fiscal and monetary policy failures; thus, demand-management policies must in the future be used more quickly, more firmly, and more effectively than in the past to prevent aggregate demand from straying into or long remaining in the inflationary zone. Whether past failures of policy that allowed inflation to obtain momentum arose from experts' miscalculations, a failure of will on the part of political leadership, a weakness of stabilization tools, or lack of public support, steps need to be taken to avoid their repetition.

1. *Ibid,* page 35.

2. Nevertheless, some mistakes in demand management are inevitable. Moreover, since demand-management policies, once having failed to *prevent* inflation, are severely limited in their ability to *eradicate* it, reliance must not be placed so exclusively as in the past upon demand management as the major or sole strategy for anti-inflation policy. There clearly are other strategies which can usefully complement demand management, and a greater effort must be made to use these effectively. These policies are outlined in the remaining sections of this chapter.

Price-incomes policy

The term "price-incomes policy" (or simply "incomes policy") is applicable to any of a wide variety of government programmes, ranging from widespread compulsory controls over prices and wages to vacuous exhortations on behalf of price stability. Their common element is that, without attempting to alter economic structure, these programmes endeavour to persuade, shame, or, in the extreme case, compel business firms, workers, and others, to avoid, reduce, or delay increases that they might otherwise have made in prices, wages, rents, dividends, or other forms of incomes. Incomes policies can be contrasted with policies designed to reduce the *ability* of firms, workers, or others to seek or achieve increases in prices or wages. The latter presumably require changes in economic structure. To be sure, the effort to persuade may sometimes involve the threat—and occasionally, to validate the threat, the action— of effecting a change in economic structure, at least as it applies to individual industries: e.g. suspending certain trade privileges, lifting or relaxing import quotas, etc. But the basic purpose of the action—if it is part of an incomes policy—is to persuade people to act differently, not merely to alter the structure in a way which restricts their ability to act.

Almost every Atlantic country has had some experience of an incomes policy during the post-war period. In the Netherlands, the activity has been continuous, through the early "guided-wage policy", the work of the National Board of Mediators, the Foundation for Labour, and, most recently, the Wage Law. Use has there been made at various times of compulsory price controls, compulsory wage controls, voluntary "guidelines", requirements for government approval of private decisions, and government authority to invalidate private decisions. Norway (through the National Arbitration Board, Contract Committee, and Expert Committee), Finland (most recently through First and Second Stabilization Agreements), and Austria (through the Parity Commission and its Incomes Subcommittee) also have records of almost continuous centralized discussion, with occasional or intermittent government intervention during the post-war period in the setting of wages and prices. The Scandinavian countries all have a

113

long and strong tradition of highly centralized wage bargaining, encouraged but not formally participated in by government, through which industrial peace has been maintained. Given the great importance of international trade for these countries, the parties can hardly avoid taking account of the national interest in reasonable price stability. But in Norway, Finland, and Denmark, government intervention has frequently reinforced the weight given to stability as opposed merely to settlement, and, more recently, even Sweden has resorted to a temporary freeze.

Germany began a system of limited government intervention through its "programme of concerted action" under the Growth and Stability Law of 1967. This has primarily involved the setting by government of "targets" for changes in the levels of prices, wages, and profits, and the discussion of these targets with representatives of employers and labour. In France, an incomes policy began to emerge as part of the Fifth Economic Development Plan (1966); price controls have sometimes been used, including the "contrats de stabilité" through which industries could opt out of controls through stabilization agreements with the government. The United Kingdom has had extensive experience with incomes policy, through its Council of Prices, Productivity, and Incomes (1957), National Incomes Commission (1962), National Board of Prices and Incomes (1965), and Prices and Incomes Acts (1966 and 1967). Wage and price freezes, powers to review and delay wage and price changes, and voluntary appeals and agreements have all been used. The United States instituted her "guideposts" for wage and price stability in 1962, and used persuasion, public criticism, and private negotiations in an effort to influence wages and prices through 1968. Very recently the government has again begun to intervene, but without explicit standards. Canada's experience (Price and Incomes Commission, 1969) was brief and never fully effective. [1]

The OECD report, *Inflation: The Present Problem,* makes a useful distinction between incomes policies based essentially on a "social contract" among the interest groups and the government, and policies based essentially on a unilateral government determination. Under the former, each participating interest makes commitments with respect to matters under its control or influence, in return for the reciprocal commitments of the others. Under the latter, the goverment may consult with the parties but does not seek their agreement or consent. Various intermediate positions are possible along the scale from the pure "social contract" to the purely unilateral. For example, even the unilateral policies attempt to appeal to the recognition (which underlies the "social contract" approach) of the common interest which all groups in society have in avoiding an inflationary spiral that only raises the levels of prices and of nominal incomes and really benefits no one.

1. The maximum amount of up-to-date information, assembled in one place about incomes policies in many of these countries appears in OECD, *Inflation: The Present Problem,* pp. 77-90.

There is a second dimension of variation among price-incomes policies. As the foregoing brief summary of countries' experience indicates, numerous combinations have been used along a scale which runs from mere government announcement of standards for desirable wage and price movements to, at the other extreme, complete compulsion. Many of the methods involve a considerable degree of voluntarism. Some authorities dismiss anything short of full compulsion as useless, on the ground that, so long as they are not compelled to do otherwise, businesses and workers will do what it is in their narrow self-interest to do. Defenders of some degree of voluntarism point to the fact that modern economies are not composed of small, atomistically competitive units, which in effect have no discretion at all. Instead, they consist of or include large and powerful trade unions and corporations, whose leaders are aware of the fact that they posess a certain range of discretion, who know that the way they exercise their discretion may influence the way others will use theirs, who are aware that their market power has either been conferred by legislative grant or is tolerated by legislative inaction, and who are quite conscious, or capable of being made conscious, of some obligation to use their power responsibly in the public interest.

The methods used in an effort to implant or strengthen the sense of obligation to act "responsibly" have been variously described (in the United States) as "ear-twisting", "jaw-boning", or "finger-pointing". They include face-to-face discussion between leaders of the private groups and government officials, the focusing of public attention on the decisions made by unions and firms, explicit government criticism of those decisions when they violate the standards and commendation when they meet them, and occasionally, threats of the withdrawal of special privileges or benefits which these groups may enjoy.

The process of education and persuasion can be strengthened if the government has authority to do some or all of the following: to appoint permanent or *ad hoc* boards of inquiry, to require advance notice of price or wage changes, to suspend such changes for a period while their justification is investigated, to require testimony or the supplying of information by those involved in such investigation, and to make specific recommendations to the parties for wage or price changes in cases reviewed.

Most students of price-incomes policies agree that, in a number of countries, such policies have had at least a modicum of success, for at least a limited time, in avoiding or slowing down inflation. Such a conclusion is difficult to prove or quantify. Nevertheless, careful observation does often support it. What is equally true is that, in almost every case, the policy has sooner or later broken down, followed by an upward surge of wages or prices.

This latter fact is not conclusive proof that incomes policies are useless. The question still needs to be asked in each case whether—even taking account of the surge that followed a breakdown in the policy—the price level may not still have been lower after the breakdown than if no effort had been made. Such a judgement is of course even more difficult to reach than the one that the policies were effective prior to their breakdown. Also needing to be answered is the question whether or not the breakdown in one or more cases was not the result of incorrect demand management policies, which created inflationary pressures that were beyond the reasonable capabilities of the incomes policy. Indeed, one familiar criticism of incomes policies is precisely that they divert attention from the necessity also to pursue adequately non-inflationary fiscal and monetary policies.

It is not possible here to review the widely varied experience with incomes policies in sufficient detail to support any definitive evaluation. The review by the OECD secretariat causes it to admit that the Organization's advocacy of incomes policies may sometimes have been over-optimistic as to their effectiveness. Nevertheless, the OECD experts remain convinced that price-incomes policies must remain an important part of the anti-inflationary arsenal in most countries, and that they need to be applied with more continuity and commitment than many governments have been able to muster. Their evaluation makes a number of concrete suggestions about some of the specific problems encountered.[1]

Many, although by no means all, economists who have studied the problems of inflation support the OECD judgement, and regret that in several countries, the use of price-incomes policies has continued to be treated as an issue of partisan politics, a circumstance which makes it impossible for such policies to attract the widespread public support essential for their success.[2]

Since governments are usually the largest single employers in their economies, and public enterprises, in some countries at least, among the most important sellers of commodities and services, it is natural that consideration should be given to the role of government wages and prices in a price-incomes policy. On occasion, governments have attempted to counter an inflation by simply holding down for as long as possible the wages of their own workers and the prices of the goods and services they sell. In the end, there has been, in almost every case, a build-up of serious resentment among the workers and severe deficits in the enterprises, which have ultimately required sudden, large, and destabilizing adjustments, particularly when private employers and workers and private entrepreneurs point to these adjustments—without fully appreciating their "catch-up" character—to justify similar changes in their own wages and prices.

The conclusions sometimes drawn from such experiences—that no attempt should be made to use government wages and prices as a constructive element in a national wage and price policy—is surely wrong. If

1. *Inflation: The Present Problem,* pp. 11-12, and 36-41.
2. An effective analysis which supports the need for incomes policies (and other policies reviewed in this chapter) was published recently by the influential US business organization, the Committee for Economic Development: *Further Weapons Against Inflation: Measures to Supplement General Fiscal and Monetary Policies,* A Statement by the Research and Policy Committee, November 1970.

governments have price-incomes policies, they should be sure that *all* of their own activities conform in the fullest extent to these policies. And they should study their own operations to find ways to make governments' own market behaviour a model for others. If there are features of private wage or price determination procedures that are particularly conducive to inflation, ways should be developed to supplant them in public enterprises. If disputed wage differentials in private employment are a source of upward pressure on the whole wage structure, the government and its workers may lead the way to their resolution, and so on. Perhaps the single most important thing is for governments to organize themselves in such a way that their wage and price decisions are systematically and continuously reviewed and explored for their impact on the development of wages and prices in the economy as a whole, and that those officials responsible for anti-inflation policy participate in all such decisions.

Some advocates of income policies argue that their success is dependent upon the willingness of the governments which attempt to use them to face up to the hard questions of an appropriate income distribution, both as among wages, profits, farm and professional incomes, and managerial compensation, and—within wage income—to the differentials as among skills, occupations, industries, and regions. As part of the social compact through which government intervention in the process of income formation is accepted by labour and business in the interests of avoiding inflation, they argue, there must be the development of specific goals for the redistribution of incomes, and an undertaking by government to use its tax, regulatory, tariff, agricultural, manpower, and other policies in a way to support the movement towards these goals. Others argue that mixing up such questions with the control of inflation guarantees the failure of an incomes policy.

It may well be that the correct answer to this difficult question differs from one country to another, or from one stage in the evolution of an incomes policy to another.

One of the conclusions of the OECD report is that there may sometimes be a useful role for the temporary price and/or wage freeze, as a means for dealing with an inflationary situation that has got out of hand. It is seen as a technique for breaking through a price-wage spiral, for restoring at least temporary stability and thereby perhaps modifying inflationary expectations, and for giving demand-management policies time to begin to take hold or a non-compulsory pirce-income policy a chance to be formulated and set in motion. This conclusion will be debated by many. There are those who find even the most temporary controls repugnant in a free society. Others fear that the availability of compulsory controls could weaken the will to take other necessary actions, particularly in the area of demand management, so that temporary controls might tend to become semi-permanent controls. Still others would argue that securing the public understanding and support that would be necessary to make even temporary controls (especially over wages) workable is no different or less difficult a task than securing the public

117

understanding and support that would be necessary to make a non-compulsory incomes policy workable. Some of these objections to compulsory controls would seem less compelling if the use of temporary controls were restricted to problem areas that appeared to constitute the acute focus of an inflationary infection.

On balance, even in those countries where reliance on free markets has its greatest support, many students of the problem are coming to believe that if inflation remains as severe as it has recently been, and if public antipathy towards rising prices should reach the point which begins to threaten national morale or political stability, no weapon in the anti-inflation arsenal should be permanently proscribed, even compulsory controls. In early 1971, compulsory price controls were in effect in the Netherlands, Norway, Sweden, Denmark, and Iceland, and had recently been used in Finland and France. Wage "pauses" or conditions of severe wage restraint were in force in the Netherlands and Ireland, and had recently been in effect in Finland.

Since the present author has participated actively in US price and wage stabilization efforts (including the price-wage controls of World War II and the Korean War, plus membership in the Council of Economic Advisers during most of the period of the "guideposts"), it may be appropriate for him to add his own conclusions about incomes policy in the United States, without, however, taking the space to support or develop them. The first four relate basically to past experience (although with obvious implications for the future). The last four look only to the future.

1. A principal weakness of the 1962-68 "guideposts" was the failure sufficiently to involve the leadership of labour, business, and public opinion in their formulation and modification, and in plans for their "enforcement". The US labour movement and business communities are not sufficiently centralized either in power or influence—nor could they become so, even if that were desirable, in so vast and varied an economy—to permit the leadership on either side to enter into "agreements" committing its side to anything. But active participation of these groups in an advisory role to government in the formulation and modification of policy might have given the resulting policy somewhat greater "legitimacy", and increased at least modestly the understanding of the parties on both sides of the nature of the problems and their sympathy with the policy's objectives.

2. The economic arithmetic of the "guideposts" was impeccable, and must basically be respected in any incomes policy. Howewer, the evolution (or the failure to evolve) of the guideposts placed too much stress on economic rationality as opposed to workability and acceptance. For example, it was no doubt a mistake to have continued to insist on guideposts which were consistent only with complete stability of the price level at a time when prices had already begun to rise more than nominally.

3. The guideposts—or, more broadly, the intervention through public and private persuasion—had a noticeable and useful impact on wages and prices, even during the period 1966-68 when demand-management policy

118

was inappropriate and highly inflationary. There was (in this writer's judgement) no damage to the allocation of resources, nor appreciable inequity —both of which were frequently charged.

4. Locating the administration of the guideposts and related interventions primarily in the Council of Economic Advisers was not ideal. To be sure, since the policy was voluntary, it benefited from a close association with the prestige of the Presidency and from the President's personal intervention at a few crucial points. Neither the Secretary of Labor nor of Commerce would have been a suitable administrator, given his office, and, in any case, the incumbents during most of the period were not supporters of the policy. A merger of the two Departments, or the Cabinet reorganization proposed by President Nixon, would provide a more suitable office in the future.

5. Given the seriousness of the problem and the inherent limitations of a purely voluntary policy, the author favours the establishment, by legislation, of a Price-Wage Review Board, with limited powers (a) to require prior notice of wage and price changes, (b) to suspend such changes for a limited period, (c) to investigate them (including power to compel testimony), and (d) to report to the public with recommendations. [1] The Board should be authorized to study and recommend—and possibly even be given limited powers of control—with respect to certain features of price-setting or of wage contracts (e.g., the conditions under which escalator clauses could be used), or to certain trade or employment practices that tended to raise costs or reduce competition. It would not, however, have power ultimately to limit or control any price or wage.

6. The President (but not the Wage-Price Review Board) should have at all times standby authority for the compulsory control of wages and prices, wholly or in any part, with the requirement that any use of this authority be reviewed by the Congress under a procedure which would permit a Congressional veto of the President's action.

7. To the maximum extent possible, the existence of a price-incomes policy (although not, obviously, the details of the policy) should cease to be considered a partisan issue, but rather come to be regarded as a regular and permanent aspect of the US stabilization system.

8. A well-developed incomes policy should be in place and working before the US economy next returns to the zone of full employment.

---

1. The author made recommendations along these lines as early as 1958. See his paper in *The Relationship of Prices to Economic Stability and Growth* (Compendium of Papers Submitted by Panelists appearing before the Joint Economic Committee), 31 March 1958 (US Government Printing Office), pp. 634-6 and *passim*.

Structural policies against inflation

Considerable difficulties are encountered in classifying anti-inflation policies, once "demand management" has been put to one side. There is often debate even about the proper definition of price-incomes policies, and beyond that, there is little agreement on how to describe the remaining policies. The heading "policies to shift the Phillips Curve" is sometimes used to include all policies other than demand management, including even incomes policies. That phrase—however it is used—implies an acceptance of the existence of a stable trade-off between unemployment and inflation which is quite unjustified. Here the term "structural policies" refers to policies designed specifically to reduce the rate of price increase when aggregate demand is high and unemployment low—as opposed to policies that tend to reduce the rate of price increase at any and all levels of aggregate demand.

One principal reason why inflation is associated with tight labour markets is that, when unemployment is low, a larger than usual percentage of those remaining unemployed are marginally qualified, if at all, for any but the least demanding forms of employment. To be sure, large numbers of qualified workers continue to enter (and to leave) the labour market, to quit existing jobs to seek better ones, or to lose their jobs in firms or industries that are contracting employment even as others are expanding it. But the total "selection" of unemployed workers that is available (or is easily known to be available) to any particular employer to fill his particular needs is considerably reduced. The job-seekers suitable for any particular job are fewer in number and thus more "thinly distributed" over the labour market. Workers newly entering the labour market, leaving their jobs, or losing them, need not wait as long to find a suitable job—thus the number unemployed due to "friction" or "turnover" at any given point in time is smaller. But employers with jobs to fill have to wait longer and try harder to discover unemployed workers who have the particular qualifications they need—thus they accumulate a larger number of vacancies. This situation is sometimes described by saying that as the unemployment rate falls, more and more of the unemployment that remains is "frictional" unemployment, even though the total amount of frictional employment also declines.

Under these circumstances, employers trying to fill vacant jobs are under increasing pressure to attempt to bid away suitable workers from other employers or industries by offering or agreeing to pay higher wages; they are willing to incur substantial costs of recruiting at greater distances; or they accept the higher costs of training, of poor performance, and of rapid labour turnover involved in hiring less suitable workers. And they raise their prices to cover these costs.

These cost-increasing and wage-raising pressures of frictional unemployment can be reduced by improving the labour market information network; by programmes of labour training and retraining which can make un-

120

employed workers more available for the particular vacancies that exist; by reducing artificial barriers to the movement of workers into vacant jobs; by aiding the geographical mobility of workers from areas where unemployment is relatively high to areas where it is relatively low; and by other measures designed to even out the geographical pattern of the demand and supply of labour.

The information network dealing with vacancies and available workers is almost nowhere as good as it might be, and in many countries exceedingly poor. It involves word-of-mouth, advertising, and private and public placement services and labour exchanges. There is a strong case to be made for having a single (and therefore public) agency as the source of all information and placement activities. Requiring that employers report all vacancies to the public labour exchange, and that they hire only workers who have registered with the exchange can greatly increase the availability of information to workers about jobs and to employers about job-seekers. And modern computers can vastly speed the matching of qualifications sought and available. Advance information on forthcoming lay-offs, given to workers and—through a labour exchange—to prospective alternative employers, can greatly reduce the time lag between discharge and re-employment. Prohibition of lay-offs without advance notice to the worker and to the labour exchange would be costly to employers; yet it might greatly reduce the net social cost of "frictional" unemployment, and at the same time reduce inflationary pressures at high employment.

The case for large-scale manpower training and retraining programmes can rest alone on human considerations, and on considerations of productive efficiency. Yet there is also a powerful case—too little understood—for large-scale training and retraining programmes as a principal means of increasing the effective mobility of labour, thereby reducing inflationary pressures at low levels of unemployment. Sweden and Canada appear to be the countries most advanced in the use of such programmes.

In societies which accept full employment as an urgent goal of social policy, it should hardly need to be said that artificial barriers—public or private—that needlessly keep unemployed workers from filling vacant jobs have no excuse for existing. Yet a vast array of such barriers exists in almost every country—the relic of a day when there was no commitment to full employment, when unemployment was in fact often massive and prolonged, and when a desire to "protect" jobs from the competition of "outsiders" was a quite understandable if never fully justifiable objective of workers. Such barriers exist in central government and local government legislation and regulations, in trade-union requirements, and in employers' hiring practices. They often take the form of the insistence upon irrelevant qualifications of age, sex, colour, residence, education, training, or experience, enforced through eligibility requirements, entrance examinations, union membership, licensing, or other methods. They have some impact on the

121

price level even when unemployment is not unusually low. But by further restricting the ability of employers to hire from among the much smaller number of available job-seekers when unemployment is low, they exert strong inflationary pressures on wages, costs, and prices.

As a first step, governments need to review and alter those inflationary implications that are inherent in existing laws and regulations relating to such matters as methods of minimum wage determination and the structure of minimum wages; apprenticeship programmes; the definition of appropriate units on the side both of employers and labour in collective bargaining; union obligations under collective contracts; the labour standards required of sellers to the government; and the nature and conduct of strikes. Moreover, the processes by which administrative determinations are made under such legislation or regulations may be as important as the laws or regulations themselves. But new legislation may also be required to get at those sources of labour monopoly or employer participation in discriminatory practices which are permitted under existing law. New or existing training programmes may also be directed especially to increasing supplies of qualified labour in areas where wage inflation has been particularly pronounced or where existing wage differentials are clearly inappropriate.

Persistent regional disparities of unemployment rates reflect another major reason why low over-all unemployment rates lead to inflation. Demand-management policies sufficiently expansionary to reduce unemployment to an acceptable level in regions with persistent labour surplus must first create severe inflationary pressures in areas of persistent labour shortage. Improved labour market information and manpower training will help to even out regional disparities; but more positive measures are surely needed, designed to assist and encourage workers to leave surplus areas, and/or to assist in creating new jobs in these areas. Government payment of transport and moving expenses for workers and their families, and assistance in acquiring new housing (and in the disposal of housing in the old location) may be expensive. Yet by reducing the costs of frictional unemployment to workers and to society they may easily pay for themselves, permitting higher levels of employment, output, and real incomes, along with a lower rate of inflation.

Immobilities and frictions in the labour market undoubtedly have some counterparts in the goods markets, although they are probably far more limited. However, better consumer information about products and prices might reduce the inflationary significance of bottlenecks in the production of particular goods and services at times when no bottleneck limits the production of substitute goods or services. Unnecessarily restrictive procurement specifications or production standards (as, for example, in building codes) can also prevent feasible substitutions of alternative materials when a bottleneck at high employment limits production of the one specified.

122

Limitations, formal or informal, on the entry of new firms into certain distributive or service trades may also create unnecessary and inflationary bottlenecks at high employment. Almost every country can find specific cases of such price-raising limitations, and many of them could be corrected.

Income supports

There is one group of policies, hard to classify even as "directed against inflation", which may nevertheless make inflation control easier. These are policies which can help to make more nearly tolerable the human costs of unemployment, and thereby make society willing to accept a somewhat higher rate of unemployment—either regularly or intermittently—as the consequence of a more restrictive management of aggregate demand. These include more generous and universal unemployment insurance benefits and/ or "redundancy payments". More humane systems of welfare payments should reduce the political pressures to absorb marginally-qualified workers into employment through a highly stimulative policy on aggregate demand. Schemes of residual public service employment for the unemployed should have the same effect.

Whether persons receiving various kinds of benefits or holding special categories of jobs are or are not counted as unemployed makes no real difference. What may make a difference is the extent to which these measures to reduce hardship arising from unemployment may reduce the readiness of the persons so assisted to accept regular employment if it becomes available. For if more generous treatment effectively removes these persons from the labour force, or makes them so satisfied to be employed in a special status that they no longer seek regular jobs, the more restrictive demand-management policy may have little impact in reducing inflationary pressures. However, it is possible to design these programmes in ways which minimize this danger. For example, the Family Assistance Plan of welfare benefits proposed by President Nixon is expressly designed to increase the incentive for persons receiving welfare benefits to accept jobs, even though the level of such benefits would be appreciably raised.

When it has become necessary to create or tolerate a temporary reduction in the level of aggregate demand in order to dissipate inflationary pressures that may have been generated during a preceding boom, action to restimulate the economy may be delayed or avoided if it is possible to increase, temporarily, the availability not only of income supplements but also of programmes of paid training or retraining activity. Stepping up such programmes during a temporary slump can also permit the supply of labour to be more closely adapted to the requirements of the subsequent expansion.

Other policies against inflation

The remaining policies that will be listed here are policies which could be described as primarily designed to reduce particular costs and prices, or to minimize their increase. They appear to have little or no direct relationship to the problem of inflation: failure to pursue these policies could not cause inflation in a society in which other causes did not exist. Moreover, because these policies would improve economic efficiency and raise real incomes, they would justify themselves even if their effects on costs and prices were to be entirely offset by a faster rise in money incomes.

Nevertheless, these policies are in fact quite relevant to the problem of inflation. One basic fact about inflation is that every increase in one price or wage leads to others, in a spreading chain reaction. Every price increase that can be avoided, or every price decrease that offsets some increase, helps to avoid the chain reaction of secondary effects. Thus, every small contribution that can be made to limiting or offsetting the rise of costs and prices becomes of considerable strategic importance. The fact of endemic inflation therefore gives special urgency to the policies here listed. Most of the kinds of changes proposed would have a one-time effect on costs and prices. But there are enough individual changes which could be made to provide (partial) offsets to inflation each year for some years to come.

International trade policies. An inflationary period is thus a particularly good time to pursue vigorously policies which will reduce barriers to international trade, either through international reciprocal action or unilaterally (and, of course, a bad time to introduce new trade restrictions). The anti-inflationary effect of the reduction of trade restrictions is not merely that of allowing lower-priced goods of foreign origin into the market, but also, in many cases, of increasing the pressures on domestic producers for innovation, technological change, managerial and organizational improvements, rationalization of trade practices, and similar changes that can help to control or reduce costs and prices. Despite the great progress made since World War II, wide room remains for further trade liberalization, not only through tariff reductions, but perhaps more significantly through the dismantling of other forms of protection: quotas, subsidies, limitations on government procurement, aid-tying, and a host of miscellaneous kinds of protection through systems of internal taxation, sanitary regulations, "quality standards", labelling requirements, etc.

Protection through quantitative restrictions such as quotas may even have some directly causal relationship to inflation, for such protection operates most stringently to limit supplies and to raise prices precisely in periods of demand. The protection given by tariffs automatically weakens as internal prices rise, helping to add to supplies just when it is most needed. The impact of quotas is just the opposite.

Closely related to the above are the next two categories, which also may involve, at least in part, the protection of domestic industries from foreign competition.

Protection of inefficient industries. In almost every country, there are "sick" or inefficient industries which governments attempt to protect and keep alive through subsidies or other methods that either raise prices or somehow reduce incentives for workers and others to shift into more productive and more rewarding employment. In many countries, special support is given, through various means, to such industries as textiles, coal mining, shipbuilding, some branches of heavy engineering, aircraft manufacturing, merchant shipping, and others. If these industries cannot become efficient through rationalization, then serious consideration should be given to developing means to assist all or a part of their workers and investors to make a successful transition to other industries where rewards are higher, thus no longer requiring consumers to support the inefficient employment of these resources by paying unnecessarily high prices for their outputs.

Agricultural policies. Shifting away from those systems of support for agricultural incomes that operate through artificially high market prices, restricted farm production, and protection against imports can make an unusually strategic contribution to anti-inflation policy. For food purchases account for a particularly large share of the expenditures of low-income families. Partly, perhaps, because food is purchased almost every day, consumers are particularly aware of and sensitive to changes in food prices. Moreover, they tend not to distinguish between real increases in food prices and those increases in nominal food prices which pay for better selection, improved quality, and pre-preparation services—all of which are increasingly important. In almost every Atlantic country, economic distress in the farm sector could much more effectively be attacked by measures to rationalize the structure of agricultural production, to take greater advantage of international cost differences, and to support the incomes of poor farmers by methods that do not unnecessarily raise the incomes of rich and efficient farmers.

Policies on competition. Policies to strengthen competition strike directly at the market power which underlies cost-push inflation. Such policies could thus contribute direct, although probably marginal, benefits in weakening the causes of inflation. Some of them, indeed, were referred to above under the heading "structural policies against inflation". However, in many cases, the real significance of competition policies is that such policies can permit the reduction of or curb the increase in particular costs or prices and thereby help to offset increases in the general price level that stem from the more basic mechanisms of an inflationary spiral. Included here are a strengthening of the conventional approaches of "anti-trust" policy (conspiracy in restraint of trade, market sharing, mergers, etc.); the re-examination of laws relating to trade practices, price discrimination, and similar matters in order to eliminate unnecessary restrictions or competition; the elimination of any

125

unnecessary regulation of *minimum* prices in such areas as transport and retail trade; the elimination of any unnecessary and anti-competitive effects of licensing provisions, building codes, government procurement regulations, and similar governmental interventions; and possibly the development of new international law and administration to deal with international restraints on competition.

Promotion of efficiency. Finally, there is a wide range of industries in every country which, although inefficient and technologically backward, survive because they provide important or irreplaceable goods or services for which no alternative source is available. Their prices, however, are unnecessarily high, and, in many cases rise more rapidly than others. They include building construction; medical care; many kinds of personal and business services, particularly repair services; some branches of retailing. Available remedies include financial assistance for rationalization, removal of obsolete legal requirements, encouragement or financial support for the development and dissemination of improved technology, alteration of structures of fees or methods of payment which provide incentives for inefficiency, and many similar possibilities.

Summary: strategies against inflation

It can well be argued that inflation has become a far more serious and pervasive problem than most economists, leaders of public opinion, and informed citizens believed five or ten years ago that it would be. Alternatively, or in addition, it may well be that the importance which informed public opinion attaches to the costs of inflation has been revised upwards in recent years. Reference in either statement is obviously not merely to conditions in 1970 and 1971, but to the foreseeable period ahead. If inflation is a more serious problem than we thought, or if the weight now given to the problem by public opinion has increased, then obviously the control of inflation must receive a larger weight than it has received up to now in the design of national economic policies.

One implication of this conclusion that inflation control must receive a greater weight in economic policy may be that some other goal of policy must receive a lesser weight. Often this is taken to mean a lesser weight for full employment as a goal of policy. The problem of inflation and its control is often described these days in terms of the Phillips Curve: as a problem in the "trade-off" between full employment and price stability. We cannot, it is pointed out, simultaneously and fully achieve both conditions. The problem therefore is to decide how much shortfall we are willing to accept in our full employment goals in order to come a bit closer to achieving stability of prices. This way of posing the problem obviously visualizes

126

demand management as the primary tool both of anti-inflation policy and of full-employment policy.

Yet it can well be argued that this way of posing the problem of inflation control is misleading and unproductive. In the first place, even if we consider price stability and full employment as in some sense alternatives, the difficulty may not lie so much in our employment targets as in our unwillingness or inability to avoid overshooting them. Whatever the target for demand management, the number-one priority in inflation control may very well be to do a better job of staying on target. For the consequences for the price level are quite different between the case in which the employment target is achieved on the average but with a wide dispersion around the average and the case in which it is achieved on the average but with a narrow dispersion of "misses." For the consequences of misses on the two sides of the target are not symmetrical. Exceeding the employment target by half a percentage point for six months or two years has a much greater impact in raising the rate of inflation than falling short of the target by half percentage point for six months or two years has in reducing the rate of inflation. And many believe that at least a prolonged "miss" on the side of too much demand may actually alter the entire terms of the trade-off, if not permanently, then for some considerable period of time.

This emphasizes the extreme importance of working to overcome both the political and the technical difficulties which have handicapped demand management up to now. Even those who believe that employment targets are too ambitious would have to agree that the effort to improve the effectiveness of discretionary fiscal and monetary policies deserves exceedingly high priority (except, perhaps, those few who conclude in advance that the problems are insuperable, and that we should settle for automatic stabilization effects alone).

Still, even with the best demand management that can realistically be expected, may not employment targets still be too ambitious and need to be lowered—either temporarily or permanently—in order to accommodate the greater weight that must now be given to control of inflation? Perhaps so, at least in some countries. There may be a few countries in which general agreement can be secured that an employment target is too ambitious. Acceptance of a lower target in such cases may be helped by simultaneously improving the income protection given to those unemployed. If, in the opposite case, there is pressure to raise the employment target, it may be easier to resist such pressure if improved income protection can be provided for those whose sacrifice of employment buys greater price stability for the rest of the community.

But posing the problem of inflation control solely in terms of the trade-off between price stability and employment goals remains misleading. For giving a higher priority to inflation control need not always mean attributing a lower priority to employment. There are other things that can give way.

One thing that might give way, at least in part, is the presumption in favour of minimum interference in the processes of private decision-making with respect to wages and prices. Acceptance of some impairment of private discretion in wage and price setting through an incomes policy (or even, at a pinch, through temporary controls) may well be a partial substitute for a higher rate of unemployment as a means of curbing inflation.

Another thing that could give way if inflation control requires higher priority is the unwillingness to re-examine the wide range of "protections" for individuals and groups that were erected at a time when full employment was neither a policy nor a reality. Prior to World War II there may have been some excuse for trade unions to restrict their membership, for governments or professional societies artificially to limit the practice of a profession, for employers to restrict hiring by irrelevant qualifications, for domestic industries to be protected in a multitude of ways from international competition, for legislative or private cartel restrictions on industrial competition, for subsidies to keep inefficient industries alive, for trucks to be protected from competition by railroads, for small retailers to be protected from competition by chain stores, for supporting the prices received by farms that were inefficient or too small but for whose owners and workers alternative industrial employment was unavailable, and so on. But in today's full-employment world these protections are not merely an unnecessary luxury but a threat to our ability to achieve broader goals. They could give way if a higher priority is to be attached to price stability.

Some of the other things that might give way in order to permit a greater weight for inflation control seem to require no sacrifice by anyone. If improved manpower policies help employers to find more readily the workers they need, and help workers to move readily into jobs (or better jobs), it is hard to identify any interest that is receiving lower priority in order to give higher priority to inflation control. The same would appear to be true of measures to improve the efficiency of construction and repair services; to slow down the spiralling increase in medical care prices or costs: or to permit buyers to substitute a different but equally effective material or part when the sellers of one specified by regulation can take no more business.

How effective strategies other than demand management can be, either individually or in combination, in helping to avoid or control inflation cannot be judged with any certainty. Therefore, a government trying to improve its economy's performance on prices would be well advised not to concentrate on a single strategy, but ought to pursue a number of them simultaneously. The OECD describes this as a "positive price policy through the whole range of government activities." Some governments have talked about such an approach, but none has ever really tried it.

If it should turn out that through such a range of policies the rate of inflation consistent with full employment targets could be reduced from (say) 4 or 5 per cent to $1\frac{1}{2}$ or $2\frac{1}{2}$ per cent, we might then well decide to trade off some part of the gain in price stability for a somewhat more ambitious employment target. However, given the present situation, it would appear exceedingly unwise to start revising employment targets upwards until the full power of the new "across-the-board approach" has been clearly demonstrated.

Postscript: learning to live with inflation

Suppose that even the best will and skill are unable to overcome the inherent difficulties of trying to do a better job of inflation control, and the rate of inflation remains in the 4 to 6 per cent range of recent years, or even accelerates. Should we then concentrate on finding ways to ease the costs and distortions of inflation? Probably yes. But this is no time to begin. For no one can seriously argue that the best will and skill have yet been applied to the problem. And until they have been and have failed, efforts to "ease the burdens" of inflation can only increase the difficulties of controlling it. Presumably the burdens of inflation will be eased by making the adjustment of all individual prices and incomes to changes in the general level of prices more prompt and automatic, through escalator clauses or sliding scales, and/or through more frequent renegotiation or recalculation of prices, wages, interest rates, and other terms and conditions which affect people's incomes. It is the relative rigidity of some prices and money incomes that create hardships for some individuals or groups and windfalls for others when the price level rises (or rises more than was expected at the time the prices and money incomes were determined).

But if such rigidities are withdrawn or eliminated, the only result can be to speed up the rate of inflation. The heart of the inflationary process lies in the impact of one price increase causing another increase causing another. To the extent that this impact is incomplete or is delayed, the spiral is slowed. Making the reaction fast, full, and automatic will cause the spiral to speed up. This does not mean, however, that if the use of an escalator provision along with very *moderate* wage increases could be successfully traded for *excessive* wage increases without escalators, government policy ought to oppose the former. Unfortunately, in many countries, strong trade unions are sometimes able to achieve both excessive wage increases *and* escalator provisions.

Some mitigation of the impact of inflation on the lowest income groups and on those least able to protect themselves—particularly the aged and disabled—may be necessary. But so long as there is to be any hope of controlling inflation, any full and automatic mitigation should be restricted to the groups most in need; for others it should be partial rather than full, delayed rather than immediate; and it should, if possible, not be allowed to be used to protect from erosion by higher prices money income gains that— if generalized to all in similar circumstances—would significantly raise costs or prices.

129

Summary and conclusions

T he argument of this paper can be summarized as follows:
1. In contrast to the stable or declining price level experienced in the Atlantic Community during the period between the two world wars, the post-war period has been characterized by a mild inflation averaging about 2 per cent a year. Inflation gradually speeded up, beginning in the mid-1960s, averaging close to 6 per cent during portions of 1969 and 1970. However, this acceleration largely reflected—both directly and indirectly—difficulties in the United States. Apart from these difficulties, no clear and continuing trend of accelerated price increases can be established, and the rate of price increase has now probably already begun to slow down, at least in some countries. However, this slowing down has been purchased by serious restrictions on economic activity and high levels of unemployment in several of the most important countries. Relative to levels of aggregate demand, the inflation rate is unprecedently high. There is, moreover, nothing in the record that would support hopes that the Alantic countries will easily or automatically return to the 2½ to 3 per cent inflation rate of the late 1950s and early 1960s.

2. The principal costs of a mild inflation consist of some arbitrary redistributions of income, and of political and social discontent which reflects both dissatisfaction with these redistributions and a tendency to assume that inflation reduces almost everyone's real income. There are further costs in terms of resource misallocation and loss of efficiency, but so far these have probably not been serious. They could easily become more serious, if the inflation rate were to stay in the 5 to 6 per cent range or to accelerate. Differential rates of inflation have, moreover, contributed to balance of payments problems.

3. During the post-war period, the Atlantic governments have deliberately and with generally good success maintained a high level of internal aggregate demand. Nevertheless, it is incorrect to conclude that inflation is due simply to "excessive" aggregate demand. This is in any case a *relative*

130

not an *absolute* matter—no unambiguous definition of "excessive" demand is possible. To some appreciable extent, the role of strong demand in recent inflation has been the result of avoidable policy mistakes. Moreover, a high level of demand impinges on economies in which trade unions and large firms possess considerable "market power", in which there are strong downward rigidities of wages and prices, and in which significant institutional, psychological, and attitudinal factors heavily influence the responses of individuals and economic groups to the "objective" circumstances. Psychological responses may be altered by the process of inflation itself, as well as by other events and developments in the political, social, and international environments. It is surely possible that inflations, once they exceed some threshold level, may accelerate independently of any change in the objective circumstances, although evidence of this is, so far, unclear. However, it is surely correct that an inflationary process tends to develop a life of its own, so that merely removing its initial "cause" does not quickly or automatically cause it to cease.

4. Inflation tends to spread from one country to another—although so does price stability. Small countries, in particular, are often unable to protect themselves from imported inflation. Forces pulling towards an international uniformity in rates of price increase operate in part automatically through the market, and in part through the response by government policies to the change in a country's balance of payments. However, forces working towards uniformity are not all-powerful; some countries' price levels get too far out of line, ultimately requiring correction through an alteration of exchange parities. Some believe that such alterations need to be made more easily and frequently, or even automatically, through "floating" rates.

5. There are many strategies for the control of inflation. They involve fiscal and monetary policies for the management of aggregate demand; price-incomes policies that attempt to influence changes in prices and wages without altering the structure of the economy; manpower and related policies that attempt to reduce the strength of the upward pressures on wages and prices at low levels of unemployment; and a whole group of miscellaneous policies that try to minimize the over-all increase in prices through securing reductions or a slower rate of increase in particular prices. Controlling inflation through demand management involves real costs of reduced employment, output, and incomes—costs concentrated on a fraction of the society. Incomes policies interfere to some extent with traditional market freedoms. Many but not all of the other policies require the giving up by some industries or groups of protections that originated in a non-full-employment environment, but that are surely less important in today's full-employment world. Improvements in the effectiviness of monetary-fiscal policies are badly needed and can be made; but, in most countries, demand management also needs to be supplemented by as many as possible of the complementary strategies.

Concluding comments

Inflation is clearly an endemic problem in the Atlantic World. It will not go away by itself, and it cannot be cured simply by avoiding future "mistakes" of economic policy. Given the understandable and desirable pressures for full employment in every country, given the increasing aspirations of every group for rising real incomes, given the tendency everywhere for the fulfilment of people's aspirations (in all areas of economic, political, and social life) to be pressed ever more aggressively and insistently, given the inevitable frictions and immobilities that exist in every economy, no country can avoid inflation merely by avoiding "mistakes". Effective control of inflation requires a determination to apply positive anti-inflationary policies across the board.

Nevertheless, the current problem of inflation in the Atlantic Community should be regarded as serious, not disastrous. Currently, inflation is slowing down. The true costs of mild inflations must not be (although they sometimes are) exaggerated. Despite frequent mistakes of government policy, the level of public understanding of the problem of inflation and of the nature of the policies needed to contain it has improved. The tools for the containment of inflation are available, even if they everywhere need sharpening and greater skill in their use, some of which will automatically come with experience. It probably remains true that the greatest obstacle to improved performance is the lack of political willpower and leadership necessary to assure that appropriate and timely action is taken. This, in turn, reflects the absence—still—of a sufficiently well-informed and concerned public opinion.

Confidence that inflation can be contained should rest on the simple fact that inflation *per se* gives hardly anyone any permanent advantage. There may be strong social advantage or strong vested interests in support of policies or institutions which in the past have been associated with inflation—but none in support of inflation *per se*. If policies can be found which will permit the social interest in high employment and prosperity to be achieved with less inflation than in the past, no organized interest will mourn the loss.

Achieving better control over inflation may well involve further expansion of the role of government in economic life. Yet to the extent that its policies succeed in containing inflation, the expansion of government's role should have the result of widening rather than narrowing individual freedoms —by helping to eliminate random redistributions of wealth and income, and by creating a more stable and secure environment in which firms, individuals, and social groups can pursue their economic, social, and political goals.

The Dollar Crisis and Europe

Louis Camu
Chairman of the Banque de Bruxelles

Summary

A great many articles have been written on a subject rich in repercussions, namely the dollar crisis and Europe. The succession of major events which led to the international monetary crisis has certainly been abundantly commented upon, but the chain of cause and effect does not yet seem to have been analysed precisely or even clearly. Although a great part of the study by Louis Camu was written during the weeks preceding the American thunderbolt, it nevertheless affords a penetrating critical analysis and an excellent survey of the logical path from monetary disorder and uncertainties to the breakdown of the international monetary system set up twenty-five years ago.

At the outset, the author examines the basis and motives of operations denominated in Eurodollars. From a simplified representation of the United States' balance of payments over the years 1949-1969, the "basis of the Eurodollar system", that is to say, the accumulation abroad of claims on the American economy, is demonstrated. This raises two main questions; first, do these claims arise because foreigners want to hold dollars, or because the Americans are hardly in a position to cover their deficit in any other way? Second, are not dollars also created spontaneously by the banking sector outside the United States?

The answers given to these questions suggest that the growth of the Eurodollar market is not governed solely by the American payments deficit and that it does not depend solely on the existing volume of external short-term commitments of the United States banking system. Various sequences showing the course of imaginary operations bring out the importance of the international money market in relation to the dimension and direction of international capital movements.

It is precisely these uncontrolled capital movements, facilitated by the existence of the Eurodollar market, which form a pattern for the author to explain clearly and consistently the atrophy of the international monetary system. Throughout his study, Louis Camu is careful to examine the incidences of international capital flows both on government monetary policies and on the foreign exchange markets. The overwhelming weight of the American money market compared with the European markets perfectly illustrates the decisive impact of American bank operations on world interest

135

rates and brings out the difficulties encountered by European monetary authorities which try to pursue a policy independent of that of the United States. In fact it is apparent that the Europeans are hardly in a position to solve the major problem of economic and monetary policy in isolation and must therefore tackle it jointly.

In this connection, the author subjoins the fundamental problems which cannot fail to be encountered by a Europe anxious to avoid fresh shocks and to preserve hard-won assets.

Another problem which is today crucial, that of the war on inflation, is lucidly studied. New analyses, particularly of the effects of the revaluation of the Deutschemark, are particularly interesting in this connection.

The last part of the study consists of a plea for the speeding up of European unification and the enlargement of the Community to include other states. In the author's own words: "The problems of monetary policy, both internal and external, with which the European countries are faced today permit of only one rational solution, namely the accelerated implementation of the project for Economic and Monetary Union. This may seem paradoxical at a moment when pessimism is all the vogue, even as to the possibilities of achieving it in the long-term. And yet, the present problems, as they have been identified, demand that it should be set up with all speed, and give it such decisive advantages that the present crisis in fact offers a unique opportunity to construct Europe."

The conditions for the viability of a "Community of growth and stability" are here perfectly summed up. The present monetary crisis itself affords an opportunity for rapid progress in integration, the advantages of which are clearly underlined. President Nixon's decisive declaration of 15 August gives the author, who completed his study in September, the opportunity to outline the new international monetary system, making it clear, however, that it is premature to try to define its exact form at the present stage. From the outset, he is opposed to the restoration of the asymmetry which has until recently characterized international relations and he goes on to raise the twofold question which must sooner or later be satisfactorily answered: first, to specify the level at which the relations of parity between currencies should be fixed, and, second, to define a fixed reference point, independent of currencies and not conferring a privilege on any of them.

In the immediate future, however, the only logical approach is to absorb inflation before re-establishing a system based on fixed exchange rates. On the subject of the new monetary reserve instrument, Louis Camu advocates the creation of a standard governed by the wisdom of the IMF erected into the role of an international central bank.

In conclusion, the author emphasizes that it is once again a matter of the political authorities adapting themselves to economic realities and not allowing the international monetary system to become one of the objects of the strategy of the world powers: "Money must not be made the star of national pride... Only the technical content is valid... This time it is up to Europe to accept this truth."

The Author

Chairman of the Banque de Bruxelles, Mr. Louis Camu is a former Chairman of the Association belge des Banques and of the Banking Federation of the European Economic Community. He is also Honorary Chef de Cabinet to the Belgian Prime Minister and a former Royal Commissioner for Administrative Reform, as well as a Governor of the Atlantic Institute.

137

Introduction

John W. Tuthill *

T he paper by Louis Camu represents the culmination of a series of studies sponsored by the Atlantic Institute during the past year. Each of these studies, within its particular realm, has pointed to the need to create common European policies and to align them closely with those of North America and Japan. The issues of technology, agriculture, trade and investment policies, and inflation have been examined not as unrelated issues; on the contrary, they have been appraised in the light of the important political directions they reveal or entail. The present study continues this broad emphasis upon inter-related political considerations.

In the first of these studies, *Europe and Technology,* René Foch analysed the reasons for Europe's inability so far to find effective ways of pooling its technological resources. He recommended institutional changes designed to stimulate greater European unity in the field of technology. According to Foch, a common technology policy presupposes the definition of a common European attitude, not only in the interest of promoting European integration, but also with the objective of improving co-operation with North America and thus strenghthening the Atlantic community.

The second study, *A Future for European Agriculture,* conducted by a panel of distinguished European and American experts, under the chairmanship of Professor Hans Wilbrandt and with Pierre Uri as rapporteur, considered the Common Agricultural Policy first from the point of view of the internal interests of the six Common Market countries. The reliance on price support, at high levels, has a number of serious consequences for the economies of the Six. It has imposed a heavy burden on national treasuries and on consumers. It has helped to create surpluses which in

* Director General of the Atlantic Institute and former American Ambassador to the O.E.C.D., to the European Communities and to Brazil.

138

turn have led to the subsidizing of exports. Other countries not only have difficulty in maintaining outlets for their agricultural products within the Common Market; they also face subsidized competition in third markets.

The study recommended price reductions which would be compensated by income subsidies "of a kind which do not retard but accelerate the restructuring of agriculture and the redirection of production". Such a policy would create more viable farming units and gradually eliminate the financial burden engendered by surpluses. It would facilitate Britain's making necessary adjustments when joining the Common Market, and at the same time attenuate the explosiveness of the agricultural issue in international economic relations.

In the third of this series of studies, entitled *Stemming World Inflation,* Professor Gardner Ackley, in collaboration with a group of distinguished European and American economists, analysed the problems of international inflation and their particular impact on the northern industrialized world. Professor Ackley cited the relatively mild post-war inflation rate of approximately 2% a year, which continued until in the mid-Sixties it began to rise rapidly, reaching close to a 6% average by the end of the decade. The balance-of-payments disequilibrium of the United States was identified as a major source of the increased rate of inflation in the industrialized countries during recent years.

Rejecting one-sided explanations and simplistic panaceas for this worldwide phenomenon, Professor Ackley discussed the causes of inflation rooted in the economic structures of modern Western societies. He proposed a multi-faceted approach towards its control, namely, a flexible use of fiscal, monetary, income, and manpower policies not merely to control the rate of inflation but also to combat its deeply engrained causes and its negative consequences for social welfare, political stability and the favourable development of the world economic community.

Published just a few weeks before President Nixon announced the wage-price freeze, the Ackley study advocated for the United States the establishment "of a Price-Wage Review Board with limited powers". It may therefore be assumed that it played a constructive role at the very moment the US Government was looking for policies designed to break the price spiral which has been so disruptive, both in the United States itself and in its relations with other countries.

The fourth of this series of studies will appear shortly, under the title *Trade and Investment Policies for the Seventies* (Praeger, New York). It is the result of discussions within an international study group, set up by the Institute and chaired by Sir Eric Roll, and an international conference which the Institute organized jointly with the Keidanren (Japanese Federation of Economic Organizations) in the spring of 1971 in Tokyo.

The study, edited by Pierre Uri, argued that early positive initiatives were required to deal with the numerous problems, such as trade policy, the tremendous growth of foreign investment and the overall effects of the mobility of capital via the multinational corporations, together with the relative immobility of the other factors of production.

In this, the latest contribution to the series, Louis Camu analyses the highly topical subject of *The Dollar Crisis and Europe*. The current crisis has come about because of the failure of North America, Europe and Japan to resolve basic problems, many of which are outside the monetary field. Nations have pursued internal agricultural policies with too little regard for the effects of such policies on their neighbours. There has been backsliding on non-tariff barriers, while little forward movement towards worldwide reduction of barriers in industrial products has developed. As the multinational corporations have increased their production of goods and services abroad, some of them, and some governments, have lost their earlier zeal as advocates of free trade. Especially during the past few years, individual nations have been faced with substantial increases in inflation. In their attempts to deal with the issue locally, some nations, in effect, have exported their inflation to others. Interest rates have varied widely among the major world money markets and little has been done to keep them in balance. During 1971, an exchange rate realignment and an overhaul of the world monetary system were needed. All the elements necessary for the eruption of a crisis were upon us and the crisis came.

The recommendations of the current paper have much in common with those made in the previous papers of the Institute. Europe cannot adequately deal with monetary problems without greater unity—and a unity which must include Britain. This will be beneficial to Europe, not merely in the short run, by enabling Europe to negotiate more effectively with North America and Japan, but also by inducing, as a result of increased efficacy, a greater European sense of responsibility regarding worldwide issues.

This theme is similar to that which runs through René Foch's paper on technology. It is also consistent with the analysis set forth by the panel of experts regarding European agricultural policy. In the discussion of trade and investment policies, again it is evident that greater European unity will facilitate the solution of problems facing the free world.

Finally, the same theme will be taken up in the forthcoming paper on *The Fragile Alliance* by Curt Gastyeger, who will examine its broad political and security implications for the future of European-American relations. The paper leaves no doubt that Europe's claim of greater

140

independence and the United States' growing emphasis on purely national interests will only increase tensions in, and promote disintegration of, the Alliance, unless both sides recognize the necessity for concerted action in all the fields that are vital for their security and prosperity.

The Atlantic Institute is particularly pleased to present the paper on *The Dollar Crisis and Europe*. Louis Camu represents the new post-war European bankers who are probably the best informed group in Europe today. He is not only fully conversant with all aspects of these problems but, in addition, has a sense of political reality which gives form and policy content to his recommendations.

Louis Camu prepared a draft outline of the paper on this subject in the spring of 1971. On 5 May he met a small group of Atlantic economists, bankers and writers at the PEP offices in London. Shortly after the beginning of the meeting, Dr. Hermann Abs, of the Deutsche Bank, was called from the room by a telephone call. He returned to report that the foreign exchange markets in Germany had been closed. The need for a basic paper was greater than ever.

On 15 August, President Nixon announced his New Economic Policy. Most of the following paper was written before that. The author has brought it up to date to take into account the action by the US Government and the subsequent actions by the other major trading and financial centres in the world. However, few changes—and none of a basic character—have been required in the text.

The Atlantic Institute is indebted to Mr. Camu and to Professor Albert Kervyn de Lettenhove, whose experience and knowledge have been most valuable in preparing the paper, for having undertaken the task of writing this study. We are convinced that the following pages will not only increase public understanding of the current problems, but will also help to point the way towards common solutions.

Acknowledgements

I am greatly indebted to Baron Kervyn de Lettenhove, Professor of Economics at the University of Louvain, who, with characteristic kindness and generosity, undertook the statistical, technical and didactic parts of this report. I am also grateful to him for his invaluable comments throughout its preparation.

I received great assistance from all those who attended a special meeting in London last May: Dr. Hermann J. Abs, and Dr. Trouvain, Deutsche Bank; Dr. M.F.E. Aschinger, Société de Banque Suisse; Mr. Raymond Bertrand, OECD; Professor Richard Cooper, London School of Economics; Mr. Milton Gilbert, Bank for International Settlements; Professor Magnifico, Banca d'Italia; Mr. John W. Tuthill and Professor Pierre Uri, Atlantic Institute; Mr. Charles Villiers, Guiness, Mahon and Co. Ltd.; Sir Geoffrey Wallinger and Mr. Roger V. Low, Bank of London and South America; Mr. Michel Grosfils, Banque de Bruxelles. My thanks are due to them for their many suggestions and comments, not all of which could be included. They are, of course, in no way responsible for any of the opinions expressed in this report.

Louis Camu

142

The creation of Eurodollars

Much has been said and written about the monetary events of the past few months.[1] While the course of events is well known, the sequence of cause and effect has not often been clearly elucidated. There seems to be room for a presentation of the quantitative data in which each factor would be given its due weight, and for a discussion of the consequences of economic policy from the point of view of the Common Market. That is the object of this survey. It was written before 15 August 1971, the date of President Nixon's speech in which he "ordered the temporary suspension of the convertibility of the dollar into gold or any other reserve asset". We do not believe that this decision invalidates the analysis or the reflections which follow. It is, indeed, rather their foreseeable culmination. At the end of this paper we shall comment briefly on the events which have occurred since it was first outlined.

The Origins

It has been repeated *ad nauseam* that the crisis of May 1971 was the consequence of the United States' deficit and that that deficit created Eurodollars, whose disordered movements made the international monetary system unstable. Responsible newpapers spoke of "the Eurodollar cancer", central bank governors asked the question "Eurodollars or paper pyramid?"[2] and statesmen warned against "the spread of inflation throughout

1. One of the best comments (written, moreover, before the May crisis) is undoubtedly that of Professor F. Machlup: 'The Magicians and their Rabbits', *Morgan Guaranty Survey,* May 1971.
2. Guido Carli.

the world as a result of the growing issue of dollars in the United States".
We must try to make a precise diagnosis before discussing the cure. We
shall therefore begin this study by recalling the mechanism for the creation
and multiplication of Eurodollars.

It is often said that from the institutional point of view, money is the
debt of a bank, and, in particular, a dollar is a debt of an American bank.
Dollars held abroad are the external debts of these banks. They originate
in public or private trade, or in financial deficits contracted by or credits
extended to the United States, their mass being mostly liquid or realizable
at short term.

This simple presentation is no doubt correct, but it is also incomplete,
and even dangerously incomplete when it comes to interpreting recent
events. It nevertheless affords a useful starting point for our survey.

The creation of claims against the United States which become external
liquidities through the American deficit can be summed up in a simplified
table of the United States' balance of trade for the twenty years from 1949
to 1969 (constructed by Professor Robert Triffin). The figures (in billions
of dollars) have been rounded off:

Income		Expenditure	
Surplus on current account	25	American assets abroad	110
Foreign assets in America	40	of which:	
Deficit	45	— direct investment	60
financed by:		— public and private loans, etc.	50
— reduction in reserves	9		
— increased indebtedness	36		

The deficit is the result of the excess of the export of American capital
over the surplus on current transactions and foreign investments in the
USA. Without going into the detail of these aggregate magnitudes let us
consider how they are financed. The deficit has brought about a reduction
in the United States' holdings of gold, but above all a considerable increase
in indebtedness. These debts are precisely dollars held abroad, monetary
claims against the American economy, and therefore the basis of the
Eurodollar system.

The supply of external dollars has a simple origin. The quantities of
dollars held abroad vary at the outset partly according to the difference
between the United States' deficit and its settlement by the use of exchange
reserves. But, on the demand side, two questions must be asked: first, do
these debts arise because foreigners want to hold dollars or because the

144

United States cannot settle its deficit? Second, do not these dollars also originate—and in very substantial amounts—from the operations of the commercial banks and the central banks without any corresponding deficit in the United States or any increase in the United States' indebtedness?

Let us proceed by examples. A European exporter who receives payment in dollars in the form of a cheque on a New York bank deposits it with his own bank. If his country's exchange control regulations permit, he may be credited either in dollars or in national currency. If he himself shortly has to make a dollar payment, or if he has no immediate need for the money and can get a higher return on a dollar deposit, he will prefer to keep it in that form. His bank will then owe him dollars and will have acquired in return a claim against a New York bank or a deposit with its American correspondent. Eurodollars are born.

The same applies if an American resident desiring a better return on his dollar deposits than his local bank can offer him—since the official regulations in fact fix certain ceiling rates—asks his bank to transfer his deposit to a foreign bank (usually a foreign subsidiary of the American bank itself).

It must be emphasized that this creation depends on an external demand for dollars, either on the part of the exporter himself—to pay for purchases—or more often because someone wants to borrow these dollars. It is this demand which enables the bank to offer an advantageous rate of interest on the dollar deposit and which therefore leads to its being created. The dollar deposits are fed at the outset by these commercial transactions by non-bankers. They do not affect the debt of the American bank, but merely transfer it as between non-resident bankers. When the dollars are held by European banks, they enable them to grant credit to start with in the same way as their national currency. For example, if a bank customer holds a dollar claim which he desires to realize immediately, the European bank will borrow these dollars in New York, effect the transfer to its customer, the creditor, but will retain a forward credit in dollars which it will relend.

Our example demonstrates part of the multiplying effect of Eurodollars by which the same deposit in New York successively finances several operations. But this deposit may pass through the hands of a number of banks before being used for trade purposes. Transfers of this kind, however, have no economic effect and merely swell the assets or liabilities of the banks operating on this market.

The Eurodollar market thus becomes a phenomenon of international credit flow and the currency used is immaterial to the source of direction of this flow.

In principle, the multiplying mechanism ceases to take effect when a borrower of dollars, or the creditor whom he has paid, converts them into his national currency. His bank then sells them to the central bank and they disappear from the market to form part of the official foreign exchange reserves; the New York deposit is transferred from the New York commercial bank to the Federal Reserve. And yet, as we shall see below, this is not always the case.

In this example, the Eurodollars originated in an export to the United States. This is not, however, even essential; an enterprise which has liquidities in its national currency, but which can get a better rate for dollar deposits, may (in certain countries) instruct its banker to buy dollars. If other transactions are in balance, this purchase made from the central bank will reduce its exchange reserves. This example shows, even better than the previous one, that the creation of Eurodollars depends not on the United States' balance-of-payments deficit, but on the desire, outside that country, to hold dollars.

What leads to this creation of Eurodollars is primarily the demand for dollar credits which principally arises, in normal times, from the need to finance that substantial proportion of international transactions which is settled in dollars. This demand calls forth a corresponding supply, thanks to the excess of liquidities (or the abundance of temporarily unemployed cash reserves) in countries where exchange control is liberal or easy to circumvent. This flexibility of supply in response to demand is, however, not unlimited. Beyond a certain point, easily disposable liquidities become exhausted; thus, in 1969, a very high price had to be paid to persuade foreigners to retain the dollars they had acquired or to buy them from their central banks so as to feed the market.

Furthermore, it is well known that the central banks maintain the parity of their currencies (under a system of fixed exchange rates) by buying or selling them against dollars when there is a desequilibrium on the exchange market. Since the United States' deficit is equal to the aggregate surplus of all the other countries of the world, the dollars which they acquire would correspond to this deficit (less what is settled in gold) if there were no Eurodollar market. The existence of this market changes the process; if foreigners want to increase their dollar holdings, the central banks will sell to them, or will buy less from them. If, on the other hand, the private holding of dollars by their nationals increases, the central banks will have to buy them, in excess of the American surplus.

Thus, the total "primary" dollars held abroad no doubt vary with the United States' balance-of-payments deficit, less the fall in its exchange reserves. But, as a counterpart to this supply, there is a private demand which will always succeed in satisfying itself at the cost of appropriate variations in the interest rate on Eurodollars. Since the private demand and the American deficit are (almost) independent, it is the amount of dollar reserves of the central banks which must be adjusted on the debit side to cover the gap between aggregate supply and private demand.

This outline description applies to the normal functioning of the market. It needs serious modification to take account of the events of 1969 and 1970-71.

Exodus and multiplication

L et us break down the financing of the American deficit in recent years to get a first picture of the factors which led to the May 1971 crisis. (In the following Table, an increase in United States debts, or a fall in assets, is shown by a minus sign (—), a reduction in debts or an increase in assets by a plus sign (+).)

Table 1

Financing of the American deficit, 1965-1971
(billions of dollars)

	Total 1965-69	1968	1969	1970	1st qtr. 1971
Variation of debts:					
— to the private sector	—16.5	—3.8	—8.7	+6.2	+2.9
— to the public sector	— 0.4	+0.8	+1.5	—7.8	—4.8
Variation of assets:					
— exchange reserves	+ 0.3	—0.9	+1.2	—2.8	—0.9
— special drawing rights (allocation)				+0.9	+0.7
Total = Deficit	—16.6	—3.9	—6.0	—4.4	—2.8

The deficit shown in this Table corresponds to the official figure on the basis of liquidities, corrected for non-liquid debts to central banks. The 1970 figures are corrected to eliminate the temporary gold deposits of the IMF with the US Treasury. The allocations of SDRs (not included in the total) are shown to allow reconciliation with the official figures. The first column (five-year total) and the last column (first quarter of 1971) are not on an annual basis.

Sources: Federal Reserve Bulletin and *Survey of Current Business* (US Department of Commerce).

Taking the whole of the period 1965-69, one is struck by the fact that the substantial deficit during this period—an average of $ 3.3 billion a year—was entirely financed by the private sector. On aggregate, the net absorption of dollars by external demand or by the Eurodollar market exactly offset the deficit. This of course represents a net absorption; certain Eurodollar operations result in conversions into other currencies and thus increase the exchange reserves of the central banks.

The bulk of this increase in demand on the Eurodollar market arose in 1968 and 1969, but above all in 1969. It is interesting to recall that the first of these years is the year of speculation in gold, culminating in the dissolution of the gold pool, and the second is the year of speculation in the Deustchemark, culminating in its revaluation. The simultaneous increase in the demand for dollars shows clearly enough that the standard was not called into question; the market was thinking in terms of a rise in gold or of the DM rather than a fall in the dollar.

The figures also emphasize that the acquisition of dollars by the central banks has no direct relation with the United States' deficit. Is this an explanation of the decision taken at the end of 1969 to activate the special drawing rights in the International Monetary Fund? The Europeans had made it a condition that the American deficit should be eliminated. Now, 1969 is precisely the year of maximum deficit. This is a curious change of attitude, the justification for which is to be found in the fact that it was the second consecutive year in which the dollar balances of the central banks fell.

In 1970 and the first quarter of 1971, the plus and minus signs changed again; the demand of the commercial banks for dollars lessened and this seems to have been the main cause of the return flow to the central banks. In 1970 the American deficit created $ 1.6 billion of dollar assets abroad, while the return flow of Eurodollars brought $ 6.2 billion in to the central banks. In the first quarter of 1971, this return flow remained the dominant factor, responsible for $ 2.9 million, compared with $ 1.9 billion for the balance of payments.

The explanation of the movements by the demand for dollars outside the USA is also incomplete. The differences in interest rates (and the deviations due to Regulation Q) induced capital flows to the United States in 1968-69, whereas in 1970-71, the same causes produced a reverse movement. The effects on official reserves are amplified by the market.

The analysis of the variation in exchange reserves, or the "central bank" aspect of the question, discloses other manipulations. Table 1 in fact shows an increase of the dollar reserves of central banks of $ 7.8 billion in 1970, whereas the IMF statistics show that their reserves of foreign currencies (excluding the Federal Reserve) increased by $ 14.2 billion.

149

There may be several explanations for this difference; the variation in sterling balances, swap agreements between central banks, creating reserves in European currencies, or the accumulation of Deutschemarks in official reserves. Swap agreements have only a paper effect on the level of reserves, whereas if the central banks accumulate DM, they oblige the Bundesbank to accumulate a corresponding quantity of dollars.

Information on these types of transactions is incomplete; only the Federal Reserve and the Bundesbank publish the composition of their foreign exchange reserves. They are also the only two central banks which publish the commitments of foreign central banks to their commercial banks. The figures in Table 2, covering the last five quarters available, are therefore incomplete and there is a possible margin of error in the residue shown.

Table 2

Variation in foreign exchange reserves outside the USA
(billions of dollars)

	I	1970 II	III	IV	1970 Total	1971 I
European currencies (identified)	—0.4	+0.1	+0.4	+0.1	+ 0.2	—0.6
Identified dollars:						
— USA current deficit	+0.8	+0.2	+0.5	+0.1	+ 1.6	+1.9
— Eurodollar return flow	+1.6	+0.6	+1.4	+2.6	+ 6.2	+2.9
Unidentified	—1.3	+2.6	+1.7	+3.2	+ 6.2	+1.0
Total foreign currency	+0.7	+3.5	+4.0	+6.0	+14.2	+5.2

Sources and definitions:

Line 1: the sum of the following terms:
— Balances (other than those resulting from support operations).
  Jan.-Sept. 1970: $ 0.8 billion, *Economic Outlook* (OECD).
  Dec. 70, Sept. 70, March 71: $ 0.6 billions, *International Financial Statistics* (IMF) and *Federal Reserve Bulletin*.
— DM balances of central banks (+ $ 1.1 billion in 1970 — $ 0.3 billion in 1971. Bundesbank: *Statistische Beihefte,* Reihe 3, Table 16, column 22 and Table 18, column 15).
— Liquidation of sterling support swap agreements. For Dec. 69-Sept. 70 the figure is obtained as follows:

  Total sterling balances (billion dollars) .... —1.6 (IFS)
  Sterling balances (excluding support) .... +0.3 (OECD)
  Support operations (liquidation) .... —2.4
  of which: Federal Reserve .... —1.0 (FRB)
            Others .... —1.4

  It is this figure of $ 1.4 billion (of which $ 0.9 billion for the Bundesbank alone, op. cit.) which is shown in Table 2.
Lines 3 and 4: *Federal Reserve Bulletin* and *Survey of Current Business.*
Line 4: obtained by difference.
Line 5: *International Financial Statistics.*

The Monetary Fund publishes, in its table on foreign currency reserves, an item of "difference" between the trend of total currency reserves and those whose source is identified: the figures are $ 6.4 billion in 1970 and $ 0.6 billion in the first quarter of 1971. These are, however, gross figures, which differ from those in Table 2 as a result of various corrections made in that table.

The "unidentified" item may embody certain errors and omissions; the total error, however, is unlikely to amount to $ 0.5 billion for 1970. This item therefore represents one of the major creations of liquidity for that year.

The main source of these reserves—the only source if the figures in Table 2 do not contain any error—is the recirculation of dollars by the central banks. It is now well known that they have increasingly formed the habit of relending to the Eurodollar market their surplus foreign currency reserves. The central banks, which were embarrassed at carrying out these operations themselves, lent their dollars on term to the Bank for International Settlements which gave them a higher rate of interest than that offered by United States Treasury Bonds, and itself lent this currency to the Eurodollar market.

Multiplication

Thus, it is not true that dollars which go into foreign exchange reserves disappear from the market. If the borrower of these Eurodollars, or the person to whom they have been paid, converts them into national currency, they will go into the exchange reserves of his central bank. The result is that two banks will show the same dollars in their reserves, the first in the form of an asset (on terme) against the BIS, and the second in the form of a current asset in New York. Indeed, if the second central bank relends its dollars on term to the BIS, the game can go on indefinitely.

It is clear that Table 2 does not directly measure the magnitude of such transactions, but only the overall effect of all operations on exchange reserves. Caution is also necessary in breaking down the figure of $ 6.2 billion, the "residue" for the year 1970. It must be remembered that it may just as well be an accumulation of reserves in European currencies as the result of Eurodollar operations. In either case, however, it represents a creation of reserves by the act of the central banks, outside the USA. This is what Professor Machlup has wittily called "the rabbit multiplier".

The conclusion must be that three factors contributed to the exceptional swelling of the foreign currency reserves of the central banks in 1970. One of the most important, $ 6.2 billion, results from the policies followed by the central banks themselves. The second, which is not independent of the first, is constituted by the return flow of Eurodollars from the private market to the official reserves; as shown by Table 2, it was the exceptional swelling of these assets in 1968 and 1969 which made possible the size of the return flow in 1970. If absorption by the private market masked the American deficit from 1965 to 1969, on the contrary, it aggravated the crisis for the central banks in 1970-71.

The current deficit on the United States' balance of payments enters only as the third factor, and seems smaller — $ 1.6 billion in 1970 and $ 1.9 billion in the first quarter of 1971, this last figure being, moreover, swollen by abnormal capital exports on the part of American firms. These findings radically change comment and opinion on the May crisis.

Private capital movements

T he Eurodollar market does not easily lend itself to measurement, since it is very hard to eliminate duplications. Only the BIS has tried. The analysis of the short-term debts of the USA, those due to commercial banks, firms and individuals, and, since 1970, part of those due to the central banks, indicates that they constitute the raw material which is exchanged and multiplied among the participants in that market. They are the "rabbits".

Table 3 shows the trend of dollar balances by type of holder (the figures for June 1971 are estimates involving a margin of error).

Table 3

Short-term external debt of the USA
(billions of dollars)

	1968 Dec.	1969 Dec.	1970 Sept.	1970 Dec.	1971 March	1971 June
Indebtedness to:						
Commercial banks	14.3	23.4	20.4	17.0	14.0	13.2
of which:						
— USA borrowing	6.0	12.8	9.7	7.7	4.4	2.4
— other purposes	8.3	10.6	10.7	9.3	9.6	10.8
Sundry	5.8	5.5	5.4	5.7	5.9	6.0
Central banks	17.5	16.0	21.7	23.9	28.7	35.3
of which:						
— liquid	12.5	12.0	17.8	20.1	25.1	
Total	37.6	44.9	47.5	46.5	48.6	54.5

Sources: Federal Reserve Bulletin, Survey of Current Business; and International Financial Statistics. For June 1971, Morgan Guaranty Trust.
The figures exclude debts to the IMF arising out of gold transactions.

The flows in Table 1 correspond to the changes in stocks in Table 3. The absolute figures, moreover, have their own interest; thus, the last lines of the table show that debts to the central banks more than doubled between December 1969 and June 1971: the accumulation of these eighteen months was more than that of the preceding twenty years.

The main interest of Table 3 lies in the breakdown of private assets. Here it is "USA borrowing" which attracts attention. This covers borrowing by the American commercial banks from their European subsidiaries, which are the main operators on the Eurodollar market. It may be wondered why they borrow. The explanation lies in the large number of banks. The subsidiary of one of them in London, for example, receives a deposit in Eurodollars or borrows them, it acquires as a counterpart to this debt, an asset with the parent house in New York, and, if it cannot be satisfied with the interest paid on this deposit, it will have to relend these Eurodollars at a higher rate. The borrower in turn will probably have a different New York bank as his correspondent; the parent house will then lose the deposit. The only way for these parent houses to ensure the permanence of the deposit is therefore to borrow these Eurodollars from their subsidiary. They can then dispose of them at very short term to make up the deficiencies of Federal Funds—that is to say, to obtain abroad the sums needed to constitute their compulsory deposits with the Federal Reserve, when they cannot find them from local banks with surplus reserves—or at longer term, directly to extend credits to their American customers.

This explanation emphasizes the fact that this borrowing by the American banks is above all sensitive to the monetary policy of the Federal Reserve and to customers' request for credits; it is a privileged way of partly evading the restrictions imposed by the monetary authorities.

This borrowing constitutes a new type of use of Eurodollars; we have seen that they could continue to finance international operations in dollars, but that, if the supply exceeded the demand, they were reconverted into national currency by a borrower, then going into the official exchange reserves and being recirculated or not. In the present case, they go off the market, while still remaining dollars; the dollar could be said to be the national currency into which they are converted.

Table 3 also shows that it is this item which has shown the widest variations and which is largely responsible for the big changes in private demand. In other words, the state of banking in the United States has been the main factor in the variation of demand; by its influence on interest rates, it has induced the banks and businesses to create Eurodollars by placing their available funds in dollars or by keeping the dollars earned by trade transactions.

154

Graph 1 on page 26 gives the quarterly figures for the last few years; it shows the apparently decisive effect of these American bank transactions on the Eurodollar market.

The index of industrial production in the United States can be regarded as a perfect indicator of the American economic situation. A rise in the index means greater demand for credits in the United States. The rise coincided with a more restrictive monetary policy on the part of the Federal Reserve. As soon as production falls, the demand for internal credits slackens. It was then found that monetary policy was relaxed for fear of accentuating the recession. The combination of these two influences is immediately felt in the liquidity of the American banks and therefore in their borrowing on the Eurodollar market. In the end, it is this last demand which entails the variation of interest rates on this market and of the supply of Eurodollars by foreigners. The graph suggests that a billion dollars additional borrowing by the American banks means a rise of about 0.6% in the interest rate, with a symmetrical effect on the fall.

Such an interpretation would, however, be too simple. We find that, up to 1970, the demand of American users for Eurodollars paralleled that of non-American users. Later, the fall in interest rates is the result of three simultaneous influences: the fall in demand by the American banks, a rise elsewhere in the world, but an increase in supply by the central banks. The relation with the first of these factors shown by the graph suggests that during the period 1970-71, these last two balanced each other. It may be interesting, in this connection, to compare the BIS estimates of the Eurodollar market with the short-term indebtedness of the United States to the private sector (excluding from the BIS figures operations in other Eurocurrencies).

Amount of Eurodollars (billions of dollars):

	1967	1968	1969	1970
BIS estimates	17.5	25.0	37.5	46.0
Table 3 *(Federal Reserve Bulletin)*	16.4	20.1	28.9	23.7

It will be seen that the figures were very close in 1967, and then gradually diverged, probably because of an increase in the frequency of transactions, each "primary" dollar financing a growing volume of credits. In 1970, the difference becomes striking; where American sources show a fall in dollar balances of the private sector, the BIS shows a further

155

Graph 1

The influence of American banking transactions on Eurodollar market rates and their relation with American industrial production

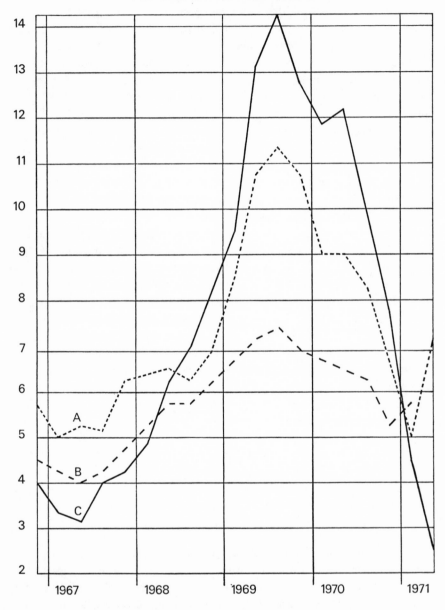

A. Interest rate for three-month Eurodollars (%)
B. Industrial production in the United States (1963=100)
C. United States borrowing on the Eurodollar market (in billions of dollars)

substantial extension of the market. This clearly shows that the role of the central banks has become essential. The dollars held in New York by the private sector could fall because they were replaced by dollars lent by the BIS or direct by certain central banks. Thus, the return flow of Euro-dollars to the central banks, shown by Table 2, is the result not only of the fall in borrowing by the American banks, but also of the growing supply by the central banks themselves.

It must also be emphasized that this supply, unlike the private supply, is not dependent on the interest rate, but is linked with the inflow of dollars into the central banks. The supply by the central banks is therefore both the cause and the effect of the fall in interest rates; the cause, because, more than any other factor, it has fed this market, and the effect because it is the fall in interest rates on Eurodollars which has led European firms to sell their dollars against national currencies.

If one looks at the trend on the European side, one finds that the money market rates in all European countries were below the Eurodollar rate in 1969; in the case of Switzerland, Germany and the Netherlands, the differences were actually more than 5%. It was therefore in the interests of European firms to place their liquid funds in Eurodollars.

In the course of 1970, the situation was gradually reversed with the fall in Eurodollar rates, while the central banks, anxious to fight inflation, hesitated to lower their discount rates to follow the market. The Europeans, therefore, from being lenders, became borrowers; according to the BIS, the indebtedness of European firms in Euro-currencies increased by $7 billion in 1970. According to the Bundesbank statistics, the net Euro-mark commitments of German non-banking firms increased by $1.8 billion and their dollar commitments by $8 billion between the end of 1969 and March 1971 (and by another $5 billion for the month of April alone). (Bundesbank: *Statistische Beihefte,* Reihe 3, Table 17).

Arbitrage of dollars against European currencies—the main motive for which was the difference in interest rates—compelled the central banks to buy back nearly $20 billion within 15 months (Table 2). The dollar was therefore quoted on the foreign exchange markets practically without interruption at a rate near the intervention floor of the central banks. The DM, on the contrary, was steadily at its ceiling rate. Such a situation, when it persists for too long, inevitably generates monetary anxieties and sets off speculative reactions. Even if the date when they will appear cannot be foreseen, the phenomenon is inevitable in a world which is losing confidence in the fixity of exchange rates.

The American Secretary of the Treasury, Mr. Connally, was therefore not entirely wrong in attributing the crisis to the fact that the economic situations in the United States and in Europe were out of phase, although the resulting exchange movements might be economically irrational. The American recession of 1969 improved the balance of current transactions and strengthened the competitive position of the United States, but it also induced a much larger outflow of capital, which weakened the dollar. Equally, Germany's basic position has weakened, following the 1969 revaluation and the inflationary pressure (which will be discussed below), but the war on inflation has also induced an inflow of capital and a further revaluation of the D-mark.

The whole of this trend can be summed up by comparing the supply of and demand for "external dollars". As indicated above, the action of the central banks is now additional to the supply derived from the American deficit. Private demand is independent of supply and mainly depends on the American economic situation. Under a system of fixed exchange rates, the central banks must absorb the difference between supply (for which they are partly responsible) and private demand.

Table 4

Trend of "external dollars"
(billions of dollars)

	end 67—end 69	end 69—March 71
Supply of "primary" dollars:		
— of American origin[1]	+10.2	+ 3.5
— recirculation by central banks	(+ 1.0)	+ 7.2
Absorption of dollars by the market:		
— by American banks	+ 8.6	— 8.4
— by other users	+ 3.9	— 0.6
As balance:		
Dollar reserves of central banks	(— 1.3)	+19.7

1. USA deficit less fall in exchange reserves.

Source: Tables 2 and 3 (some of the figures in this table are approximations, as we have already seen).

This table clearly illustrates certain essential factors of the situation, even if it disregards others, particularly the increased velocity of frequency of transactions, which enables the same amount of "primary" dollars—as recorded here—to finance a larger volume of credits—as shown by the BIS figures.

The post-March 1971 figures are still incomplete (the figures in Table 3 are estimates). It is known that the central banks must have absorbed another $ 1.5 billion in April, and the Bundesbank alone $ 2.2 billion in the first days of May before the exchange markets closed. It can be estimated that at the end of June, the central banks had absorbed some $ 26 billion since the end of 1969, and even that is a net figure; to get the amount of gross purchases, more than $ 4 billion must be added, which subsequently came back to the Federal Reserve against European currencies (liquidation of swap agreements), or against gold, SDRs or claims against the IMF. It must, however, be remembered that part of these $ 26 billion had been created by the central banks themselves.

Before we leave this aspect of the question, we should also recall the difference between the wave of speculation in 1969 and that in 1971. In 1969, capital from other European countries and from the United States was attracted to Germany by the prospects of a speculative gain (the "errors and omissions" item of the United States' balance of payments records a capital outflow of $ 2.4 billion during the first three quarters of 1969), but the Eurodollar market was relatively little affected. In 1971, on the contrary, capital flowed simultaneously into all the European countries, and the Eurodollar market supplied the bulk of the flow, the direct United States contribution being $ 1.3 billion only in the first quarter of 1971 ("errors and omissions" in the balance of payments). This contribution was no doubt higher in April and May. We certainly seem to find here, for the first time, a loss of confidence in the dollar compared with all other currencies. It is the standard itself which is called into question.

Before we discuss the choices which this situation leaves open to Europeans, we must first clarify the internal monetary effects both of capital movements and of the acts of the central banks.

Internal and external liquidities

T he object now is to examine the combined effects of the American deficit and of capital movements on the internal liquidity of the European countries.

As recalled above, the internal monetary effect primarily depends on the total currencies bought and sold by the central bank. Whether these currencies are then converted into gold or claims on the Monetary Fund or other assets in no way changes the internal effect on liquidity. Thus, from this point of view, it is immaterial whether the bank agrees to finance the American deficit by retaining dollars, or declines to do so, for instance, by demanding payment in gold.

For the Common Market countries, net purchases of dollars by their central banks can be estimated at some 13.2 billion for the year running from March 1970 to March 1971: this figure corresponds to the total increase in their foreign exchange reserves over the period, plus the winding-up of identified swap agreements, plus the repayment of IMF credits, less the allocation of SDRs. The period adopted here avoids the uncertainty of the figures for the first quarter of 1970 (winding-up of very large unidentified swap agreements) and the speculative capital movements of April-May 1971.

The importance of this figure is that it relates to purchases by the central banks, the normal counterpart of which is a creation of "primary currency"; not only do these purchases add to the stock of money, but they increase the liquidity of financial intermediaries and open the way for the multiplying effect of credits. Thus the comparison which best brings out their significance is not with the total stock of money, but rather with the currency of the central bank in circulation: this is shown in Table 5.

160

Table 5

Primary currency and balance of payments
(billions of dollars)

	Notes in circulation March 1970	External creation of primary liquidity March 1970-71
Germany	9.1	+ 8.3
Belgium	3.5	+ 0.7
France	12.8	+ 1.6
Italy	8.9	+ 1.7
Netherlands	2.6	+ 0.8
		+13.1

The second column represents the variation of total foreign exchange reserves, adjusted for the winding-up of swap operations (Germany and Italy), the repayment of a credit to the IMF (France), compensatory financing of the Treasury (Belgium) and the allocation of SDRs.

Sources: International Financial Statistics, Federal Reserve Bulletin, Bundesbank.

It will be seen that, over this period, the central banks of the Six must have absorbed some $ 13 billion out of the $ 19 billion representing the total world increase in these balances during the period (Table 2). For all of these countries, except France, the impact on internal liquidity has exceeded 20% of the primary money in circulation. In each case, therefore, the central banks, in their desire to combat inflation, have had to make use of the compensatory policies available to them to neutralize this inflow; open market operations, increasing the bank reserve ratio, reducing discount facilities, etc.

The situation of Germany is obviously the extreme case, and we shall therefore look more closely at the effect of the balance of payments on internal liquidity. This will give us occasion to consider the consequences of the operations of central banks, commercial banks and business firms in relation to the Eurodollar and Euro-currency market.

During the year from March 1970 to March 1971, Germany's basic balance (current transactions and long-term capital) showed a surplus of $ 0.6 billion, while the inflow of short-term capital amounted to $ 7.6 billion. These movements created corresponding debts abroad, which can be broken down as follows:

	(billions of dollars)
Banks' commitments in Euro-DM	+2.2
(of which, borrowing by German firms) +1.6	
Firms' commitments in Eurodollars	+0.5
Other private commitments (net)	+0.2
Unidentified investments by foreigners	+4.7
Total	+7.6

The first item indicates foreign capital which has come into Germany and stayed in the banks. It represents an increase of foreign exchange reserves, but not the direct creation of money. It nevertheless increases the liquidity of the banks who can extend further credit on the basis of these deposits. It will be seen that the greater part of these Euro-DM created by foreigners has been borrowed by German business firms from the foreign banks which owned them. At this point there is no variation in foreign exchange reserves, but the actual creation of money (a foreign deposit becoming a national deposit) and an increase in the flow of expenditure (a business firm only borrows to finance supplementary expenditure).

Thus, so long as German firms can borrow abroad, the prohibition of the payment of interest on foreign deposits remains ineffective; the holder will obtain interest by lending on the Euro-DM market, where rates are kept up by the demand of German firms. In fact, for these firms, debts in DM involve no exchange risks.

The borrowing of firms in Eurodollars (the only part of the capital movements which can be attributed to Germans) has been much less. Operations of this kind correspond to the classical case where there is an increase both in foreign exchange reserves and in the stock of money.

It may be taken that the unidentified investments by foreigners consist mainly of the purchase of short-term bills and notes on the money market. These increase the foreign exchange reserves, the liquidity of the German sellers and, directly or indirectly, that of all financial intermediaries. The recent prohibition of this kind of purchase would also tend to throw foreign assets on to the Euro-DM market, which would limit their internal monetary effect, especially if German firms no longer had access to it.

The figure of $ 4.7 billion given for this item is arrived at by difference. It involves a margin of error owing to another policy followed by the Bundesbank, which has in effect encouraged the commercial banks to place the foreign currency they acquire back on the Eurodollar market, by promising to redeem them at term at an agreed rate. Thus, in the case of a foreigner buying a bill or note in Frankfurt against dollars, the seller will be credited in marks, but his bank, as a counterpart to this debt, would lend on the Eurodollar market. In this case, the stock of money would have increased (without any variation in the foreign exchange reserves, the Bundesbank having temporarily rejected the dollars), but the bank, as a counterpart to the new deposit, would extend credit abroad rather than at home. The internal credit multiplier cannot take effect, but the external multiplier takes effect: the borrower of these Eurodollars from the German bank may use them to buy marks, thus raising the same problem again.

This policy may therefore prove ineffective. This is no doubt why the Bundesbank has recently made less use of it. Although the amounts involved in these operations are not published, an indication of them can be found in the net foreign currency position of the German banks. In June 1969, when this practice was vigorously followed in the face of the inflow of capital, the net assets of the banks were more than $ 1.8 billion, whereas after the 1969 revaluation, the net position was in deficit and has constantly remained so ever since, which shows that these operations have become less important than the banks' borrowing in Eurodollars.

These swap operations are akin to the recirculation of Eurodollars referred to above. However, while the external effects are the same, these operations at least have a justification from the point of view of national monetary policy, that the others which also bring the internal multiplier into play, have not. [1]

Since the D-mark began to float at the beginning of May 1971, the Bundesbank has been regularly selling dollars on its foreign exchange market. Inconsiderable in May, these net sales (i.e. after deduction of redemption from the commercial banks under previous agreements) amounted to more than $ 2.3 billion in June. Here the internal effects are those of a direct reduction of primary liquidity. The dollars thus pumped back into the Eurodollar market find their way to the reserves of the Bank of France or the Bank of Japan; selling dollars has the same external effect as lending them.

So long as there is concern about the dollar (expressed by the expectation of succesive revaluations of other currencies) any attempt to keep dollar assets out of a country will merely send them to another country.

1. These "swaps" are not shown in Tables 2 and 4, since the dollars involved do not enter into foreign exchange reserves.

163

The seller exports his surplus liquidity problems, to the detriment of his neighbours, close or distant. From the point of view of international solidarity, it would be preferable to keep the incoming dollars in the foreign exchange reserve so as to rid the market of floating capital in dollars and trying to convert itself into another currency, and to settle the problems of excess internal liquidity which it has created by open market sales of national bonds. (In the German case, the proposed policy assumes that the Bundesbank does not wish to raise the level of the revaluation of the D-Mark; we shall revert to this point below.)

This policy of operating through national bonds may, however, come up against a major technical difficulty, namely the narrowness, or the virtual non-existence, of a national money market, and the consequent inability to absorb sufficient open market sales. This is, moreover, why the Italian central bank regularized the liquidity of its internal money market by methods akin to open market operations on the Eurodollar market. In Belgium, too, Treasury borrowing (and repayments) on the Eurodollar market have fulfilled a similar function.

It thus seems extremely valuable, from the point of view of the monetary policy of the European countries, to have access to an international capital market, whose resources are large in comparison with the size of the national market.

The experience of recent years, however, shows that the Eurodollar market is too large and subject to too powerful exogenous influences to play this role effectively.

Two distinct problems arise here; the first, the size of the market, could be fairly easily solved at the present stage. Thus, the figures in Table 4 show that if the central banks had abstained from recirculating, the market would have been drained of its speculative funds (they would all have been converted into other currencies) before the spate of dollars involved the closing of the foreign exchange markets. The decision announced by the central banks of the Group of Ten to discontinue these operations is therefore an important step towards a solution (unless the Bundesbank increases its dollar sales!). The central banks in this group, however, are not the only ones, nor perhaps even the main ones, concerned. If, for the others, the profits to be made on the Eurodollar are more important than their responsibility to the international monetary order, they must be given access to investments elsewhere with a comparable return, for example, US Treasury Certificates, not negotiable, but liquid. And if, moreover, the central banks of the Group of Ten could wind up their Eurodollar operations as and when the Bundesbank sells

164

dollars on its foreign exchange markets, we should avoid renewing the supply of speculative capital.

The second problem, which is harder to solve, lies in the fact that the weight of the American money market is overwhelming compared with that of the European markets.. Table 5 clearly shows that capital movements of the order of $ 10 billion presented the European countries with acute liquidity problems which, with fixed exchange rates, were at times almost insoluble. Now, Table 4 and Graph 1 show that the American banks absorbed and then rejected amounts of this order over a short period. These $ 10 billion (taken by way of example) represent nearly 30% of the primary money of the Common Market whereas they constitute little more than 3% of advances by American commercial banks to the private sector ($ 297.6 billion in December 1970). The movement of funds which might endanger the monetary stability of Europe therefore represents less than the normal variation of the amount of American credits from one month to another.

The graph, moreover, clearly shows the decisive impact on interest rates of these operations by the American banks. It has been emphasized in this connection that it was in fact the Federal Reserve policy which determined the interest rates ruling on the European money markets. Central banks which tried to follow a different line of action found it nullified by the international market and were finally obliged to bring their discount rates into line. This page of history is too well known for it to be worth recalling the details.

Like sorcerers' apprentices, the operators on the Eurodollar market —non-bankers, the commercial banks, the BIS—have failed to perceive the dangerous effect of the dimension generated by the accumulation of these partial movements. The central banks have not thought of co-ordinating their efforts to arrive at the dimensions required by the credit flow, its source and direction.

This indifference—or incapacity—is all the more curious since all the operators on the Eurodollar market were conscious of the influence of leads and lags in movements provoked by lack of phasing, themselves amplified by the market.

Since the flow of Eurodollars outside the United States is virtually unlimited and the dimension of the market is, in practice, independent of the United States' deficits, the phenomenon of modifications in the timetable of buying and selling or of payments was recognized as the most immediate cause of movements.

It is impossible for Europeans to solve this problem of economic and monetary policy in isolation; they must tackle it by joint action; how can they create a European money market big enough to ensure the flexibility of national policies, and at the same time sufficiently independent of the United States?

We shall revert to this question after discussing the other problem that is so crucial today, the war on inflation. Naturally, we are concerned here only with the international aspects of its causes and effects.

The problems of inflation

On 3 May 1971, the five German Institutes for Economic Research published a joint report demanding that the D-Mark should be floated with a view to its subsequent revaluation. This publication immediately set off the wave of speculation which compelled the German Government to follow these proposals.

The reasoning of the Institutes for Economic Research was, however, only partially based on the inflow of foreign currency into Germany in the preceding months. Their main concern was the war on inflation. They stressed the international interdependence of prices; price increases abroad enabled German firms to raise their export prices, while the rise in the price of imported goods gave industrialists the same freedom of manoeuvre on the internal market. In these conditions, the only way of preventing the rise of internal prices is to revalue the currency, ideally by allowing the exchange rate to rise in harmony with the rise in foreign prices. Thus prices in marks could remain stable in spite of their rise expressed in terms of dollars.

Before criticising this position, let us say at once that concern with the problem of inflation is fully justified, as shown by the trend of price indexes given in Table 6.

These indexes are not always strictly comparable to each other and too much importance should not be attached to slight differences between one country and another. It is, however, clear that, during the first wave of inflation in Europe (1963-66) the Germans succeeded in maintaining much greater price stability than their Common Market partners or than the Americans. The trend of the last two years, on the other hand, shows a much greater acceleration of the rise in Germany than elsewhere, except

Table 6

Trend of internal prices
(Average annual growth rates)

	Industrial wholesale prices		Cost-of-living Index	
	1963-1969	1969/1 - 1971/1	1963-1969	1969/1 - 1971/1
Germany	0.6	7.5	2.6	4.5
Belgium	2.2	4.0	3.8	4.0
France	2.2	6.0	4.0	5.5
Italy	1.8	14.5	3.3	5.0
Netherlands	2.5	2.0	5.0	5.0
USA	2.2	3.7	3.2	5.5

Source: Main Economic Indicators (OECD). For France, Belgium and the Netherlands, manufactured products. For Germany and Italy, average of consumer goods and investment.

in Italy. And the figures for the last twelve months show that if the price push is slowing down in several European countries, it is, on the contrary, becoming accentuated in Germany. If during the earlier period it was justifiable to say that the Germans were importing price inflation, this no longer seems true for the last two years.

Now, these two years include the effects of the changes in monetary parities in the autumn of 1969. The revaluation of the D-mark lowered the cost of imported raw materials, and, to a lesser extent, of manufactured products. The trend of internal prices is no more satisfactory in Germany, in spite of the revaluation, than it is in France, where, on the contrary, devaluation has involved the automatic rise of import prices.

This suggests that the present causes of German inflation are rather to be found in the internal situation. In this connection Table 7 indicates certain significant explanatory factors.

Table 7

Trend of unit labour costs, 1969-1971/I
% variation 1969/I - 1971/I

	Industrial production	Industrial employmt.	Product-ivity	Hourly earnings	Labour costs	Labour costs in $
Germany	+14	+6	+ 7.5	+28	+21	+32
Belgium	+12	+1	+11	+23	+11	+11
France	+12	+3	+ 8	+21	+12	+ 1
Italy	+ 3.5	+5	— 1.5	+35	+37	+37
Netherlands	+24.5	0	+24.5	+18	— 5.5	— 5.5
USA	— 2	—6.5	+ 4.5	+12.5	+ 7	+ 7

Source: Main Economic Indicators (OECD).

168

The unreliability of these figures must again be stressed.[1] The margin of error is, however, not enough to invalidate the conclusion that there are major differences in the trend of unit labour costs.

Except for Italy, which is manifestly a special case, where social tensions have led to veritable industrial stagnation, Germany is the country where labour costs have risen fastest; these results confirm and explain the trend of prices of manufactured products shown in Table 6 (which were given on an annual basis).

The figures in Table 7 strongly suggest that the price rise in Germany at present depends on the trend of internal costs and is no longer induced by the rise in external costs. The attempt to arrest price rises by currency revaluation seems, in these conditions, to be the application of a remedy which is not appropriate to the present malady, on the pretext that it is the same malady as that of five years ago.

Too much importance should not be attached to the last column in Table 7, which adjusts the trend in the light of parity changes. The situation at the beginning of 1969 was not in fact one of price equilibrium and it is clear that the Germans (like the Italians, indeed) at that time had the benefit of a competitive advantage, or, if is preferred, that their profit margins were higher when they sold at the same prices. Nevertheless, Germany's basic balance is in slight deficit since 1968 (net long-term capital exports exceeding the surplus on current transactions) and the trend (in dollars) of prices and costs for the last two years will not tend to restore a surplus.

It must not, however, be concluded from this that the price rise and revaluation will endanger Germany's balance of payments. Reference must be made here to another aspect of the international interdependence of prices, which is neglected by the German analysts. They reason, in effect, as though they were dealing with a small country passively submitting to the influence of external prices. This is no doubt true for raw materials, but Germany is today, on a par with the United States, the world's first exporter of manufactured products. For the Common Market countries (and for many others too) Germany is far and away their most important trade partner and the prices of German industrial products determine those of the European market.

---

1. Hourly earnings do not necessarily represent the total trend of wage costs (employers' contributions to social security may have increased faster): the employment data refer to workers and not to hours worked. It is also probable that the categories covered are not identical from one country to another. Minor differences in the trend are therefore not significant.

The consequence of this has been that the 1969 revaluation of the D-mark has created a margin of manoeuvre for the other European exporters; the Belgians, the Italians and the French have taken advantage of it to follow the rise in German export prices. This rise was, moreover, very necessary in Italy, in view of the rapid climb in costs. It is particularly significant that, ever since the second quarter of 1970, the French index of average export values (expressed in dollars) has been higher than before the French devaluation and has gone up by a further 4% since then.

Such indexes are, however, relatively insignificant. Thus, the German index of average export values has only gone up by 1% since the 1969 revaluation, while a price index based on a large sample of exported manufactures shows a rise of 7%, which is much more plausible in the light of the trend of internal prices. Such indexes are, however, not available for the other countries.

The shortcomings of the statistical mechanism make it difficult to reach positive conclusions here. It may, however, be suggested that the revaluation of the mark alone is relatively ineffective in checking the rise of German industrial prices. In fact, more than half Germany's imports of manufactures come from her Common Market partners. If these partners, as seems probable, align their export prices with German prices, the revaluation will mean a rise in the price of imports in dollars, rather than a fall in the price in marks. (This obviously does not apply to raw materials, the price of which remains fixed in dollars). This same policy on the part of the other European firms moreover enables German industry to keep its export prices in pace with the rise in its internal costs without losing markets.

This analysis suggests that European trade in industrial products is in practice based on a mark standard rather than on a dollar standard. In these circumstances, the revaluation of the mark leads to the export of German inflation; it creates an upward thrust of prices in neighbouring countries, directly in the case of imports from Germany, and indirectly by giving national industries the latitude which allows this rise.

In the years of the great pre-war depression, currency devaluations were spoken of as a means of exporting unemployment, and the post-war monetary system tried to prevent the return to such practices. Today the conflict between the objective of internal equilibrium and the objective of international solidarity has taken another form. In a period of depression a country which wanted to follow a policy of full employment on its own had to devalue its currency. Nowadays, a country which wants to pursue a policy of price stability on its own, would have to revalue its currency.

170

The foregoing analysis, however, suggests that the German situation does not fit into this simplified pattern; change of parity might well serve to export inflation, but it is ineffective for combating price rises originating from the increase of internal costs.

To come back to the European point of view, the problem which emerges from the above discussion is that of capital movements in a context of inflation. If the war on rising prices must make use primarily of the weapons of monetary policy (in the European setting there are too many institutional restraints on budget policy for it to have the necessary flexibility), it is then necessary to be able to protect oneself against sudden inflows of capital which may diminish its effectiveness. This remains true, even if inflation arises primarily from internal pressures and if, in consequence, the excess liquidity caused by the balance of payments constitues an instrument of propagation rather than of initiation.

It must no doubt be recalled at the same time that capital movements may serve essential objectives of the allocation of resources and that even shifts of liquid funds may constitute a major instrument of monetary policy.

This is not all; a further dimension remains to be added to these difficulties, namely the balance-of-payments prospects of the United States. If we have stressed the fact that the current deficit was hardly responsible for the recent crisis, the fact nevertheless remains that the cumulative effect of the deficits of the past few years is one of the causes of today's difficulties. It is clear that, in the monetary sphere, the United States weighs so heavy that its evolution will be one of the main elements of the world in which, through necessary adjustments, an equilibrium leading to expansion must be re-established.

After considering this point, we turn to the internal problems of the Economic and Monetary Union within the Common Market (including its enlargement) and to a discussion of the policies which might today promote its objectives.

The prospects of the United States' balance of payments

T he only question so far has been that of financing the American deficit and particularly of the bank movements which should equalize the final balance of all transactions. We shall now consider these different transactions; their trend is shown in Graph 2, using the new presentation adopted by the *Survey of Current Business* since June 1971.

Net exports of merchandise largely determine the balance of current transactions. It may therefore be concluded from this that the increase in the net income which Americans earn from their past investments almost makes up for the deterioration in the current non-trading items (grants, transfers, tourism etc.).

The striking feature here is the fall in the surplus over the last few years. The American recession of 1970 improved exports by a bare $ 1.5 billion only and it is highly probable that a recovery in the USA in 1971, coinciding with a slowing down in expansion in Europe, will bring about a further deterioration in current account. The year 1970 represents the most favourable cyclical moment for an American surplus; that is the measure of the weakening of the basic position since 1964.

This trend can only partly be explained in terms of prices. Table 6 showed that internal wholesale prices had hardly risen in America any more than in Europe (and not at all, if allowance is made for the trend of the last two years). Nevertheless, average unit export values have risen slightly more for the USA (20% between 1964 and 1970) than for France and Germany (13% between the same dates). As we have seen above, however, these figures are not very significant. Whatever may be the reason, the fall in the export surplus and the disappearance of the surplus on

Graph 2

United States' balance of payments

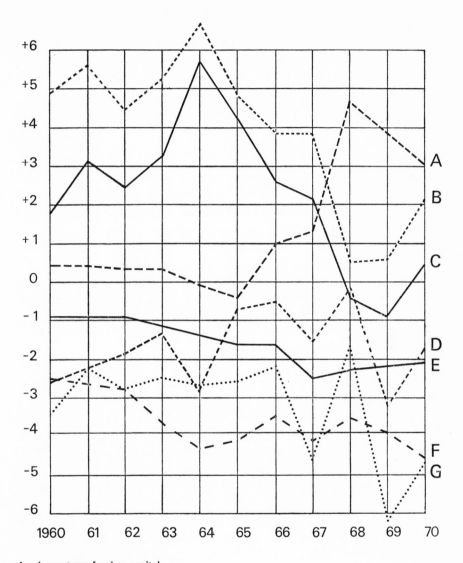

A. Long-term foreign capital
B. Merchandise
C. Current transactions
D. Short-term capital
E. Public capital (United States)
F. Long-term capital (United States)
G. Basic balance

current transactions must be taken as probabilities in considering the prospects for the next few years.

Alongside capital movements, two items display great stability. First, public capital (from which early repayments have been subtracted), the net exports of which have moved slowly from $ 1 to 2 billion; second, long-term exports of private capital, the bulk of which consists of direct investments. Here again, the amount is growing fairly steadily, from $ 2.5 to 4.5 billion. Already for some years past, the United States, in an effort to redress its balance of payments, has been imposing limitations on these movements, especially towards Europe; the figures bear witness to the scant success of this policy and there is little reason to think that any fresh effort in this direction would meet with much greater success.

Long-term foreign capital, after remaining for a long time at an almost insignificant level, rose spectacularly in 1968, under the combined influence of the Wall Street rise and the efforts of the American unit trust investment funds. A new current certainly seems to have been created, capable of surviving the rise which generated it, and even the setback to the biggest of these funds. It is no doubt reasonable to expect this type of investment to continue at an average rate in the order of $ 3 billion a year.

Short-term capital is, of course, the most volatile element in the system. The item "errors and omissions" which regularly shows a deficit, has been added here. These unidentified outflows increased considerably in 1969 (speculation on the mark) as they will no doubt do again in 1971 and for the same reasons. The other movements are rather tending to fall, no doubt in so far as short-term financing by the Eurodollar market has replaced credits granted from New York. Except in moments of monetary uncertainty or wide disparity in interest rates, this item could tend to balance out.

Adding up these different factors, the extrapolation obtained would be that of a deficit in the basic balance of the order of $ 3 billion a year in "normal" periods. This figure is a little above the average for the early 1960s, but far below the rate for the last four years, when it has been more than $ 4 billion. And it can be expected to be more than $ 8 billion during the first half of 1971, which is certainly not a normal year. It should also be emphasized that this estimate does not allow for the elements of steady deterioration noted above; thus, it implicitly assumes that the efforts at recovery which the present situation will no doubt force upon the United States Government will in fact be made.

This estimate also implies a certain scepticism as to the vigour with which such measures can be pursued[1]. It would indeed be necessary to bring about a surplus on current transactions of at least $ 5 billion a year to ensure that the overall position was in comfortable equilibrium at term, without imposing any restrictions on capital exports. But these $ 5 billion, which carry such great weight in international payments, are a mere trifle in an economy whose dimensions, as measured by GNP, exceed $ 1,000 billion[2], It is hard to imagine an American government pursuing a policy of internal deflation or renouncing the objectives of its world political strategy for the sake of such a slight difference. In what follows, we shall therefore start from the assumption that if the Europeans do not want to go on accumulating dollars, it is up to them to take effective action. In other words, all that can be hoped from the American side is policies which bring the external deficit from its present catastrophic level to a "normal" level.

In any event, these are no more than assumptions. Even if they contain a considerable margin of error, they are those which appear most probable, and therefore, those which should be taken into account when framing a policy.

1. It may be recalled that this study was written before the announcement on 15 August 1971 of President Nixon's measures. The introduction of the 10% surcharge on United States imports—coupled with the other measures designed to strengthen the competitive position of American producers as against imported products—might make the hypothisis which follows somewhat more plausible.

2. The $ 5 billion fund for the redressement of the American balance might have a much greater effect if it called into question the whole system of international relations.

European economic and monetary policy

T he last part of this study is designed to draw conclusions in the matter of economic policy from the facts and assumptions set out above. We shall start by stating the central proposition and then go on to analyse its components and try to justify it.

The problems of monetary policy, both internal and external, with which the European countries are faced today, permit of only one rational solution, namely the accelerated implementation of the project for an Economic and Monetary Union. This may seem paradoxical at a moment when pessimism is all the vogue, even as to the possibilities of achieving it in the long term. And yet, the present problems, as they have been identified, demand that it should be set up with all speed, and afford it such decisive advantages that the present crisis in fact offers a unique opportunity to construct Europe.

Four propositions are submitted in this connection. The aim is to introduce in the Common Market countries:

1. exchange rates jointly flexible against the dollar;

2. the rapid elimination of margins of fluctuation between Community currencies;

3. common regulations for movements of external capital;

4. a common programme for combating inflation.

Each of these points is closely bound up with the others, and each of them contributes to the whole. Their significance and their implications will be brought out seriatim. They must be looked at as a whole, and they lose their meaning if they are regarded individually.

1. The flexibility of external exchange rates

Technically, flexible rates mean that the central banks are no longer obliged to buy in all the surplus dollars offered on the market when the rate reaches the lower limit of the narrow variation authorized.

This constitutes, at the present stage, the only available method of avoiding an undesired accumulation of dollars. With fixed exchange rates there is no alternative; the American deficit and the use of the dollar as currency denomination of the international credit flow will inevitably be reflected in the increase in the dollar balances of the central banks. The analysis indicates two other possibilities: financing by the private market and the reduction of American foreign exchange reserves. Neither of these now offers any solution. Once the dollar is challenged, we can hardly expect to see the rapid reconstitution of vast private balances which was experienced in 1967-68. It is highly probable that the new external dollars created by the American deficit will fast accumulate in the currency reserves of the central banks.

Furthermore, the foreign exchange reserves of the United States had fallen in June 1971 to $ 13.5 billion of which $ 8 or 9 billion must be regarded as non-disposable; this represents a minimum gold stock which the United States wishes to conserve at all costs. No doubt Belgium and the Netherlands could succeed in converting part of their surplus dollars into SDRs or other assets, but that is because their demands are small enough that they can be satisfied. All that a massive demand presented by the Europeans could obtain would be to make the dollar officially non-convertible. This would introduce further trouble and could aggravate the lack of confidence without in any way changing the substance of the problem.

This aspect is, in any event, a minor one; it has been emphasized above that the monetary effect (and the inflationary effect) are precisely the same whether the central banks accumulate gold or dollars. So long as inflationary pressures exist in Europe, external economic policy should be aimed at eliminating the balance-of-payments surplus which is the counterpart of the American deficit. Since one can hardly rely on the effectiveness of the exhortations which the Europeans have been addressing to the United States on this subject for at least seven years past, it is now up to the Europeans themselves to take the necessary action.

With a flexible exchange system, the Europeans are masters of the surplus which they desire (or which they are prepared to accept) in their external transactions. The net purchases (or sales) of foreign currencies which the central banks made for each period would become one of the crucial decisions of Community economic policy. If the central banks do not buy dollars, private transactions will necessarily balance out and the American deficit will be reduced to the surplus which the rest of the world is prepared to accept.

In present circumstances, it is clear that the consequences of a floating rate would be a depreciation of the dollar or an appreciation of European currencies. This is a prospect which industry would contemplate without pleasure. It is not very pleasant deliberately to weaken your own competitive position. The Europeans would like the Americans to do away with their deficit , but, implicitly, without losing any of their own surplus, which is manifestly impossible. Whether the dollar falls or European currencies rise, the effects are exactly the same on the markets of Europe, the United States and the Third World. Economically speaking, there is no difference between the two, any more than there is between the European surplus and the American deficit. There can be no reduction in the one without a symmetrical diminution of the other and it is perfectly futile to want to maintain the one and to eliminate the other.

In a situation of this kind, it is quite idle to try to apportion responsibilities. An interdependent economic system is like a Newtonian universe, in which each star exerts its own influence and is subject to that of others; each contributes its share to the trajectory of all. The economic universe, however, embodies an asymmetry to which the economists have long called attention; pressure for adjustment is primarily exerted on the deficit country because of the loss of its foreign exchange reserves. In the present case, however, the universe is symmetrical so long as the Europeans accumulate dollars as a counterpart to the American deficit. If they do not want to continue, it is then up to them to take the initiative.

All this is evident, and would not be worth repeating, were it not for the blindness on this subject which is too common in Europe. If one looks for a moment at the alternative ways of eliminating the American deficit— protectionism on the internal market, the withdrawal of troops from Europe, the end of aid to the Third World—would it really make the Europeans any happier? If the end of the Vietnam War would reduce the American deficit, it would also reduce the surplus of the Europeans, whose industry profits indirectly from the military commitments of the United States. And it is enough to see the competition among the Europeans when an American firm contemplates building a factory, to realize that nor is it satisfactory to eliminate direct investments, with the creation of jobs and the possibilities for restoring regional balance which they entail.

A controlled flexibility of exchange rates which, we repeat, would leave the Europeans masters of the external surplus they are prepared to accept, clearly seems to be the preferable solution, as the one which introduces the least disturbance into international political relations. Just as it is the most adaptable. We are reasoning now in terms of full employment and of the war on inflation, in which the elimination of an external surplus is one of the effective instruments of economic policy available. But there is nothing to say that such a situation must be permanent, and, in different circumstances, the political authorities of the Community might on the contrary desire a surplus and instruct the central banks to buy foreign currency on the market.

At the international level, a system of this kind, if it lasted long enough, would end by creating a European monetary bloc; a certain number of currencies would become linked to European currencies, the rest remaining tied to the dollar. The choice would be made in the light of predominant trade relations. Once again, the result would be the same whether it was the dollar or the European currencies which floated. It is clear that such a solution is not without its disadvantages, but it is hard to see any choice which does not have greater disadvantages. In particular, it avoids the return to tight controls, the memory of which is highly irksome, even if it demands regulation of the movement of external capital.

2. *The solidarity of Community currencies*

It is clear that a greater flexibility of exchange rates would very soon become incompatible with the functioning of the Common Market if this system applied to the reciprocal relations of the Community currencies. Technique teaches us that, on the foreign exchange market, each central bank maintains the parity of its currency against the dollar. If the permitted margin of fluctuation is 1% (which is the case under the IMF agreements) the difference between a currency which is strong against the dollar and one which is weak against the dollar may reach the limit of 2%. And if these currencies reverse their position in the course of time (the strong becoming weak and vice versa) the theoretic maximum difference could reach 4%. The European Monetary Agreement system involves smaller margins of variation against the dollar (0.75%) but the fact remains that the possible fluctuation between European currencies is still twice the possible fluctuation against the dollar.

There is hardly any need to stress the irrational character which such an arrangement assumes when the creation of a monetary union is contemplated. It is therefore quite natural that one of the first steps envisaged should have been to reduce the margins of fluctuation between European currencies.

The problem assumes further gravity as soon as the margins of fluctuation against the dollar widen. All the disadvantages experienced today with the floating mark, among others in the functioning of the agricultural market, would be multiplied. The method of intervention of the central banks will have to be modified, and this is true even on the basis of the decisions taken last February and reopened by the floating of the mark on 9 May.

The system contemplated by the Werner Committee, of reducing the margins between European currencies was, it is true, complicated, since it assumed that the interventions of each central bank would at all times be co-ordinated with those of the others. One market may be a seller while another is a buyer, and the central banks will have to react to a weighted combination of net supply and demand on the group of markets. In spite of its inherent difficulties, it is no doubt technically feasible to apply this mechanism, but it is understandable that the central banks should have asked for an experimental period.

In the longer term, what is envisaged is something much more simple: the suppression of the margins between European currencies, and the conversion of the "Organization of Central Banks" (to use the expression of the Werner Committee) into a veritable European Fund which would directly carry out exchange transactions on the various European markets.

From the point of view of widening the margins of fluctuation as against the dollar, it would be much simpler to cut short the transition period and to proceed to create this agency as quickly as possible, limiting the margins of fluctuation between currencies from the outset to the minimum technically necessary so long as real unification has not been achieved. In this way, the slightly greater uncertainty introduced into exchange with the dollar area would have its counterpart in a reduction of risks in intra-European transactions.

As an immediate step this would require the German authorities to fix their exchange rates in relation to their European partners. And at this level, confirmed by the revaluation of the mark in relation to the other Community currencies, movements would become united in relation to the dollar.

The virtual suppression of margins between a group of currencies (assuming that exchange operations between them no longer took place via the dollar) would modify the functioning of foreign exchange markets. Operators are very sensitive to minimum differences of rates which facilitate adjustments. In practice, private operators who must in any circumstances

180

buy or sell to meet their trading or financial needs choose the best moment, that is to say, the most favourable for their operations; thus, a slight fall will induce purchases and a slight rise will induce sales, with an automatic effect of return to equilibrium.

With virtually fixed rates, the benefit of this mechanism is lost. It is, however, only a question of slight differences in the timing of operations. The reasons for buying or selling (trade transactions, investments, borrowing) are not sensitive to the margins of fluctuations; the supply of and demand for a currency on a market is not affected by them over a longer period. Thus, with fixed rates, the central banks would no doubt have to intervene more often, buying one day and selling the next, but it may well be thought that the net effect on a year's buying and selling would be insignificant.

If this technical aspect has little importance, the influence on the conditions of monetary policy would, on the contrary, be more significant. Recent years have shown that differences in interest rates constitued one of the means of regularizing liquidity on a market, funds flowing to the market where the yield was highest. The reduction of the margins of exchange fluctuations would make this mechanism more sensitive by doing away with the need for term cover, with the costs involved. The interest rate would thus become a much more sensitive instrument within a fixed interest rate zone; where a difference of, say, 1% was necessary to induce movements of funds, $\frac{1}{2}\%$ or $\frac{1}{4}\%$ would be enough. At this point, the level of the discount rate (which becomes a Community decision) is the instrument of cyclical policy, and small deviations from this average rate become the instrument for regulating liquidity on the regional markets. Experience of the functioning of these new mechanisms would have to be acquired gradually.

There remains the more general problem. The solidarity of European currencies implies mutual support, that is to say the backing of the weakest by the strongest. This is not, however, linked to the virtual suppression of margins, but comes into being as soon as the margins of fluctuation between European currencies are reduced compared with the margin of fluctuation in relation to the dollar. Thus, if the dollar were weak on all European markets except Milan, the Bank of Italy would have to induce a fall in the dollar on its market too, that is to say, it would have to sell enough to modify the equilibrium on that market. It could not accept the risk of this drain on its foreign exchange reserves except with a guarantee of support from the other central banks, whose policy compelled it to sell dollars.

181

The abolition of all margin of fluctuation does not change the essence of the problem, though it may affect its intensity in the very short term. The Community countries, in accepting the principle of smaller margins among themselves than in relation to the dollar have, in fact, already accepted this solidarity. Its application should, moreover, not involve any additional burden, if one accepts the point of view defended above that minor fluctuations (in the context of the $\frac{1}{2}\%$ margin) have no influence on supply and demand over a period of a few months.

It may be provisionally concluded that, faced with the prospect of the widening of the margins of exchange rates, the Community countries should either abandon the Common Market, whose functioning is not compatible with significant and continual variations in the currencies of the group, or turn resolutely in the direction of monetary unification. At this stage, the more radical solution of the prompt installation of institutions and an elimination of margins of fluctuation within the Community is technically simpler, without involving additional economic costs. It would, moreover, be of great political effect. We must now examine the other conditions for achieving it.

3. *The regulation of external capital movements*

The system so far envisaged, of exchange rates fixed between European currencies and floating in relation to the dollar, may meet the objectives of economic policy to control the surplus of the basic balance and to create liquidities by external relations. In the event of an inflow of capital, however, it would do so only at the cost of a rise in the exchange rate (a fall in the dollar) which might be unrelated to fundamental economic equilibrium. Exchange rates cannot be left to the mercy of speculative influences and if one has to buy too many dollars to avoid a rise in the rates, one loses control of internal liquidity.

The system proposed here is therefore valid externally only so far as it is completed by measures which lessen the attraction for holders of liquid funds to shift them into or out of Europe.

In this connection, the Commission of the Community has proposed directives, and, without approving them formally, the Ministers have declared their readiness to apply them where this has not already been done. Some of them are designed to lessen the attraction for foreigners of short-term investment; they can no longer earn interest on their bank deposits and will no longer have access to negotiable securities on the money market. Other provisions would limit borrowing abroad by banks and business firms. Finally, the reserve ratios on foreign deposits would limit the credits which the banks could extend on this basis and would at the same time make those deposits less profitable. Belgium, which has for many years practised the system of the double foreign exchange market, has remained self-consistent; she has strengthened the barriers dividing the trading market from the financial market.

For the immediate future, when substantial floating capital has flowed into Germany, such measures should encourage it to flow out, though only if its holders no longer believe in the possibility of an exchange profit. In July, the Bundesbank seemed more anxious to sell dollars, for reasons of currency control, than the speculators were to sell their marks, and the consequent rise in the mark justified their "wait and see" policy.

If the problems of the spring of 1971 were to arise again in the future, these measures would no doubt be effective enough to make it unnecessary to generalize the system of a double foreign exchange market, already criticised because of the controls which it requires. There would indeed be less reason to expect the forthcoming devaluation (or revaluation) of a European currency if a Community exchange rate reflected the overall situation of the Union, which, by definition, would be more stable than that of any of its members. In addition, a progressive and gradual variation in exchange rates (as would be the case under the contemplated system) rules out the possibility of substantial short-term profits: it is only the prospect of a sudden change in parity, with the capital profit it brings, which justifies the loss of three or six months' interest.

In the long term, moreover, these measures raise another more fundamental problem. As defined here, they would reduce the mobility of capital both within the Community and away from it. Now the unification of the European capital market and money market is an important factor in facilitating the internal balance-of-payments adjustments of member countries. It is an instrument which cannot be forgone and whose development should, on the contrary, be favoured by fixed internal exchange rates.

A unification of internal capital markets, while maintaining certain external percolation, involves the application, not of general directives of the type referred to above, but of Community regulations identical in each member country. Just as the Common Market, in the field of merchandise trade, required the existence of a common external tariff, so the Monetary Union, for its complete fulfilment, requires the existence of a common definition of authorized external operations. Since it must be possible for this definition to be flexible, it then becomes necessary to contemplate transferring this regulation-making power to a sole authority.

With this problem, however, we enter into the long-term field, and the mechanisms described above can start to function without being subjected to the serious delay involved in the unification of external exchange regulations which is the condition of complete internal mobility.

4. *A common programme for fighting inflation*

We have tried to show above that the revaluation of a country's currency was not an effective instrument in the war against inflation. There is, moreover, no guarantee that flexible exchange rates, even used in number, will be any more effective. The most that can be said is that a group of countries whose foreign trade is less than half the total is in a stronger position to follow an autonomous policy and to resist impulses from outside.

In practice, exchange policy does not seem to be the appropriate instrument here, and other weapons are needed to combat a price rise caused mainly by the rise of internal costs.

At the present juncture, the importance of a common policy on this point is rather to eliminate a decisive objection to any project of union. Solidarity among currencies can be accepted only at the cost of solidarity in economic policies, and particularly in the creation of internal liquidities by credit, both public and private. It would be purposeless to organize a common external system if its effects were to be destroyed by internal divergences.

The stress is here laid on monetary policy, as one of the sole instruments in fact available to governments, but the experience of recent years shows that its effectiveness remains limited in the face of cost inflation. Even if governments can give each other no assurance that they can effectively control the rise of their prices, the definition of common policies to be pursued in the short term would already be a significant step forward. And it should not be impossible in the autumn of 1971, since all governments are nearly equally concerned about cost inflation. They would no doubt be prepared to submit to the criticism of their colleagues, and even to their prior agreement, the measures they propose to take in the fields of fiscal and monetary policy.

It is clear that this is not necessarily satisfactory; policies pursued in the context and in the light of Community interests will not always be more successful in attaining their objectives than purely national policies. This is, moreover, only the short-term aspect of the fundamental problem for the survival of the Economic Union, namely, the parallel evolution of the Community countries.

They need not all have the same growth rate of GNP or of GNP per capita, or of nominal wages, nor need they even all follow similar cyclical trends. Indeed, to take this last point first, the fact of being out of phase, the effects of which on capital movements between Europe and the United States are under discussion, would be much less serious inside the Community. Between economies with a similar industrial structure, and whose products can fairly easily be substitued for each other, the fact that economic cycles are out of phase may well result in violent movements in trade balances, but they are easily equalized by appropriate policies, and the temporary disequilibria they provoke can be handled in the context of mutual assistance. They are in fact movements which are inherently reversible. Furthermore, the growth of intra-Community trade, which raises its share in the GNP of participants, and the integration of big firms, which tends to make the investment cycle more uniform, suggest that lack of phasing will become less marked with the passage of time.

On the other hand, it is important to prevent the development of too wide a gap in the trend of costs, since this would really imperil the future of the Union. A fundamental disequilibrium arising out of too great a difference between internal and external costs, can be corrected only by a readjustment of exchange parities.

In a monetary union which maintains a flexible exchange rate with the rest of the world (or a large part of it), this question can hardly arise in relations with the rest of the world. It may nevertheless arise inside the Community. The exchange rate would in fact reflect the average position of members, or at least a deliberate policy based on this average position. But if the governments of member countries were incapable of mastering the rise in costs, these would be in danger of growing steadily faster in one country than in the rest. The fact that this country was tied to an average exchange rate which was too high would then involve it in a deficit tending to become permanent. Under today's normal circumstances of money wages which do not fall in the event of under-employment, the result would then be a level of unemployment in that country which might be socially intolerable.

Conversely, since the external exchange rate would reflect the average situation of member countries, it would be too low for the country whose rise in costs had been appreciably less than that of its partners and this country would be in danger of experiencing an excess of effective demand which would, on the contrary, involve an inflationary push.

These dangers must not be exaggerated. Economies show considerable powers of adjustment and a great many exchange rates have not had to be changed for more than twenty years. Furthermore, it may be hoped that

185

the progress of economic integration will strengthen the automatic side of adjustments.

Trade union claims already take account of the external competitive position of their sector. This type of attitude could develop with the proportion of production exported, even in the big countries. The adaptability of industrial structures to the trend of demand is another problem which may be grave in certain regions. The solution is not to be found in the use of such a typically macro-economic instrument as exchange rates.

The lasting remedy of disparity by devaluation means that it must be possible to impose on the masses indirectly a reduction in the standard of living which they cannot be made to accept directly. With economic integration and the consequent greater proportion of imported products in total consumption, and with agricultural policy in particular, it is probable that that form of monetary illusion which is attached to a nominal amount of wages expressed in national currency will disappear. At this point devaluation loses much of its effectiveness as a means of adjusting the level of costs.

One might conclude by suggesting that the only danger for a union undertaken now might arise out of cumulative disparities in cost structures. This danger will diminish over the years, though only slowly. The risk involved in an immediate decision is therefore not much greater than it would be in five or eight years' time. The risk is, however, sufficient to make it necessary at the present stage to avoid an irrevocable and final commitment never to vary the internal parities of the Community. But it is not, however, so great that the immediate advantages which the Union would bring should be renounced.

Public opinion has recognized in recent years that national markets were becoming too narrow to allow all the economies of scale made possible by modern technology. The recent theory of optimum monetary zones transposes this conclusion to the monetary level. The optimum size will be reached at the moment when the advantages of a fresh extension counterbalance its disadvantages.

The concrete application is difficult, and no practical attempt has yet been made to measure the optimum dimension. Nevertheless, the speed at which financial integration is proceeding suggests that, here too, economies of scale are important and that the change is along the same lines as in industry, where the optimum dimension grows steadily with time.

It may also be noted that the decisions which might be taken by countries outside the Union to link their currencies to European currencies rather than to the dollar, but without assuming the internal obligations of the Union, would strengthen these advantages. The situation of these outside countries would not affect the determination of the exchange rates or the policy pursued in this connection, and they would, moreover, remain free at any time to modify their exchange rates in relation to the Union.

Such extensions can only have a favourable effect on the optimum dimension. While it is impossible to reach precise conclusions on this point, it nevertheless seems highly probable that the present dimension of the Common Market, in view of the character of its member countries, is not greater than is desirable. Does the enlargement of the Community raise any problems?

The enlargement of the Community

I f, in the autumn of 1971, the United Kingdom and other EFTA members decide to join the Common Market, how will that affect the propositions set out above? What about the allied problems of sterling balances and external payments as far as Britain is concerned?

We must say at the outset that the question of sterling balances does not seem likely to cause any special difficulty in the functioning of the Union. The amounts held in the sterling area appear to be remarkably stable. Central bank holdings rose to $ 5.6 billion at the end of 1970, climbing from $ 4.3 billion at the end of 1968, but having fallen slowly from the level of $ 6.5 billion in 1964. These changes primarily reflect the balance of payments of external members of the sterling area. Private balances are even more stable and fluctuate around $ 2.5 billion ($ 2.6 billion at the end of 1970). Balances, both official and private, held in other countries are falling slowly but steadily: they amounted to no more than $ 1.6 billion at the end of 1970, having fallen from $ 3.2 billion at the end of 1964.

There is therefore no problem of sudden and unstable capital movements. Neither should there be any problem of currency management, in view of the consolidation agreements already made. The facts show that the variation in sterling assets arising out of the surplus or deficit of member countries of the area are much smaller than the short-term capital movements connected with British trade itself and its financing.

The problem lies not in the situation of the pound sterling as a reserve currency, but rather in the balance of payments of the United Kingdom herself. The only sterling balances which have shown variations are those arising out of the support given to the Bank of England by the other central banks. These credits amounted to $ 5.3 billion at the end of 1968 and fell back to less than $ 5 billion in March 1971. During four of the five years from 1964 to 1968, the United Kingdom, which (like the United States) is normally an exporter of long-term capital, had a deficit on her current account. After the 1967 devaluation, and under the influence of deflationary measures, the balance of payments recovered in spectacular fashion and this, combined with a renewed inflow of short-term capital, made it possible to repay the advances of the central banks at the same time as a great part of the International Monetary Fund credits.

If Great Britain had been part of a European Union during the period 1964-1968, it is clear that her membership would have created internal disequilibria and the tensions connected with them. This objection disappears with the restoration of the external situation since 1969. The lesson should not, however, be forgotten. The United Kingdom can enter the Union only on the basis of a realistic exchange rate which ensures that her industry can derive full benefit from the extension of its markets and its integration with Europe. The problem will, however, only arise in a few years' time (and not even necessarily as early as 1973), and it is idle to speculate today whether the present rate satisfies these conditions. In any case, at the present stage, no irrevocable and final commitment should be entered into with regard to fixed parities within the Union.

In so far as the British economy is, on average, faster to yield to inflation than the continental economies (which is in any event by no means certain), the British Government should also accept the necessary degree of co-ordination of economic policies. It has, moreover, expressly undertaken to do this. France and Germany today represent the two extremes of the range of concepts of economic policy. The United Kingdom, standing between them, would not make problems more difficult to solve, but might, on the contrary, add her weight to the necessary compromises.

The Vice-President of the Commission, Raymond Barre, has recalled in recent speeches that a Community of ten cannot have the same character as a more restricted group in which much more complete political and institutional integration is conceivable. The machine would be made even more cumbersome and many decisions of detail made more arduous, even if the choice of basic guidelines were no more difficult. There is in practice a whole fund of Community experience at administrative level whose importance should not be underestimated even if ministers disagree; it is reflected in a better understanding of and respect for the point of view of other partners, learned in the course of long discussions. There will be a whole new apprenticeship in life in common which will have to be served, and this will take time and will temporarily halt progress in the functioning of institutions.

Must it be concluded that enlargement means renouncing certain objectives which would otherwise have been within reach? That is less certain, for if we want to be realistic, we must go the whole hog; it has been known for many years that the maximum objectives set in a period of European euphoria are beyond reach for some time to come. It was General de Gaulle who tolled the death knell of illusions by his intransigence on the principle of national veto and the policy of the empty chair. The tactics which had succeeded for one party could be used by others. In fact it was the slow retreat of the Community idea before the resurgence of nationalism which impelled the ministers, at their Hague meeting, to wish to proclaim a great leap forward, without, however, having secured their bases, and this omission became sadly evident during the monetary crisis last spring.

These reflections suggest that the whole nature of the Community and the objectives of integration which can reasonably be assigned to it, will not be fundamentally changed by enlargement.

Conclusions

The whole of the foregoing analysis assumes that the member countries of the Common Market will pursue the objectives which may be defined roughly as follows:

— an external equilibrium satisfying the needs of growth without inflation, allowing for normal capital exports and programmes of aid to developing countries;

— control of the effects on internal liquidity of short-term capital movements;

— the pursuit of European integration and the advantages which may be afforded by a "Community of growth and stability";

— the reinforcement of the international monetary system, pending the success of negotiations for its reform.

In the light of these objectives, four instruments of economic policy have been proposed, which, if they could be used exactly, would enable them to be achieved simultaneously.

Without reverting to the considerations set out above, it may be emphasized that in this 'mix', the flexibility of external exchange rates is a medium-term rather than a short-term instrument. In other words, the central banks (or the European Fund) should pursue a policy of stability and should allow only small and gradual variations, just enough, at the present stage, to eliminate the surplus deemed undesirable. This surplus is, moreover, not large, and a sufficient widening of the margins of fluctuation would probably be adequate in the short term. It would be time enough to discuss a further widening if the first one failed to achieve its objective.

It is clear that such measures are not without their cost. More flexible exchanges would, in particuliar, involve an onerous uncertainty for a num-

191

ber of trade and financial transactions, and that is why we have pleaded above for very wide zones with internal exchange stability. The fact remains that at the stage where the deficit of international payments has been concentrated for too many years in the countries whose currency has become the main instrument of reserves, such a solution seems to be the lesser evil. It is to be hoped that a sweeping reform of the international payments system may make it unnecessary to divide the world into monetary zones. But for that purpose the privilege of the dollar, which allows such a long and substantial departure from payments equilibrium, must be abolished. Flexible exchange rates would moreover enable the Europeans to press harder for such a reform.

From the external point of view, the success of the proposed policies would be measured by the fact that exchange rates should not greatly vary so long as they are flexible and that they should not remain flexible too long. Unless, as an increasing number of American economists believe, this system discloses so many advantages in experience that it is finally preferred to that of parities kept fixed for long periods.

Within the Union, the suppression of margins of fluctuation between currencies would require an experimental period. Even if it is not thought that there is one single rate which represents equilibrium and if it is accepted that satisfactory adjustments are possible for a fairly wide range of rates, there is no guarantee that the Community economies are at present within this range or that their evolution will allow them to stay there. (Thus, it is possible that, if the D-mark were substantially revalued, the price advantage enjoyed by French industry would be too great for economic equilibrium; it may nevertheless be politically necessary.) Time must also be allowed for the development of the instruments of private transfer which would allow current deficits to be settled without calling on the central banks and thus relieve the operation of mutual support. Time will also be needed for the integration of money markets to provide the central banks with an effective and precise instrument for regulating liquidity on the various markets. This running-in period will no doubt be the most difficult. It is also at this stage, moreover, that there is the greatest danger of disequilibria developing in costs. Most of these risks can be avoided only if time is allowed for the gradual installation of the instruments of the Economic and Monetary Union.

At the time the decision to set it up was taken, it was no doubt premature. There had been no time to measure all the implications and the political and psychological preparation was insufficient. And that justifies the prudence of the Werner Committee and the even greater prudence of the Council of Ministers. Hence the decision to proceed by fairly long and gradual stages, to define only the first stage precisely, and not to enter into any binding commitment until the end of that stage.

At the same time, the external crisis which began to loom as early as the autumn of 1970 suggested that the Europeans would not be allowed the necessary time to follow this line of deliberate progress, and that they were in danger of finding themselves very quickly faced with problems which would challenge the whole nature of the decisions of principle just taken. This is unfortunately what happened and what immediately revealed the lack of mental preparation.

Today we are at the crossroads. If the Europeans are incapable of showing a common front to their external problems, the crisis will have split them so widely that the establishment of the Union will be seriously, if not indefinitely, postponed. And yet the crisis itself affords an opportunity for rapid progress in integration, the advantages of which it emphasizes. The choice now lies between expediting the stages recommended by caution or remaining defenceless in the face of the crisis and at the same time, renouncing, for a long period to come, the next stage in the construction of Europe.

Six months ago, the gradual solution seemed much the more reasonable. Today it would be equivalent to a renunciation. But to go ahead we must act with a solidarity which we do not yet feel, we must trust our partners that this solidarity will not be found wanting in the face of difficulties, and we must plunge into a universe we have not completely explored. This involves a risk. Let us hope that our "kings, princes and governors" will have the courage to take it and the determination to succeed in the venture.

Tumult

The foregoing pages were written before 15th August. On that date President Nixon addressed the nation—that is a euphemism—he addressed the world, or that part of the world for which currency, the international monetary system, trade, tariffs and treaties have a meaning.

He announced various measures designed to reduce unemployment, to stop the rise in prices and to protect the dollar against the attacks launched by international currency speculators.

The dollar—but above all, the Eurodollar—is no longer convertible in the proper sense of the word, either against gold, or against drawing rights, or against any other currency. The key currency bows out.

Some people have pointed out that the country which invented the Bretton Woods agreements and stood surety for them has unilaterally repudiated them. The foregoing analysis saves us from dramatizing the event. The dollar had already become inconvertible *de facto ;* the most that has been done is to make the situation official.

Past bilateral commitments (swap agreements) will be honoured when they fall due. But no new ones will be entered into automatically. In future, neither the International Monetary Fund nor the central banks nor the commercial banks nor international trade can count upon a fixed relationship with any monetary instrument whatsoever.

Europe blamed the dollar for its pre-eminence in the monetary system, its abundance in transactions and its supremacy as currency of intervention. There will be no more supremacy. Europe can make its choice—and can even suggest a new international monetary system.

Europe maintains that the dollar is overvalued in relation to gold—that old standard of reference—and overvalued in its own economy because of inflation and rising prices. Let Europe draw its own conclusions as to the parity of its currency in relation to the dollar. It professes to be affected by the prodigious volume of dollar claims which it is accumulating, and which it is, moreover, multiplying by the action of its central banks. Let Europe itself limit what it complaints about, by the law of the market, by floating parities or by controls.

And since the other source of Eurodollars is the American balance-of-payments deficit, recourse has been had to the primary method of protectionism—import taxes, with preference and tax privileges for national products. The decision is logical when the country records a major deficit this year and, for the first time since 1893, finds its trade balance in deficit —by way of a trial shot—to the extent of $ 2 billion.

This grand design, this rebellion against the movement, no doubt lacks subtlety and imagination, but strength was needed to counter the facts.

The United States triggered off spectacular reactions all over the world, urgent meetings of councils of ministers, conferences of financiers, categorical statements and protests and conflicting positions. But in fact there have so far been few changes (we are writting on 1 September 1971).

From the monetary point of view, the dollar has depreciated slightly on those markets—Great Britain, France for the financial dollar, Switzerland, Belgium, Italy and Japan—which have not so far accepted its floating between 2 and 5%. On those which had already adopted it—Federal Germany, the Netherlands—the earlier depreciation has very slightly increased (6 to 8%).

A singular recognition of confidence in this embarrassing and highly criticised currency,—supported by judgement of the power of the economy which uses it and the state which manages it—the lack of confidence is only an average of 3% of the estimate believed to be forced on the world by American imperialism.

Paradoxically, this confidence does not serve the ends of President Nixon's "new economic policy", while serving the idea which the United States may form of the soundness of its currency when it breaks the bounds of the monetary system.

No doubt this evolution does not really reflect the gravity of the break.

The gold exchange standard, based on the two complementary elements of the unlimited convertibility of a reserve currency and fixed exchange rates between the key currency and other currencies, is dead and done with. Its disadvantages—the privileged position of the dollar and the explosive development of the Eurodollar market—were only too evident.

It can be taken for certain that this state of asymmetry in international relations will never again be accepted: the future international monetary system to be set up will have to recognize this.

It is, moreover, premature to try to trace the exact lines of this new system today. The most that can be done is to outline them.

The problem is twofold; first, to specify the level of relations of parity between currencies and, second, to identify a fixed standard, independent of currencies and not giving any currency a privileged position.

No one today could reasonably answer the first of these questions: in any event, how is it possible to assume a situation of equilibrium of prices and costs between economies gangrened with inflation?

In these circumstances, there is no chance that an exchange rate which is valid today will still be so tomorrow. The only logical approach is to absorb inflation before trying to re-establish a system of fixed exchange rates.

That will take time; that is why we do not see any possible return to fixed rates for many months to come.

There will be increasing pressure for this "return to normal": the adverse influence on trade and international investment of a system of more or less floating and more or less directed currencies will be more and more painfully felt each day.

For it is not correct to believe that floating exchange rates establish a market rate for currencies resulting freely from the volume of transactions. The central banks necessarily intervene, since they cannot tolerate exchange rates which momentarily affect their country's economy, credits and trade. Only the Bundesbank in Germany has, since the mark was floated, tried to limit its interventions on the dollar market.

A period of transition will set in, which will be called controlled floating—this is less pejorative than "crawling peg", though not very different. During this period controls will develop simultaneously, the authorities having a special propensity to protect themselves as soon as a new system is tried out.

Furthermore, controlled or flexible floating will not accommodate itself any better than fixed parities to the massive flows which shook the old system and it will therefore be necessary to step up penalization by exchange rates and to resort to regulations.

At the present moment there is no country, France, the Netherlands, Great Britain, Switzerland, which has not taken control measures, and the whole spectrum of techniques has been used. Europe of the Six provides the example of great imagination and variety—yet one more obstacle to its monetary unification.

For long-term capital, the market will be fettered, which will render more difficult the international flow of investment which is so essential to development. For the short term, compulsory deposits, the abolition of interest payments and the prohibition of the holding of external balances will slow down movements and the transformation which might result from them.

Belgium, which has for a long time practised the system of different exchange rates for trade transactions and for financial or capital transactions, has maintained the double market, but has allowed the former to float. France has adopted the Belgian system, but without floating for the commercial market. The system was recommended by the Common Market Commission, because it is the one which requires fewest controls and which could be extended in a unified manner, provided an identical procedure were adopted for determining the nature of operations.

Other countries have partly adopted this system by a distinction between security currencies and trading currencies. There is thus a danger of seeing very different restrictions introduced in the course of a fairly long experience of floating. Although floating was regarded as the price for a certain economic freedom, paradoxically it will lead to the reverse.

The second question—defining a new international monetary order and fixing a universally valid standard to which all currencies will be linked, and creating an instrument for the settlement of debts and claims—can only be answered later. Various plans exist, among which a choice will have to be made: the return to the worship of the golden calf? or the intellectually more satisfying definition of a standard governed by the wisdom of the IMF, erected into the role of an international central bank: the SDRs?

The standard, as we have said, can no longer favour one given currency area at the cost of another. It must also be a vehicle for transactions not only between central banks, but also between private operators on the international capital market. The plans so far worked out fail to meet this second requirement.

In all this process, Europe, on the road to economic unification, will have a special part to play. Internal monetary solidarity should not only safeguard the essence of the Common Market, but will also serve as a —geographically limited—model for the wider mechanism to be subsequently set up.

This European solidarity can, however, only be constructed on the recognition of realistic exchange rates. But we are bound to recognize that the present trends do not favour a return to equilibrium; speculative movements still mask—for how long to come?—the relative strengths and weaknesses of the EEC currencies.

Monetary solidarity between the Common Market countries does not immediately demand wholly fixed parities, as provided in the Werner Plan, or immutable parities. So long as the economic policies of the EEC countries are not co-ordinated, adjustments must be possible. But solidarity should manifest itself by an appreciably narrower flexibility within the Community and an appreciably wider one towards other currency areas, the United States and perhaps Japan.

Again, the Netherlands and Belgium have shown an original example by tying their commercial parities to a rate of flexibility close to that of the IMF. They maintain sufficient stability for transactions between the two countries and float in relation to the rest. Extended to the other Common Market countries, and, overall, extended to Great Britain and the countries applying for membership in an enlarged Europe, this system demands the creation of a reserve fund for co-ordination, intervention or stabilization, financed by governments or by central bank reserves as a protection against disequilibria which might shake the system, arising either out of economic conditions or out of massive movements of liquid funds in search of a higher return or with renewed hopes of revaluation. The extension of the Benelux system might give rise to a Eurocurrency established around pivot exchange rates which would take the place of the Eurodollar in international operations. The market techniques of London, as well as of Zurich, would very soon take advantage of this possibility.

Once again, it is up to the political authorities to adapt themselves to economic realities. The international monetary system must not be allowed to become one of the objects of the strategy of the world powers. You cannot play about with money without profoundly dislocating the economic and social forces, and even the civilizing force, which are the valid basis of these world policy games. Money must not be made the star of national pride or the pride of a finance minister. Only the technical content is valid—even if in order to respect it we have to renounce the fiction of national sovereignty in the monetary field. This time it is up to Europe to accept this truth.

There are plenty of other fields where the strategy of international politics can flourish. May I cite Talleyrand, who wrote to King Louis XVIII from the Congress of Vienna, "Sire, I have greater need of cooks than of diplomats".

Europe and America at the Crossroads

Curt Gasteyger

Deputy Director of the Atlantic Institute

Summary

1.   Rarely in history has the world experienced more change and greater fluidity on so global a scale and within so short a time as in these early seventies. In such a world, which is moving form bipolar confrontation and super-power predominance into a more subtle constellation of political pluralism and economic interdependence, European-American relations also are exposed to new stresses and strains.

By a singular coincidence, Western Europe, as a result of its gradual unification, is rapidly becoming economically more powerful and politically more self-conscious at a time when the United States is going through a period of economic crisis and political reappraisal. Inevitably, this will mean for both sides a difficult period of adjustment. They may come out of it as closer partners or fiercer rivals.

Europe and America have indeed reached the Rubicon: the point at which they can either resign themselves to a further deterioration of their formerly prospering relations, or set out for new shores by recalling their common interests and mobilizing their common imagination. The recent monetary crisis could serve as a catalyst and has also clearly shown that Japan must be involved more and more in this process of a *relance atlantique*.

2.   This process will have to start with the recognition that interests and concepts in North American and West European policies have become more differentiated, diversified and partly even contradictory. These divergences of views and interests are complicated by the fact that in some instances they are hardly less manifest within Europe itself than between the two continents. Whether Europe and America will find a *rationale* sufficiently strong to enable them jointly to override the "breaking-point" of discordance, discrimination and disintegration, will depend largely on how they perceive their own long-term interests in a rapidly changing, highly competitive and extremely complex environment.

3.   After reviewing the uncertainties and changes in the foreign policy of a "declining Western Alliance" and the manifold tasks that are going to face an enlarged European Community, this paper concludes with a number of

concrete proposals both in the field of practical policies and on the institutional level. They should not only give a new impetus to European-American relations but should also make them a major stabilizing element in the international system as a whole.

a. *Reappraising European security*

The nature and preconditions of European security have undergone substantial changes. The power relationship on the continent is gradually shifting in favour of the Soviet Union, while European-American relations are moving into a new and yet uncertain direction.

It therefore becomes all the more important to maintain in Europe the kind of balance of power which, for the last 25 years, has been the basis of its security and stability. This can be done by broadening the scope of intra-Alliance consultations, by strengthening Alliance mechanisms in compensation for potential force reductions, and, above all, by broadening American *political* commitment to Europe.

b. *Institutionalizing the Eurogroup*

The still unofficial Committee composed of the Defence Ministers of ten European countries should be made a permanent institution within the Alliance and its functions should be gradually broadened so as to promote more European co-operation in the defence field.

c. *Europeanizing "burden-sharing"*

To alleviate the problem of "burden-sharing"—a constant source of trans-Atlantic irritation—efforts should be made towards its "Europeanization". This could be achieved by a multilateral long-term agreement among the main European allies.

d. *Co-ordinating Western* Ostpolitik

This implies mainly three things:

—a basic understanding of the long-range implications for Western Europe as well as for Atlantic relations of a further expansion of East-West relations in general, and the forthcoming European security conference in particular;

—a common review of Western trade policies towards the Communist countries;

—a concept which would pay particular attention to the political and economic future of Eastern Europe in a changing European context.

e. *Joint management of environmental problems*

The problems of industrialized society are becoming predominant on the domestic scene of West European countries, North America and Japan. Dealing with them jointly can yield the most efficient and least costly solutions. At the same time it can help to avoid the kind of distortions in international trade which purely national solutions will almost inevitably create.

f. *Working towards a new concept of development policy*
A review of Western development aid policy is overdue. Efforts should be made to achieve a higher degree of multilateral co-ordination, so as to make it both more efficient and more farsighted.

g. *Making Atlantic co-operation a stabilizing element of the international system*
Europe will have to become more aware that a diminution of America's influence in important parts of the world can also affect its own interests. It may therefore wish to complement or combine policies in areas where the United States is disengaging. This external challenge could force the Community to create the kind of institutions capable of meeting such new responsibilities. In deciding that they should pursue their external policies wherever possible along lines of basic common interests, Europe and America must recognize that a more comprehensively conceived Atlantic co-operation not only benefits them but will constitute a major stabilizing and supporting element of the international system as a whole.

h. *Reforming Western organizations*
The enlargement of the EEC will highlight the urgency of readjusting the aging structures and broadening the insufficient capabilities of Western international organizations. While each of them has its own merits and functions, none of them is able any more, either collectively or individually, to deal effectively with the manifold new tasks and challenges the Western industrialized countries are confronted with. Sooner or later a reform of existing institutions or the creation of new ones will become imperative.

i. *Regular Atlantic summit meeting*
In view of their growing complexity, more and more issues can be dealt with only at the highest governmental level. Summit meetings of heads of governments from major European countries, the United States and Canada should therefore become a regular institution of Atlantic relations. Preferably, they should take place about once a year. Such meetings, particularly if prepared by a standing Atlantic committee of experts of wide-ranging competence, could pave the way for important decisions—or at least for a broad consensus—on central issues which no bilateral, sectoral or departmental approach can handle any longer.

j. *Drawing in Japan*

Japan should be included whenever appropriate in consultations on the growing range of problems it shares with Europe and America. While for the moment this is true mainly for economic, trade and monetary matters, the possibility of exchanging views on political and security matters should, at a later stage, be envisaged as well.

The author

Curt Gasteyger, a Swiss and by training an international lawyer, was Director of Programmes at the International Institute for Strategic Studies in London from 1964 to 1968. He is now Deputy Director of the Atlantic Institute.

Introduction

by George W. Ball*

n spite of all the talk of a polycentric world, one must still begin any assessment of the health of Atlantic relations by deciding what the Soviets are up to. Yet, appraisals of Soviet intentions cover a broad spectrum.

At one extreme are those who see the Cold War as a deliberately fabricated Western myth. The Kremlin never wished or intended to extend its influence beyond the present boundary between East and West; all it wished was an East European buffer to protect Russia against a *revanchist* Germany.

At the other extreme are the unreconstructed anti-Communists who see no essential difference between the USSR of Joseph Stalin and that of Brezhnev and Kosygin. The Soviets, in their view, are still engaged in a Communist *jehad* designed to overwhelm the West, and any diplomatic traffic with the Kremlin is a bargain with the devil.

These are, of course, the fringes—the overstated biases that cannot form the basis for serious policy. It is somewhere between them that one finds two differing assumptions deserving careful scrutiny.

Of these, much the more comforting is that the Soviet Union is no longer caught up in an imperialist drive, but is now reconciled to the *status quo*. Frustrated by an obdurate Western resistance, it has, over the years, gradually shed its expansionist ambitions, having lost its fear that the West threatens its East European empire. Because it is preoccupied with its struggle with China, its obsessive concern is to secure recognition of existing geographical and political boundaries on its Western flank, abandoning any hope of dominating Europe. Thus, for the first time since the advent of the Cold War, the West, by weaving an increasingly intricate web of bilateral arrange-

* Former American Under-Secretary of State 1961-66

205

ments between nations on the two sides of the Iron Curtain, should be able to stabilize relations with Moscow and the other East European capitals, create new security arrangements with the Soviets as a substitute for the present opposing power blocs and, at the end of the road, achieve the reunification of Europe from the Atlantic to the Urals.

That in the course of this process America will progressively withdraw its military presence—and indeed its political influence—from Europe is, to those who hold this view, no longer a cause for anxiety; for in the new environment of *détente* the nations of Europe should live happily together—in spite of the fact that they have never been able to do so in their long and sanguinary history.

Though many intelligent people have embraced this analysis, I find it a dangerous basis for Western policy—grounded, as it is, on wishful hypotheses and implausible inferences. It is, as I see it, far more prudent and realistic to assume that the Soviet leaders have not so much changed their long-range strategic objective of gaining political dominance over the whole of Europe as revised the tactics by which they hope to achieve it. Having tried for years to break the political will of the West, expressed in the Western Alliance, they no longer see hope in frontal pressure. Instead, following lines of least resistance, they have chosen to expand their power and influence around the southern flank of Western Europe into the Mediterranean. Once the Suez Canal is reopened, they will deploy the massive naval power they are now frantically building to extend their presence and influence into the Red Sea, the Persian Gulf and, ultimately, the Indian Ocean, thus joining their fleets in all the oceans to form a cordon around the whole underbelly of the Eurasian land mass. It is on this geopolitical postulate that one can find shrewd logic in Moscow's recent political support for India and Bangladesh; the expected reward may well be the prospect of forward bases in one or the other of those countries.

If this thesis is too sweeping for everyone's taste, if it seems too reminiscent of Admiral Mahan and the nineteenth century, one need not accept it fully to conclude that the Soviet leadership still cherishes large European ambitions and that the Kremlin's softening line towards the West is merely a tactical move. That Moscow is deeply preoccupied with China seems indisputable, and there is ample reason why the Soviets should wish to avoid trouble on two fronts. At the same time, it is reasonable to believe that the Soviets might have taken a milder line with the West even were there no two-front nightmare, since they had ample reason to conclude that their policy of continued pressure was bankrupt; it simply consolidated Western resistance, whereas *détente* would encourage those forces of fragmentation and rivalry that have plagued the continent for centuries.

206

But, whatever the Kremlin's *rationale* may have been, the significant fact is that—for the moment at least—the Russians have ceased to scowl and growl at Europe, and the resultant change in atmosphere is beginning to weaken the Western will to resist the extension of Soviet influence. There are many reasons why that result should not be unexpected: the advent of a post-war generation with little recollection of the Stalinist years, the loss in authority and self-confidence of the United States as a result of the Vietnamese imbroglio, the acceptance of parity in nuclear weapons which has diminished the credibility of the American deterrent, and the normal desire of people to achieve that state of grace which is vaguely thought of as "normality"—as though there could be anything normal in a world where one third of the whole population is still locked behind an Iron Curtain and the Wall still stands in Berlin.

Nor does there seem serious doubt that the Soviet Union is now deliberately concentrating on two objectives essential to its strategy of domination. First, it is striving to encourage the removal of the American presence and influence from Europe. Second, it is doing everything possible to block West European efforts to build effective institutions for common economic and political action, while stimulating those ancient habits and practices of myopic nationalism, which, always at cross purposes, reduce the power and influence of Western Europe to something substantially less than that of any of its parts.

To encourage the forces of fragmentation in Europe, the Kremlin has, once again—as it has done so often—played what it has long regarded as its trump card—its control of access to Berlin. It has taken advantage of the understandable yearning of the West German people for easier relations with their East European neighbours—and particularly their friends and relatives in East Germany—to gain acceptance of the *status quo* and encourage the Federal Republic to look eastward.

To exploit fully the European yearning for "normality", it has renewed its call for a European Security Conference, recognizing that the attractions of even an illusory *détente* operate with differing degrees of force on different national units in the European system; in fact, contrary to the normal principles of magnetics, they seem to exercise the strongest attraction in inverse proportion to mass.

Though informed Americans perceive these dangers of mischief in a European Security Conference, the Government in Washington is understandably reluctant to express a firm, negative view against the frenetic desire of several European governments to get such a conference underway. Perhaps we should be more forthright. I suspect we should, for, seen from the Western side of the Atlantic, a meeting between the nations of the Western Alliance and the Warsaw Pact can be expected to work largely to the Soviet advantage; since, though the West European nations will inevitably appear in disarray, the discontent that lies below the surface in many East European countries will be ruthlessly stifled by Soviet discipline.

At the moment, discussion on the Western side is largely limited to petty arguments as to the level at which the Conference should begin, and the rate at which progress should be made towards summitry; but that does not go to the heart of the problem, which is the symbolic meaning given to the Conference both in Europe and America.

What disturbs the more hard-headed circles of American thought is the fear that certain sectors of European opinion will regard the fact that the Conference is held as more important than any substantive achievement or lack of achievement. Thus, the convening of the Conference is likely to trigger a considerable euphoria—encouraging the wishful belief that the Cold War has indeed ended, that major military exertions are no longer needed to maintain the security of the West, and that every East-West problem can now be worked out in a spirit of mutual accommodation.

Unhappily, similar reactions in Europe and America can be expected to interact on one another to yield a dubious result; for today the United States no longer sees its world responsibilities either with clarity or common conviction. Since the early years of the Republic there has always been a school of thought that regretted America's coming of age—attaining that stage of maturity when it had to assume responsibilities beyond its own hemisphere. And today, particularly in the United States Senate where it counts, there is a tendency to pick up and echo the Venusburg music of *détente* as it floats over the water from Europe, replaying and amplifying it in an American idiom. So far, through bipartisan crash programmes and political discipline, the American Administration has managed to stand off those factions that would precipitately withdraw American troops from Europe, but it would be foolish to assume that such efforts can be endlessly repeated. They would be dangerously undercut by the sonorous though empty *communiqué* of a European Security Conference, with all the false sounds of harmony that it is likely to produce.

Yet, let there be no mistake about the consequences. Once the Congress tastes blood by passing legislation to withdraw American forces from Germany, American influence in the Eastern Hemisphere will decline rapidly. And next will come mounting pressures to remove—or at least substantially curtail—the American Sixth Fleet in the Mediterranean, thus effectively tilting the balance. For it is the conspicuous power and presence of the Sixth Fleet, reinforced by the knowledge that American forces are promptly at hand in Germany, which effectively deter the Soviet Union from applying its military strength in Egypt to reopen the Suez Canal unilaterally, isolate Israel, and gain hegemony of the south littoral of the Mediterranean.

Admittedly, these are gloomy forebodings; yet they have not led to fatalism. It is not so much America's inveterate optimism as the fact that Americans still hold firmly to the hope that Europe will recognize the twentieth century and pull itself together. Uniquely welcome in this otherwise lamentable season has been the decision of the British Parliament to adhere to the Rome Treaty, since it could make the critical difference. To many Americans, it is an article of faith that, once the formalities of adherence are completed and Britain's role in Europe has become an accomplished fact, the British will apply their special genius for political pragmatism to the gradual shaping of European institutions—not only economic but political—that will permit Europe to speak without the current cacophony of voices and to play more than the regional role to which its present obsolete structure condemns it.

All these points and many more are made with grace and persuasiveness in Dr. Gasteyger's paper. It is a measure of his perspicacity that he has identified—as others on both sides of the Atlantic have failed to do—the shrewd assumptions underlying the Kremlin's deceptively benign European policy—that its best hope for dominance is to create the conditions in which the possession of superior arms is more effective than their use. Thus, if America could only be induced to remove its presence and influence, if the drive towards European unity could be checked and the old forces of rivalry and fragmentation revived, the Soviet Union would clearly emerge as the strongest power in the whole of Europe, visibly equipped both to threaten and punish the individually weak states of the West. Once that should occur, the scamper of frightened nations to make peace with Moscow could become a stampede.

New challenges for the Atlantic world

*We live in a world which may become tragic—
and what is tragedy but comedy that has mis-
fired? Or it may become wholly comic—what
is a comedy but a tragedy which has lost its
dignity? But whatever else it is at the moment,
it is absurd.*

Peter Ustinov.

R arely in history has the world experienced more change and greater
fluidity on so global a scale and within so short a time than in these
early seventies: the decline of American influence and the expansion
of Soviet power, the entry of China upon the international scene and the
enlargement of the European Communities, the emergence of a politically
self-assured West Germany and an economically powerful Japan, the crises
of alliances and non-alignment alike, the break-up of a major Asian
country, Pakistan, the end of the post-war monetary system, the spread of
international inflation and the sudden doubts about the consequences of
unlimited economic growth and the way of life that goes with it.

Established policies, doctrines and dogmas are challenged or thrown
overboard, the "outlaw" of yesterday becomes the potential partner of
tomorrow, former adversaries are striving for co-operation that occasionally
verges on "collusion", and small allies risk becoming embarrassing obstacles
when the more powerful weave new relationships.

Does all this mark the end of the epoch that began at the end of World
War II or does it signal the dawn of a new age? Or is it little more than a
period of transition in which, behind the spectacular shifts, the main elements of the post-war system—the military predominance of the two super-
powers, strategic deterrence, the importance of political alliances, regional
economic integration and the primacy of nationalism—remain basically
intact? Nobody can tell for sure. We do not know in which direction these

210

manifold changes will take us. To a great extent our uncertainty stems from both confusioh about priorities and objectives in Western policies and limited knowledge of the motives and intentions of the Soviet and Chinese leaders. Common interests have become blurred and common principles questioned. Has *détente* with the Communist world become more important than the promotion of new forms of economic and political co-operation in the West? Is the United States attaching more importance to a rapprochement with China than to alleviating its strained relations with Japan and other non-Communist countries in Asia? Or do the Atlantic countries expect to achieve more security through bloc-to-bloc negotiations than by way of closer co-operation within the Alliance? While in most cases the first alternative does not exclude the second, it seems that, at present, preference goes to the first, not only, one suspects, because it appears more promising but also because it is new and hence more spectacular.

Although hardly begun, this era of negotiations and new openings, so resoundingly announced around the globe, has already developed its own paradoxes. Whoever compares the painfully slow search for a more balanced and appropriate monetary system or the trans-Atlantic recriminations over burden-sharing, to the considerable effort, patience and forbearance invested in the negotiations with the Communist world cannot help feeling that many Western countries are better at dealing with their former enemies and present rivals than with their own friends and allies.

It is in this climate of rising expectations towards the East, impatience or weariness in the West, that an American president and members of his cabinet can compare the current negotiations with their allies with a "poker game", and a French president intimate that the "foundation of the European edifice" is the Franco-Soviet entente. To be sure, critical reappraisal and innovation are overdue for many almost sacrosanct policies and institutions. But present trends go well beyond this. They seem to call almost everything in question, whatever its past or present merits. The "untouchables" of yesterday have become the fashionable policies of today: from Washington's dialogue with Peking to Bonn's negotiations with East Germany, from attacking the dollar to questioning the desirability of European political integration, from accepting strategic parity with the Soviet Union to establishing protectionist barriers and preferential areas. Only the future can tell whether these *volte-faces*, this general "farewell to yesterday", will be beneficial for everybody concerned. At the moment it simply announces the end of the (Western) international system as we have know it—a system which, in spite of its well-known and criticized shortcomings, inequalities and rigidities, has permitted widespread economic development and overall political stability.

If this is so, questions arise as to whether another, perhaps better, system is in the making, whether there are new visions and impulses which will lead us to a safer, more just and prosperous world, to new institutions better equipped to cope with the many and serious challenges that confront our societies, whether we can achieve more security at lower cost, more freedom for everybody with less risk of super-power intervention—or whether, for lack of imagination and political resolution, the international system will simply become more diversified but less stable, less rigid but also less predictable, with the emphasis more on national interests than international co-operation, with the inherent risk of "collective chaos" promoted by what somebody aptly called "competitive decadence".

At breaking point?

In this situation of general flux, changing priorities, shifting power and disintegrating solidarity, in a world "between detribalization and retribalization" (McLuhan), the future of European-American relations in general and the Alliance in particular has become uncertain.

Without an imminent threat from outside—or perhaps precisely because of this absence—the Atlantic world is faced with the most serious crisis from within. What some observers have been predicting for years has now become true: an almost simultaneous eruption of several hitherto latent disputes, a collision of diverging interests and an emergence of mutual antagonisms. The dollar crisis of 1971 was only the climax of a series of monetary crises in Europe that has been practically uninterrupted since 1967, fostering nascent protectionist trends, nurturing temptations in the United States to disengage partially from Europe, and sharpening mercantile rivalry from Japan to Canada and to Europe. Because all of these developments are interdependent and escalate by acting upon each other, their cumulative effect could shatter the fabric of the Alliance beyond repair.

In more than one sense, the Alliance has reached the Rubicon: the point at which it can either resign itself to the rapidly growing deterioration of formerly prospering relations among its European and North American members, or set out for new shores by mobilizing their common imagination and appealing to their common interests. The former is easy and appeals to a *laissez faire* attitude that more often than not conceals a lack of leadership; it would correspond to the centrifugal, "do-it-yourself" tendencies now so prominent and fashionable on both sides of the Atlantic. It would be an appropriate expression of nationalist resentments which have always been short-sighted in perspective and disruptive in action.

212

But it would be wrong and hardly helpful simply to criticize these attitudes, however unpleasant. They have become an important element in Atlantic relations. They can provide the necessary incentive for a more sober reappraisal of some "Atlantic shibboleths" which have so often bedevilled European-American relations. If properly used, they can serve as a catalyst in generating a new kind of relationship, the basis of which is a community of solid interests rather than lofty ideals, the recognition of mutual interdependence rather than the feeling of one-sided dependence.

Nearly a decade ago the Atlantic Institute invited a distinguished group of politicians to examine in depth the political and economic relationship between Europe and North America. Their study resulted in the publication of *Partnership for Progress,* a systematic effort to come to grips with some of the pressing problems of the early 1960s. *Partnership for Progress* set goals in specific policy areas, and at the same time provided practical guidelines for their implementation. Its main theme was that a strengthening of the bonds among the Atlantic nations, to which, in many instances, Japan, Australia and New Zealand must be added, would serve the interests of all but could not be achieved without a comprehensive approach and a co-ordinated effort.

There is no reason whatsoever to retract these recommendations. Quite the contrary: developments in the sixties and the manifold changes in the first two years of the seventies have made them even more valid than they were ten years ago. It can well be argued that, had they been followed, the Atlantic world would hardly find itself in the disarray that it does now. Admittedly, the economic gap between the two continents has narrowed considerably, and the Kennedy Round has been a major success in liberalizing international trade. But, in the absence of a broader politico-economic framework, the first development has introduced new tensions in Atlantic relations which are magnified by the mushrooming of "multinational enterprises", and the second is being seriously threatened by protectionist tendencies on both sides of the Atlantic.

Thus, most, if not all, of the issues raised ten years ago are not only as timely as they were then, but have acquired new dimensions. They have become more complex because of their wider implications for a greater number of countries and problems and because of their growing interdependence. This is true for the far-reaching economic and political consequences of the enlargement of the European Communities, for the world-wide repercussions of the dollar crisis, for the changing strategic relationship between the two super-powers, the United States and the Soviet Union, and its impact on European security, for Western Europe's desire for greater independence from the United States and greater rapprochement

213

towards Eastern Europe and, following from both, the potential tensions this may create within the Alliance. Thus, new and complex factors of conflict and dissension have emerged over the last ten years. They could drive the two continents further apart or, conversely, force them together to find common answers to what are mostly common problems.

This paper proposes to examine the general condition of European-American relations, as seen from the United States, Europe and the Soviet Union, and their likely evolution in the near future. Rather than presenting ready-made answers to the numerous problems facing the Atlantic nations —an undertaking much beyond the capacity of a single author—the study attempts to show that, in spite of growing diversity of interests and the legitimacy of national identity, most of these problems have to be tackled and solved together.

Community and diversity of interests

T he central and supposedly immutable pillar of a close Atlantic relationship has been the assumption of a broad, if not total, community of interests between Western Europe and North America: from the determination to cultivate and defend the common cultural and historical heritage to the maintenance and strengthening of common political institutions and values, from a shared faith in free trade and the market economy to a broad identity of security interests and a common perception of the Communist world in general and Soviet policy in particular. On this basis of overall consensus it seemed natural that the United States would support the economic and political unification of non-Communist Europe and that, in turn, Europe would accept American leadership. Where disagreements or dissensions remained they were muted or kept under control by the rigid discipline or prevailing solidarity that the "cold war" was generating.

Little seems to be left of this impressive nomenclature of common interests. Perhaps they have never been as "common" as numerous and repeated declarations and affirmations on both sides of the Atlantic induced us to believe. As a result, Atlantic solidarity was thought to be stronger, more durable, and less vulnerable to strains and stresses than it was in reality. If this is so then one can hardly fail to notice a remote resemblance to what happened in the Communist world. There also the much feared—and respected—"monolithic unity" which the Communist countries professed to have, turned out to be more a fiction than a reality. To a certain extent the two—the professed solidarity here and the imposed unity there—were contingent upon each other. They stood and fell with the rise and gradual disappearance of mutual fear and mistrust.

215

Whatever uniting effects the "cold war" may have had among the Western countries, their importance should not be overrated. Sooner or later they were bound to be superseded by other developments. Over the years, Europe's economic recovery and growing political self-confidence led to as much competition as co-operation, and to as much rivalry as partnership. In turn, American strategic predominance was almost bound to generate as much shared responsibility with the Soviet Union as it provided security for Western Europe. The various waves of *détente* blurred the neatly defined community of interests still further. It softened the dividing lines between East and West and opened up new roads of communication, co-operation and penetration, thus reviving old bonds and forgotten loyalties.

As a result of all this, interests and concepts in American (meaning both the United States and Canada) and (West) European policies became more differentiated, diversified and partly even contradictory. The European Communities developed an agricultural policy which hardly corresponded to the expectations that had led Washington so actively to support the creation of the EEC. Nor could it be happy about the preferential area which over the years emerged from the piecemeal embroidering by Brussels around the Mediterranean shores. And unless the United States adjusts and revises its highly conservative commercial policy towards the Comecon countries, it is to be feared that here too it will come into conflict with the very active *Ostpolitik* of EEC business-men. Last but not least, it can be safely predicted that with or without a newly devised monetary policy, Atlantic relations in this field will be much more vulnerable and sensitive than they have been in the past twenty years.

In the political realm, too, actual or potential divergences of interest have become more frequent and visible. The tedious and embarrassing haggling over a more balanced sharing of defence expenditure is merely the symptom of a deeper malaise: namely, a growing gap between the views on how to assure European security and hence a dwindling agreement on defence requirements for the seventies and eighties. It was inevitable that in the age of global nuclear confrontation Europe's position would be different from that of the early post-war years when the United States was practically invulnerable to Soviet attack. Once this was no more the case and deterrence had become mutual, Europeans began to doubt the credibility of American protection and the plausibility of Soviet aggressiveness. The changes and reversals in American strategic doctrines —from massive retaliation to limited war, from arms control to flexible response, and from crisis management to controlled escalation—were too frequent and rapid to make any of them particularly convincing. Proclaimed unilaterally, these doctrines were more a rationalization of changing American political perceptions and strategic expediency than the expression of common Alliance requirements. In consequence, they more often than not failed to convince the Europeans that their own defence contribution was as indispensable a part of Western security as it was said to be. Until recently (about the time when the common Nuclear Planning Group was set up) little was done to dispel this impression. Western Europe had to accept the unpleasant fact that while vitally depending on American nuclear protection it was, in strategic terms, becoming less important for the security of the United States. It was only a small though fallacious step to conclude from this that the latter now depended more on an understanding with the Soviet Union than on co-operation with Western Europe.

Changing security perceptions and interests were surely instrumental in Western Europe's, and particularly West Germany's, attempts to improve relations with the Communist countries in the East. In rediscovering Eastern Europe politically and economically the West European countries are not, of course, turning their backs to the Atlantic. Rather they have become Janus-headed in their political orientation, with all the ensuing uncertainties and doubts, frictions and misunderstandings. This, of course, is true not only for Western Europe's broadening political horizon but for the behaviour of all those on the rapidly changing international scene. As the diversification of interests progresses and new relationships emerge, as the unifying element of an external threat recedes and the dividing force of national interest reasserts itself, participation in, or allegiance to, a specific alliance or a regional bloc seems less important, and more conditional.

In a world which has moved from bipolar confrontation and superpower predominance into a more fluid constellation of political pluralism and economic interdependence, the fabric of interests and loyalties of which alliances are made is also subject to changes and stresses. An alliance built on the fundamental principle of free and equal association is more vulnerable to such developments than any other organization. This is because its very purpose, the organization of common defence and the co-ordination of the underlying policies, requires a minimal degree of mutual understanding and common purpose. They can only emanate from a broadly shared perception of interests. NATO's search for new goals and purposes which are common to all of its members, its expansion into new fields of activity—such as environmental problems—are prompted by the hope that this might uncover yet untapped fields of such common concerns. It is expected that they might sustain or supplement the dwindling community of interests in the traditional fields of security and foreign policy. All these efforts, whether controversial or beneficial, artificial or ephemeral, may generate new forms of co-operation and fresh bonds of community. Yet, in the long run, they cannot make up for the continuing diversification of interests which no freely constituted alliance is able to survive indefinitely. Whether the Western countries in general and the members of the Alliance in particular will find a rationale sufficiently strong to enable them jointly to override the breaking-point of discordance, discrimination and disintegration, will depend largely on how they perceive their own long-term interests in a rapidly changing, highly competitive and extremely complex environment.

American policy in transition

E verybody would agree that the foreign policy of the United States has entered a new phase. Hardly anybody would agree on the direction in which it is going to move. Is change going to prevail over continuity? Is it simply an adjustment to existing political realities or a departure for new frontiers? Is the country going to resign itself to a more equitable distribution of power while insisting on a more equal sharing of responsibilities? Are purely national interests going to predominate over international commitments? And finally, is Alliance solidarity still stronger than the temptation of dealing more and more directly with either the Soviet Union or China or both?

Reducing or reshaping foreign commitments?

There is probably no general answer to these questions. The explanation for this is simply that American policy has become less predictable. This is evidenced by the variety of judgements about the future of the United States as a world power. Is the United States about to retreat from the global role it assumed after World War II, as a growing number of observers, both American and non-American, believe? Does this mean a return from super-power status to that of a traditional rank-and-file great power with wide but limited commitments, special but no global responsibilities and a willingness to share with other powers of similar or equal rank the burdens of this world? Or is it going even beyond such a diminution of status by opting for a yet more sweeping revision of its overseas engagements, an ill-tempered curtailment of its foreign aid, a moᵣe or less voluntary abdication as the central banker of the "capitalist world" and a narrow-minded insistence on its national interests?

That these questions can be raised with some justification is an important fact in itself. It shows how rapidly views about the United States and the perception of its status and policy have changed. Washington bears at least part of the blame for this. While President Nixon's two annual reports have brought welcome and necessary clarifications of American foreign policy and objectives, the actual course of events has greatly blurred them again. To conclude from this that the United States is on its way out as a super-power and bidding farewell to a world-wide role would, however, be both rash and fallacious.

We are probably all too much under the effect of the American fiasco in Vietnam, the recent dollar crisis and the defeat in the United Nations over Taiwan, of external debacles and internal debates which, though noteworthy and significative, are in most cases nevertheless ephemeral. To be sure, the United States is likely to cut down peripheral commitments, rationalize costly but non-vital engagements, and attempt to share responsibilities where this is politically feasible and economically favourable (while such "political burden-sharing" recommends itself first of all, of course, with the allies, it does not exclude a possibly only tacit understanding with rival powers such as the Soviet Union). But all this is still far from renouncing vital interests, strategic predominance and economic weight: the autumn of 1971 has in many and not always very diplomatic ways made clear that the United States has no intention of doing so.

What Washington has failed to do so far, however, is to make clear what kind of international system it wishes to promote and what role it expects to play in it. Until recently, that is as long as American political, strategic and economic superiority was neither challenged from without nor questioned from within, there was no urgent reason to make any special effort to elaborate such a concept. Everything seemed to be relatively clear, the lines between friend and foe neatly drawn and the notion of power still identified with political-moral superiority. Although suspicious of spheres of influence and balance-of-power concepts, the United States had tacitly assured itself the former and was openly supporting the latter. "Perhaps the most striking illustration of America's faith in the efficiency of the balance-of-power principle is the decision to allow the Soviet Union to attain parity in nuclear weapons. The hope behind this gamble seems to be that once a nuclear equilibrium between the two powers has been obtained, a dynamic and therefore potentially explosive

220

situation will defuse and turn static."[1] This is not only, as the observer rightly states, a unique instance of a country which deliberately reduces its advantage over a rival for the sake of attaining an equilibrium or at least (mutual) sufficiency. It also reflects a clear propensity towards whatever contributes to strengthening the *status quo* and its promotion in politically central areas. The United States overrated stability (or rather its durability) and underestimated the dynamics of political and social evolution. It was only the latter years of the Vietnam War which shattered confidence in the almost unlimited usability of political, economic and military power and revealed the limitations of modern technology in the exercise of this power.

Difficult adjustment to a more difficult world

The effect of this crisis of confidence in what were believed to be the very pillars of American superiority was magnified by the rapid and almost simultaneous changes in the international environment. While Washington was perhaps taken less by surprise than others, it was certainly most affected by these events. Wherever it turned there was change instead of stability, uncertainty instead of predictability, challenge instead of loyalty, disintegration instead of co-operation: from Vietnam to the United Nations, from Japan to Western Europe, from the Middle East to Latin America, from the Indian sub-continent to the expanding Soviet fleet and the impact of China's appearance on the world stage.

It was to be expected that these changes and challenges, disappointments and frustrations would deeply affect American attitudes on foreign policy issues. The spectrum of reactions to the present situation and views on the future course of action is inevitably broad. It is hardly calculated to reassure whoever is looking for, if not leadership, at least guidance. It is symptomatic of this state of thorough soul-searching, critical reappraisal and quest for a new "foreign policy identity" that a highly intelligent review of American post-war policy should end with the following conclusion: "The ordeal the (American) society faces today is not simply how to disengage from a disastrous imperial war (*sc.* Vietnam), but how to dismantle the empire—together with the imperial bureaucracy,

1. Richard Pipes, "Russia's Mission, America's Destiny", *Encounter* (January 1971).

the war machine, and the industrial superstructure of the warfare state—before it destroys the nation".[1]

Such thinking expresses unmistakably a deep dissatisfaction with the present policy. It has reached such a degree that, as President Nixon emphasized in the presentation of his second (1971) State of the World Message, the major danger today is no longer over-involvement but rather isolationist under-involvement. From this point of view it is only to be welcomed when the President tries to "strike a proper balance; correcting both the excesses of the past and the over-reactions of the present".[2]

But is the doctrine, which bears the President's name, enough to cope with this difficult task? Is it, as one of its American critics points out, essentially a negative concept reacting to the excesses of the past but offering little leadership and historical direction"?[3]

While this is probably true, it does not fully meet the point. What is still more serious than insufficient leadership emanating from Washington is the deficient overall understanding of how seemingly separate issues are interrelated, act upon each other and hence can only be solved if treated as part of a whole.[4] Such a deficiency is by no means unique to present American policy. But it is here that it makes itself felt most strongly and has the most serious world-wide repercussions. It is not simply that the left hand often does not know what the right hand is doing. Sometimes neither is aware of the consequences this has for the whole body. Thus the overture towards China, welcome as it may be, makes sense only if it is an integral part of a broader concept of stability and security in the Far East, likely to be supported by the other Far Eastern countries as well. A partial withdrawal from Europe, if it should become unavoidable, is again tolerable only if carried out within a newly agreed strategic framework which also encompasses the politico-economic implications of such a step. These are considerable. They go well beyond Senator Mansfield's concern about the balance-of-payments deficit or insufficient burden-sharing by the Europeans. By now it should have become clear that one of the most dire mistakes is to deal with the troop reduction issue in purely or predominantly military terms. For much too long both European security and the balance of power have been treated as if they were only a question of force levels, equipment or strategic

1. Ronald Steel, "Did Anyone Start the Cold War?", *The New York Review of Books* (2 September 1971), p. 28.
2. Zbigniew Brzezinski, "Half Past Nixon", *Foreign Policy*, No. 3 (Summer 1971), p. 5.
3. *Ibid.*, p. 13.
4. J.W. Tuthill, "Strategy Drift in the Atlantic", *Atlantic Community Quarterly*, (Summer 1971).

mobility. To measure the degree of security by these or similar criteria is about as misleading as to judge economic stability by growth rates.

There are at least two major politico-strategic consequences with which an application of the "Nixon doctrine" to Europe (and other parts of the world), i.e. a reduction of American overseas commitments, must reckon: first, an increased probability of nuclear proliferation, second, a shift in the overall balance of power with likely repercussions on the political orientation of various countries and regions. Washington's attempts to prevent nuclear weapons spreading to smaller countries was defended on the grounds that their security was basically assured by the military might and the geographical omnipresence of the super-powers. The present Administration's intention to reduce overseas commitments and place greater emphasis on national or regional defence efforts must inevitably conflict with its (and its predecessor's) dislike of independent nuclear forces in general, a French and, *a fortiori,* a European nuclear force in particular. In an age in which the atomic bomb is still the supreme weapon, it is difficult to see how one can deny its possession to allies while at the same time either reducing the security guarantees for their protection or exhorting them to look after themselves—or both. From the more or less mild pressure on its allies in East and West to sign the Non-Proliferation Treaty (NPT) follows, one would have thought, the obligation to play a key role in maintaining the kind of international system which is least conducive to nuclear proliferation. The Nixon doctrine—or whatever name one might wish to give to this general trend of retraction—does not, however valid its reasons and honourable its intentions, point in this direction. An American disengagement from strategically and politically important areas cannot, therefore, be separated from the overall situation within which it is happening. In other words, it should be related to the kind of world order the United States wants to see evolve and help to support. Consequently, it must decide what weight and credibility it will in future give to its foreign commitments in order to secure a stability sufficient to prevent an uncontrolled arms race both among the major powers and the—until now— non-nuclear countries.

Balance of power revisited

Closely connected with this is the concern about possible shifts in the balance of power which a retraction of American power might engender. Again this is a problem which cannot be left to the generals or even the politicians alone. The basic interest of the United States with regard to

Europe was, as Hans Morgenthau asserts, "the maintenance or, if need be, the restoration of the balance of power".[1] It is precisely this broader issue of maintaining a more or less stable balance of power that is at the bottom of any American engagement. This is not, of course, to say that there can and should never be any disengagement. All that is suggested is that it should be seen in the overall context of a changing international system whose contours, in terms of who is going to exert most power in what parts of the world, are far from being clearly defined.

Thus, it is perfectly legitimate to assert that the menace of Soviet aggression was exaggerated in the early days of the "Cold War" and has gradually disappeared since. But it is equally legitimate to raise the question as to whether Moscow's current impressive military build-up in Eastern Europe could have other functions than those of threatening the West and policing the East. There are good reasons to believe that the purely military objectives of this build-up *vis-à-vis* the West have indeed receded into the background. Moscow's post-war objective on the continent after all has not been its overall military occupation but its political domination. Stalin wanted his country to become—and remain—the strongest power in Europe, unmatched and rivalled by nobody. His successors have departed little from this objective. From their point of view, a permanent American presence on the continent, no less than a politically united Western Europe, or both, cannot be looked upon—and treated—as anything other than a challenge to the very foundation of Moscow's predominant position and, consequently, Soviet security in Europe. This has nothing, or very little, to do with "military aggressiveness", "Communist expansionism" or "ideological subversion". Rather, it is the kind of *Realpolitik* that embraces all the political, economic, strategic, geophysical and psychological factors that determine the policies of the great powers and influence those of the smaller ones.

The Soviet Union has always been ambiguous about a total American withdrawal from Europe This for at least two reasons: it would substantially weaken the framework which has helped to "contain" Germany, and it would increase the pressure on Moscow in turn to withdraw its forces from Eastern Europe. On the other hand, the Soviet Union has never left any doubt that it will always resist the creation of a politically united Europe—especially one with a potential common nuclear deterrent. The crux of the matter, however, is not so much whether a distant European confederation can some day take the place of the withdrawing GIs, but whether and to

1. Hans J. Morgenthau, "Western Europe", in Abdul A. Said, ed. *America's World Role in the 70s* (Englewood Cliffs, New Jersey: Prentice Hall, 1970) p. 43.

what extent the American presence on the continent will remain an essential element of the central strategic balance and thus vital to political stability in Europe. To the outsider and, as we shall see, the Soviet observer in particular, the uncertainties and shifts in the political mood of the United States do raise, rightly or wrongly, doubts as to the permanency and reliability of American commitments abroad. We can therefore assume that the Soviet Union, too, considers a partial American withdrawal from Europe as increasingly likely. By pressing so hard for the definitive "legalization" of the *status quo* on the continent, it not only wants to facilitate economic co-operation between East and West and get a freer hand *vis-à-vis* China. It also aims at making the political-military situation in Europe, including its own predominance in Eastern Europe, appear as generally accepted and thus stable and secure: a situation which invalidates the rationale for an American military presence and calls for its reduction. Any substantial withdrawal of American forces would re-establish the Soviet Union's position as the undisputed political-military power on the continent. It could then offer itself, possibly by way of the all-European commission which a European security conference is expected to set up, as the guarantor of order and stability in Europe.[1]

If our assumption of the essence of Soviet policies and its effects on the continent is correct, then the question of the nature of American presence in, and links with, Western Europe goes much beyond the military realm. It becomes less a matter of the size and strength of American forces, important as they are, than of the overall political concept on which their presence rests. This point has been stressed by a number of observers on both sides of the Atlantic. It has, however, gained new momentum and force as a result of both the changing power relationship in Europe, alluded to above, and recent trends in Western Europe with their repercussions on Atlantic relations.

We are realizing that neither the overall nuclear equilibrium between the two super-powers nor the relatively stable military situation in Europe guarantees a static political relationship between East and West. Doubts

---

1. In a symposium organized by the Moscow journal *International Affairs,* a participant discussed the question of "establishing a mechanism which, as arms and armed forces are cut back (in Europe), would take over the function of safeguarding the continent from the threat of 'spontaneous combustion', that is, measures ruling out the possibility of any accidental outbreak or deliberate fabrication of armed incidents". According to him, "a permanent agency for security and co-operation in Europe will apparently (*sic!*) assume some of these functions, while others may require the establishment of other ancillary agencies". The speaker left open, however, who would determine the author of such "deliberate fabrication of incidents" and how he should be punished. Cf. *International Affairs,* No. 11 (Moscow, 1971), p. 67.

about American strategic commitments and the erosion of Atlantic relations accelerated by an excessive reassertion of national political and economic interests on both sides could demonstrate how quickly this much-praised stability can deteriorate.

Never before has the interdependence of economic, trade and monetary issues, and these security and political problems become more clearly visible than in connection with America's attitude towards Europe, and Europe's ties with North America on the one hand and its future relationship with the Soviet Union on the other.

The Soviet perception

Before proceeding to an examination of the European situation it may be worthwhile considering how the Soviet Union visualizes the future of the Western capitalist world. This is neither an exercise in doubtful "sovietology" nor is it, for once, a cry of alarm about the growing military potential of the Soviet Union. For too long the West has been focussing almost exclusively on its own perception and interpretation of possible Soviet intentions. In turn, it cared surprisingly little about how the Western world presented itself to Russian eyes and, on the basis of this perception, what policy recommended itself to the Kremlin leaders. Whether this perception objectively reflects reality or not matters less than the fact that Soviet politicians think it does—and act accordingly. If this is so—and we have every reason to assume that it is—then it may be useful to get a somewhat clearer picture of the general trend and direction of Soviet thinking about Western Europe and its relationship with North America.

Unflattering view of the West

To start with the conclusion: it is not a very flattering view that Moscow holds of the present developments in, and future prospects for, the "capitalist world" in general, and the "state of the Alliance" in particular.[1] Its main tenor is that the Western state system is at present going through a "serious crisis". This sounds, of course, a familiar note since,

1. A very useful description of Soviet views, on which part of this analysis is based, is given by Gerhard Wettig, "Die gegenwärtige sowjetische Politik der europäischen Sicherheit", *Aus Politik und Zeitgeschichte* (Bonn, 6 March 1971).

by any Marxist-Leninist doctrine, "capitalism" is bound to be in a "serious crisis" until its final doom. However, without undue pessimism, nobody can deny that at the present juncture the Western world actually *is* going through a crisis whatever its causes and outcome may be. It is on these two points that the Soviet analysis is of some interest because it reflects a more sober and less doctrinaire approach. Contrary to traditional Communist teachings, the causes of the present crisis in the West are not solely nor even primarily attributed to the well-known economic and social failures of the capitalist system. The emphasis seems to lie rather on political symptoms, on what is seen as a process of political disorientation and deterioration among the Western nations. In other words, Soviet observers tend to judge events in our part of the world very much in terms of traditional power politics with its interplay of emerging and declining political forces and its overall effect on the balance of power.

Thus, the utmost importance is attached to the "retreat" of the United States from overseas engagements. It is seen as a consequence of internal problems and external failures of American policies. The position of the United States has changed all over the world, notably in Asia and Europe. Here it has changed above all because "European realities themselves have changed... thanks to the successes of socialism in a vast geographical region—from Rügen Island in the Baltic to the Rhodope mountains in the Balkans".[1] Henceforth, the United States is going to pursue a basically defensive policy of simply conserving the positions it still holds, at minimal cost and without generating new ideas or taking new initiatives.

The decline of the United States' authority on the one hand, and the growing economic and political self-assertion of Western Europe on the other, are going to reduce the influence of the former without adding more weight on the global scale to the latter. These contradictory trends are likely to have the effect of "mutual neutralization" weakening the impact and influence on world affairs of both sides. Washington has made and will make a number of concessions to its European allies without getting much in return; it agrees, for instance, to the convocation of a "European Security Conference" in whose usefulness it does not really believe. On the other hand, the Europeans in their relationship *vis-à-vis* the United States will remain halfway between military dependence and economic independence, between a grumbling resentment against the American challenge and a lack of unity to counter it effectively, between solidarity as political allies and rivalry as economic competitors.

---

1. N. Polyanov, "European Realities and Prospects", *International Affairs,* No. 9 (Moscow, 1971), p. 7.

Still, according to views expressed in Soviet publications, there is a growing divergence of opinion in the West as to the basic premise of the Alliance, i.e. the Soviet threat. While the United States uses this threat as a means to "discipline" its allies, these allies do not take it seriously any more. At the same time the existence of "nuclear parity" between the two super-powers is reducing still further the credibility of American nuclear protection. This situation, Soviet observers assert, makes it even more urgent for Western Europe to come to terms with the Soviet Union. It is clear that the growing estrangement between the United States and Europe is further accelerated by such events as the present monetary crisis.

As regards the European scene, Moscow notes, quite correctly it would seem, a diversification of political tendencies at the root of which is a revival of individualistic national interests. This development is complicated by a split between what they label as "Atlanticists" and "Europeanists". The former remain basically in favour of maintaining close links with the United States and a kind of "partnership" whose precondition is European political *integration.* The "Europeanists" in turn place more emphasis on improving relations with Eastern Europe (including the Soviet Union) and hope for "European *reunification*" after the weakening or eliminating of the political element in West European integration.

It matters little how accurate this analysis is, though one has to admit that in several aspects it pretty well reflects reality. What counts, of course, is the fact that such views are held by a number of influential Soviet specialists. They are therefore likely to influence Soviet policy-makers. Even more relevant is the particular focus of these views: they concentrate very much on what is thought to be a general decline of the Western political system and the consequences this could have for Western Europe's political orientation. Accordingly, the Soviet leaders see themselves *vis-à-vis* a United States which, while militarily and economically still strong, lacks political will-power and outward-looking imagination; an Atlantic Alliance which is torn by serious clashes of interests and weakened by a dwindling American commitment and Europe's unwillingness to make up for it; and a Western Europe which is cautiously reviewing its political orientation by openly questioning American political leadership in the West and tacitly accepting Soviet military hegemony in the East. It is an environment which could provide the Soviet leaders with ample opportunities for action.

Europe: between economic power and political impotence

A presentation of Soviet perceptions of Western "disintegration" and an indication of what conclusion Soviet politicians might draw from this is in no way meant to revive the spectre of a recklessly expansionist Soviet power. To promote European integration not as an end in itself but in defence against either a Communist take-over or American supremacy is hardly the basis on which Europe's future should be built. The last ten years are evidence that some important parts of the European fabric which were woven in the rough climate of East-West confrontation did not survive well in the warmer winds of *détente*. The sad fact is, however, that so far European co-operation has made most headway when prompted by external pressure rather than internal insight. It would be somewhat paradoxical if the United States, after having mostly unsuccessfully tried to promote European integration as a political ally, now became a much more successful "federator" as an economic rival.

Also, one should not overrate what the Soviet Union can actually do. It is plagued with a number of serious internal and external problems. They range from the latent unrest in Eastern Europe to open hostility with China, from a still growing technological gap *vis-à-vis* the West to worries about dissenting intellectuals and resentful nationalities. Furthermore, the Soviet Union is engaged in a battle on two fronts, each with at least two major actual or potential rivals: Europe and America in the West, China and Japan in the East.

For whatever comfort this may give the Europeans, it does not answer the question about the place their continent is going to occupy in the future international system in general and *vis-à-vis* the two super-powers in particular. Obviously, the Europeans themselves hardly have more than a vague idea about it, let alone a concept on which to work. This is more than paradoxical, it is dangerous. One is reminded of the man who fell from the sixth floor of a building and, as he passed the third floor, confidently remarked, "So far everything has gone pretty well". Never has there been a stronger economic giant with less political will-power stumbling into the future in the expectation that what has gone well so far will also go well tomorrow.

After Britain's entry the EEC will be the world's largest trading unit. Its population will be greater than that of either of the two super-powers and its GNP will be two thirds of that of the United States, leaving far behind that of the Soviet Union, not to mention China. But the almost total dichotomy between such economic size and political weakness is likely to remain: "The European Community can be said to be playing a major role in the world economy without awareness of that role, and without application of political energy or time to defining specific objectives in relation to the world as a whole... The Community itself cannot be said to have a foreign policy, or even a foreign economic policy. It does influence other countries through its actions internally as well as externally, but the foreign effects usually seem to be afterthoughts, or even accidental."[1]

In these terms Europe is becoming a "Japan of the West" or even less: while Japan is already a political unit and is awaking to its growing political responsibilities, the members of the European Community are "re-nationalizing" what were agreed to be common policies. In so doing they weaken still further whatever is left of the Commission's policy-making power. Nothing could have demonstrated more glaringly this process of dwindling authority than its almost total absence during the monetary crises in 1971.

The trend towards re-nationalizing Community Europe, towards a co-ordinated but not integrated *Europe des patries,* continues. The hopes which the summit meeting in The Hague in 1969 generated have not been fulfilled. It could hardly be otherwise. Chancellor Brandt's prediction that the future forms of European co-operation would be below the level of supra-nationality but above the level of normal diplomatic consultation was not borne out by subsequent events. This was to be expected: a procedure that falls between integration and co-operation tends almost inevitably to revert to the level of rulings made on a national and state basis. Faced with the choice between short-sighted but expedient

1. Harold B. Malmgren, "Europe, the US and the World Economy" (unpublished paper prepared for a conference at the City University of New York, 8-9 October 1971), p. 7.

national interest and long-term and inconvenient international or supra-national interests, the members of the Community have so far almost automatically opted for the former. They have thus recaptured the essence of national sovereignty of whatever dubious and conditional value, leaving Brussels the accumulated weight of "supra-national" bureaucracy.

Britain's entry will make the EEC larger and undoubtedly stronger as well. It remains to be seen if it will make it politically more powerful. It will, to be sure, necessitate a very difficult and complex process of mutual adjustment and adaptation. This process happens to coincide with a period in which not only the monetary and trade system of the non-Communist industrialized world is in a state of flux and uncertainty, if not genuine crisis, but also the international system as we have known it since 1945 is entering a new era.

For Europe this certainly means new strains and frictions; it could also mean an almost unique chance to reappraise its present organization and future position in such a rapidly changing world. In this "new world" it will be faced with more serious competition and rivalry than ever before: not only with a militarily and politically dominating Soviet Union on the continent but with a highly competitive and dynamic Japan, an emerging Chinese political and economic giant and, last but not least, a United States for which partnership does not exclude competition and which common allegiance to the Alliance does not prevent from putting national interests first again.

Huge tasks and insufficient institutions

The monetary crisis in 1971 has revealed that European-American relations are more fragile than most people would have thought, and that European economic integration is less consolidated than one would have hoped. As it is crises which make and move history, it could well be that both the fragility of Atlantic relations and the vulnerability of the European position will catalyse a redefinition of the former and a strengthening of the latter. With luck they would provide the necessary impetus for Europe not only to overcome its present disarray but also to formulate common future policies.

In so doing it is faced with a whole gamut of problems ranging from civil violence and social unrest to rising costs for environmental protection; from finding a new equilibrium of forces and clearer delimitation of authority within the Community to working out satisfactory relations

232

with REFTA (rest - EFTA) and the other peripheral countries (Spain, Finland, Yugoslavia); from returning to fixed parities to reforming the international monetary system; from managing jointly the problem of foreign investment to pooling resources for the promotion of advanced technology; from proceeding to a common commercial policy towards the Communist countries to defining a mutually beneficial relationship with Japan and organizing a more efficient multilateral policy towards the Third World; from making European defence less costly and more rational— through better co-operation in the West and continuing negotiations with the East—to maintaining a more or less stable balance of forces on the continent which, in turn, can only be achieved by reasserting the essentials of Atlantic co-operation.

This is a long but by no means exhaustive list. It makes us aware to what extent, hardly thought possible five years ago, problems have accumulated. Faced with this mountain of problems and issues, one looks in vain for the appropriate mechanisms and organizations which could help tackle or even solve them. Nothing of that sort exists either at an Atlantic or at a European level, in spite, or perhaps just because, of the multitude of specialized bodies spread all over the area. For lack of an overall framework within which these problems could be handled, they are referred to the traditional, mostly outdated, and always time-consuming negotiations of *ad hoc* bi-, tri- and multilateral meetings: much of their time is inevitably devoted to the most pressing day-to-day problems, and little, if any, to a comprehensive examination of the underlying fundamental issues and their interdependence with, or interaction upon, other problems.

Perhaps this is the way international politics goes. It is little consolation, however, because it rarely goes well. At the same time it has, with no immediate threat from without or imminent disaster from within, strangled almost every initiative in the last decade to inject new strength into the aging structures of existing organizations or to create new ones. Europe is now paying the price for having failed, in the sixties, to equip itself with the kind of institutions it will need in the seventies. Even the EEC is no real exception to this: the "supra-national" authority of the Commission which was supposed to grow in the last decade has been gradually whittled down. It became the first and foremost victim of an outdated but revived nationalism: instead of broadening its competences as a function of the ever-increasing complexity of common tasks, the member countries have preferred to narrow them down. "If for tariffs it is normally the Community which negotiates," one of the Commission's members, Mr. Deniau, points out, "this is not the case any more for

233

exchange rates, even if they are, as the Treaty says, 'matters of common interest' (*matière d'intérêts communs*). As for questions of defence, they are specifically excluded from the Treaty." This leads M. Deniau to conclude that not only will the Governments have to look at these problems in a more comprehensive way but the Community itself will be forced to "redefine itself".[1] There are two major developments which will be crucial in this process of "redefinition": first, the imminent enlargement of the Community, and second, the changing nature of Atlantic relations in general and European security in particular.

It is symptomatic of the present state of European affairs that nobody dares to predict whether the entry of Britain and other countries into the EEC will mean little more than a numerical increase of its membership, or the addition, beyond the gain in economic weight, of a new political dimension. If it effects the latter, as it should, then the enlargement cannot be coped with simply by structural reforms and legal adaptations, by nominating additional commissioners and swelling the already over-sized bureaucracy. The quantitative jump from six to seven, eight or ten will, to use Marxist terminology, almost inevitably create a new quality. This new quality is bound to affect the Community's perception of its political identity and status. If nothing else, the enlargement should further the Commission's efforts to gain broader legitimacy within the member countries and induce the Community to assume greater responsibilities outside. Neither can be done as long as there is no clear understanding as to who is going to do what on which level and within which framework, which areas require integration, as distinct from those where either co-operation, harmonization or simple co-ordination is either possible or adequate.[2] Nobody can dispute any more that the number of subjects that can only be dealt with at a European level, is constantly growing: "in other words, certain functions should now be performed at the 'European level' rather than the national level because that is the level that corresponds to the dimension of the problem and not because of some compulsion to push to the European level anything and everything that the concept of 'Europe as a power' might seem to imply".[3]

It would seem, therefore, that one of the foremost and urgent tasks of the growing Community is to reach an agreement which, above and beyond the technicalities and formalities of enlargement, defines the areas,

1. Jean-François Deniau, "Nécessités américaines, vertus européennes", *Le Monde* (19 October 1971).
2. I am indebted to Miriam Camps for very stimulating and useful comments on this point. See also her article "European Unification in the Seventies", *International Affairs* (London, October 1971), p. 671-678.
3. *Ibid.*, p. 675.

both in terms of substance and priority, which come under its authority. The convenient and superficially "realistic" slogan *L'Europe se fera en marchant* only makes sense if this Europe gets some better idea about the direction in which it is supposed to march ; the equally non-committal programme of a *Europe à la carte* is justifiable only, if at all, if everybody agrees on the menu from which these European dishes should be chosen.

Whatever choice is made, it will determine the kind of institutions which will have to put it into action. Here, it seems, the Community is faced with one of its most difficult and delicate problems. Contrary to the stipulations of the Treaty, and contrary to the expectations of the early EEC years, the process of decision-making in Brussels has become more and not less cumbersome, less and not more efficient, complicated and confused by an increasingly blurred criss-cross of national, international and supra-national competences, interests and influences.

It would certainly be over-optimistic to expect from the process of enlargement a complete overhaul of the EEC's structural insufficiencies and a general broadening of its competences. Nevertheless, it provides a propitious, if not unique, occasion for a wider-ranging reappraisal. There are at least three major interrelated issues which urgently require a common approach; not only because they have wide implications for Europe itself but also because they are directly relevant to European-American relations: a durable settlement of the monetary crisis because of its repercussions on European stability and American credibility; a common concept for the forthcoming European security conference because of its potential impact on East-West relations and the Soviet posture in Europe; and a common accord on the essentials of European defence co-operation because of their relevance for the future of European-American strategic relations.

The essence of European security

It will, in fact, become increasingly difficult to visualize how an enlarged Community with armed forces of two million, thousands of advanced aircraft and several hundred combat vessels, can pay so little attention to the common management of defence. This neglect seems all the more out of place as the costs of arms production and maintenance are bound to rise in about the same proportion as the pressure for a reduction of defence expenditure; and as the balance of forces on the continent is shifting in favour of the Soviet Union, while its strategic "parity" with the United States could affect the latter's credibility which so far purported to rest precisely on American superiority; when internal unrest could add new elements of insecurity and lead to additional social spending; and finally, when economic recession or stagnation is reducing the still substantial cake out of which defence budgets have been cut so far. Defence planners will have to face a formidable task. Over the last twenty years they could almost automatically rely on continuing economic growth and accordingly adjust their own budget upwards. For the first time now it looks as if the customary upward trend in defence expenditure (at least in absolute terms) might come to a grinding halt; it will certainly slow down considerably. While NATO has so far managed to survive political *détente* fairly well, it may still have to prove that it can also outlive economic stagnation.

Proposals for better, more efficient and less expensive European defence co-operation abound. And so do the arguments against it. To date, the latter have almost always prevailed, the few exceptions only confirm the rule. It is not the purpose of this paper to put forward new proposals in one sense or the other.[1] It is, however, difficult to imagine how long Western Europe in general, and the enlarged Community in particular, can afford to turn a blind eye on the growing limitations of national defence capabilities and the potentials of common defence efforts.

The answer will greatly depend on what the Europeans consider to be the essence of security in the years to come or, in other words, how they think the changing international environment is likely to affect Europe's security requirements.

To an increasing number of people the answer seems to be clear: as there is no evidence of Soviet aggressive intentions there is no direct threat and therefore adequate security. What is more: the longer the Soviet Union does not show any sign of aggressiveness, the denser the network of economic and cultural interchange becomes and the more "normalized" the status quo appears, the less arms and armed forces are thought necessary in Europe. Militarily speaking, there is some truth in these assumptions. It would be politically unreasonable and economically wasteful to maintain the same levels of armament in times of *détente* as were thought indispensable in times of tension. What is, however, much more difficult—as negotiations on mutual and balanced force reductions (MBFR) may prove —is to determine the point at which such quantitative reductions affect the quality of the political basis on which security rests. It presupposes both an organizational underpinning and the kind of force levels which help to preserve the credibility of deterrence and maintain the political framework

1. See Walter Schütze, *European Defence Co-operation and NATO* (Atlantic Paper No. 3, 1969) and René Foch, *Europe and Technology* (Atlantic Paper No. 2, 1970).

within which defence can be organized and arms control measures negotiated.

Any reappraisal of European defence efforts and requirements will thus have to take into account the political dimension of security. In other words, the role and function of any given military potential has to be seen not only in terms of its defensive or potentially offensive function but also in terms of its place in the overall political context.[1] It is a commonplace but still useful to state that the importance and impact of "military power" goes beyond the military realm. This is all the more true in situations where the actual use of this military power between the blocs has become unlikely. The fact that the desirability and feasibility of force reductions in Europe is being considered mainly in military and financial terms shows a deplorable unawareness of their political implications. While there are perfectly legitimate reasons for discussing the effect of such reductions on the credibility of deterrence and capability for defence, one should not underrate their less obvious but nevertheless highly relevant impact on the overall distribution of power in Europe. It is one thing to "bring home" some American divisions and let the Europeans make up for them; it is quite a different thing to determine how this could increase the relative weight and influence of Soviet power on the continent.

West Europeans have so far been rather sanguine about such possible consequences: "Although the overall military situation has developed in favour of the Soviet Union, it has at the same time become almost a dogma in the West to believe that the (Soviet) threat has nevertheless declined" (Nerlich). This paradoxical situation can only be explained by the fact that the Western threat perception is determined by two elements: first, that war between East and West is unlikely, and second, that the *status quo* in Europe is in no way affected by shifts in the strategic balance. This view does not take into account the *dynamics* of a shifting balance of forces which could engender a process of political re-orientation and adjustment in various countries; the *political consequences* of such a shift in other fields than that of military security, opening up new options for Soviet policy in Europe; and the *growing political-strategic asymmetries* in the position of the two super-powers *vis-à-vis* Europe. In a situation like this the difficulty lies not so much in the organization of *military* defence against an unlikely aggressor but in designing the *political* framework for dealing with a power whose military superiority on the continent, indefinite in duration and still growing in extent, is casting its shadow on the whole of Europe—and beyond.[2]

1. For the following I draw on ideas which Uwe Nerlich, Foundation for Science and Politics, Ebenhausen/Munich, has developed in several unpublished papers.
2. Cf. Curt Gasteyger, "The Fragile Balance", *Interplay* (New York, March 1971).

The Chinese seem to be more aware of such a trend than most Europeans. They can hardly welcome the prospect of a Soviet Union which has not only succeeded in legalizing the *status quo* in Europe but whose military strength may no longer find a counterbalance after an American disengagement. It would be a Soviet Union without any immediate rival on the entire Eurasian continent whose weight would be felt in Peking as well as in Bonn, Paris or Brussels. Seen in this light it hardly seems a coincidence that Peking should have taken such a basically positive attitude towards the enlargement of the EEC. It probably sees in such a development precisely what it should and could be: a strengthening of Europe's position on the chessboard of power, in the pattern of checks and balances.

European-American relations reviewed: some proposals

It is in this world of shifting power balances, greater political pluralism and growing economic and technological interdependence that Europe and America have to redefine their relationship. They will undoubtedly find that it has become more complex and complicated too. The sources of friction, competition and dissension have increased. But so have the opportunities, indeed, the necessities for co-operation. They too will have to tackle the difficult task of reconciling the centrifugal forces of political pluralism with the countervailing constraints of economic, technological, social and strategic interaction. In so doing, they will have to realize that while it may still be tempting to "go it alone" they cannot do it any more without serious consequences for everybody. No doubt, greater self-assertion and more flexibility in Atlantic relations are still possible. In some cases they may even be desirable. An act of independence, however, no longer is.

The proposals below are based on this central fact of Atlantic relations. They follow from what has been said about the current political situation in the Atlantic world. They are by no means exhaustive. They merely point to some topical issues to which both Europe and America will have to address themselves in the near future.

The issues

1. Reappraising European security

The dynamics of a changing power relationship in Europe re-emphasize the importance of maintaining the balance of power on the continent which has been the basis of West European security and stability in the last

25 years. It is in this broader context that the future role of the Alliance, still the only multilateral political link between Europe and America, and the nature of the American presence on the continent have to be seen. Since a sweeping reform of the Alliance is highly unlikely, efforts should be made to broaden further the areas of overall political *consultation* within the existing institutions. They should be linked to the review of Western international organizations and the consultations on foreign policy issues suggested later on.

In particular, the *Eurogroup*—the still unofficial committee composed of the Defence Ministers of ten European States (Belgium, Denmark, Federal Republic of Germany, Greece, Italy, Luxembourg, Netherlands, Norway, Turkey, United Kingdom)—should be made a permanent institution within the Alliance and its functions gradually broadened. It would then provide the platform for regular consultations on the growing number of common political-military problems and might also encourage closer bi- or multi-lateral co-operation among its members in the defence field. Such a strengthening of the *Eurogroup* would be an important step towards creating the kind of framework within which the greater weight of Europe in the Alliance can find a more adequate expression and which is conducive to its assuming wider responsibilities for its security.

2. *Strengthening the Alliance mechanisms in anticipation of force reductions*

The need for closer co-operation and more flexible mechanisms on the *military level* could become greater if and when NATO force levels should be reduced. This is so because such a reduction of forces (be it unilateral or the consequence of an East-West agreement) will call for a greater degree of intra-alliance co-operation, consultation and trust if the credibility of deterrence is to be maintained. To put it differently: a reduction in quantity should be compensated by improvements in quality, both with regard to the underlying political-strategic concepts and the operating mechanisms.

3. *Broadening American political commitment to Europe*

As the balance of forces in Europe tends to shift in favour of the Soviet Union, American presence in Europe as an indispensable part of this balance will remain highly important. In a period of *détente* the *political* commitment of the United States to maintain the present equilibrium in Europe becomes more relevant than force levels and military equipment. Such a political commitment can, however, be assured only if and when the United States is fully involved in any process that could alter the present situation (such as a European security conference).

4. *Europeanizing "burden-sharing"*

As long as the issue of "burden-sharing" remains a source of irritation in European-American relations, efforts should be made by the West European allies to "Europeanize" what so far has remained basically a bilateral German-American and German-British affair. A longer-term multilateral agreement emanating from such an intra-European understanding would put the issue on a more stable basis favourable to long-range planning. At the same time it could help to make the West European countries feel more involved in the security of the northern and southern flanks as well.

This is all the more important since a "Europe of the Ten" will no longer be a "Europe of the central front" alone: henceforth attention will also have to be given to the special defence requirements of the European periphery, i.e. Northern Europe and the Mediterranean.

The United States in turn should recognize that its military presence in Europe cannot be treated as if it were simply a balance-of-payments problem. It is, of course, a major part of the United States' global policy to maintain the kind of international system which corresponds best to its own security and economic interest. Within this objective, the US presence is one of the most efficient resource allocations in America's overall military expenditure: the strain it entails for the balance-of-payments should become manageable again once this imbalance is redressed.

5. *Co-ordinating Western* Ostpolitik

There are three major issues in the field of East-West relations which call for better co-ordination between Europe and America:

—A basic understanding of the long-range implications of a further expansion of East-West relations in general and of the forthcoming Conference for Security and Co-operation in Europe both for Western Europe and for Atlantic relations. While much has been said and written about the security conference, insufficient thought has been given to its actual agenda and to the Soviet proposal that it should lead to a permanent security organization. It is for the former that concrete proposals on specific issues should be worked out. Besides testing Soviet intentions, such proposals could greatly contribute to identifying the areas where East-West co-operation is desirable and actually possible.

241

—A common review of Western trade policies towards the Communist countries.

As the enlarged European Community gropes towards a common commercial policy and the United States cautiously adjusts its own trade policy towards the Communist countries, some guiding principles should be laid down in order to avoid a clash or a mutually detrimental rivalry between the two.

—A concept which would pay particular attention to the political and economic future of *Eastern Europe* in a changing European context. The Berlin agreements are likely to end a troubled phase in the history of post-war Europe. Now that the *status quo* on the continent has been formally legalized the question must be asked as to what is going to happen to Eastern Europe and East-West relations after Berlin. It is here that the necessity of a co-ordinated Western *Ostpolitik* is particularly evident. Purely bilateral approaches would not only weaken the impact of such a policy *vis-à-vis* Communist Europe but would almost inevitably have a divisive effect on the still fragile fabric of West European political co-operation.

6. *Jointly managing environmental problems*

The problems of industrialized society are becoming predominant on the domestic scene of West European countries, North America and Japan. The United States' "lead-time" with regard to some of these problems (urban problems, transport, pollution) is rapidly disappearing; by now they have become of equal concern to Europe and Japan as well.

The solution of these problems will demand tremendous resources and absorb an increasing amount of political energy. Hence the tendency of the United States to reduce further its overseas commitments, and Europe's inclination to become still more inward-looking. Either trend can have an additional divisive effect on Atlantic relations if the two sides do not recognize that they are faced with largely the same problems. Dealing with them jointly can yield the most efficient and least costly solutions. At the same time it can help to avoid the kind of distortions in international trade which purely national solutions will almost inevitably create.

7. *Working towards a new concept of development policy*

A major common responsibility of the Atlantic Community remains efficient development aid. The downward trend which can be observed in some major

242

countries, above all the United States, has not only to be reversed. Above and beyond this, efforts should be made to achieve a higher degree of multilateral co-ordination so as to make it both more efficient and farsighted. This requires a thorough revision of present aid policies lest they neutralize or compete with each other. It would have to evolve a concept as to how the developing countries should be integrated into the world economy, what place they should occupy in it, and what kind of industrialization would serve both their own interests and those of the rest of the world.

8. *Making Atlantic co-operation a stabilizing element of the international system*

Europe will have to become more aware that a diminution of America's influence in important parts of the world can also affect its own interests. Thus "as America's strategic and diplomatic influence diminishes in Japan and Korea, India and Pakistan, Indo-China and Latin America ... the Europe of the Ten may come to feel that interests of theirs previously safeguarded by their ally have become exposed".[1] In several instances these interests are exposed to rising Soviet or Chinese influence. Europe cannot remain indifferent to this, particularly when it happens in areas so vital to its economy and security as the Mediterranean and the Middle East. It will therefore have to recognize the extent to which, on a global level, its own interests are tied to, or contingent upon, American policy.

But beyond this Europe may wish to complement or combine policies in areas where the United States is disengaging. This could spur European aspirations gradually to assume in some specific areas more responsibilities itself. This external challenge would, in turn, force the Community to create the kind of institutions capable of meeting it.

Europe and America have therefore to decide whether they see their interests best served by pursuing separate and possibly even conflicting policies (the EEC's Mediterranean policy—a kind of first step towards a European foreign policy—points in this direction) or else by proceeding if not in accord with then at least not in opposition to each other. This may involve consultations on reciprocity in, or sharing of, responsibilities at an early stage of the policy-making process. The United States, which as a super-power has frequently abandoned the habit of sharing political decisions, will have to resume it again; in turn, the EEC as an emerging economic power must find the appropriate mechanisms through which it can effectively

---

1. Hedley Bull, "Europe and the Wider World", *The Round Table* (London, October 1971), reprinted in *Survival* (London, December 1971), p. 404.

take part in this process of common consultation. In so doing, the two sides must recognize that a more comprehensively conceived Atlantic co-operation not only benefits them but will constitute a major stabilizing and supporting element of the international system as a whole.

Setting priorities

All these actions are important, most of them are urgent. They cannot, however, all be tackled at one and the same time. A clear order of priority should be followed, difficult as this may often be.

Ideally, the order to follow would be to start with what is the core of Atlantic relations: the re-organization of the enlarged EEC and the concomitant redefinition of economic-political relations with North America and, in a different way, with Japan, including of course a reform of the monetary system. From here one could move to the "outer circles": the developing of common approaches to the problems of modern industrialized society, the elaboration of common attitudes on European security and East-West trade, a review of the policies towards those areas where common political and economic interests exist and the search for an overall concept of development policy towards the Third World.

Mechanisms

1. Reforming Western organizations

The enlargement of the EEC will highlight the urgency of readjusting the aging structures and broadening the insufficient capabilities of Western international organizations. While each of them has it own merits and functions, none of them is able any more, either collectively or individually, to deal effectively with the manifold new tasks and challenges the Western industrialized countries are confronted with. Sooner or later a reform of existing institutions or the creation of new ones will become imperative.

2. Regular Atlantic summit meetings

In view of their growing complexity, more and more issues can be dealt with only at the highest governmental level. Summit meetings of heads of governments from major European countries, the United States and Canada should therefore become a regular institution of Atlantic relations. Preferably, they should take place about once a year. Such meetings, particularly if prepared by a standing Atlantic committee of experts of wide-ranging competence, could pave the way for important decisions—or at least for a broad consensus—on central issues which no bilateral, sectoral or departmental approach can handle any longer.

3. *Drawing in Japan*

Japan should be included whenever appropriate in consultations on the growing range of problems it shares with Europe and America. While for the moment this is true mainly for economic, trade and monetary matters, the possibility of exchanging views on political and security matters should, at a later stage, be envisaged as well.